CHINA'S GLOBAL PRESENCE

CHINA'S GLBAL PRESENCE

Economics, Politics, and Security

EDITED BY
DAVID M. LAMPTON
AND
CATHERINE H. KEYSER

American Enterprise Institute for Public Policy Research
Washington, D.C.
in collaboration with the Institute of Southeast Asian Studies

David M. Lampton is president of the National Committee on United States–China Relations. He has served as director of the China Policy Project at the American Enterprise Institute. Catherine H. Keyser is pursuing graduate studies at Columbia University; she was the research assistant for the China Policy Project at AEI.

Distributed by arrangement with

UPA, Inc.
4720 Boston Way
Lanham, Md. 20706
3 Henrietta Street
London WC2E 8LU England

Library of Congress Cataloging-in-Publication Data

China's global presence : economics, politics, and security / David M. Lampton and Catherine H. Keyser, editors.
    p.   cm. — (AEI studies; 466)
    Includes index.
    ISBN 0-8447-3643-0.   ISBN 0-8447-3644-9 (pbk.)
    1. China—History—1976- 2. China—Forecasting. 3. Twenty-first century—Forecasts. 4. Taiwan—Forecasting. I. Lampton, David M.
II. Keyser, Catherine H. III. Series.
DS779.215.C48   1988
951.05'8—dc19   87-27077
                                                                  CIP

Printed in the United States of America

The Institute of
Southeast Asian Studies

The Institute of Southeast Asian Studies, which collaborated with the American Enterprise Institute in producing the studies in this volume, is a regional research center for scholars and other specialists concerned with modern Southeast Asia. Its research focuses particularly on the multifaceted problems of stability and security, economic development, and political and social change.

The institute was established as an autonomous organization in May 1968. It is governed by a twenty-two-member board of trustees comprising nominees from the Singapore government, the National University of Singapore, the various chambers of commerce, and professional and civic organizations. A ten-member executive committee oversees day-to-day operations; it is chaired by the director, the institute's chief academic and administrative officer.

The ASEAN Economic Research Unit is an integral part of the institute, coming under the overall supervision of the director who is also the chairman of its Management Committee. The unit was formed in 1979 in response to the need to deepen understanding of economic change and political developments in ASEAN. The day-to-day operations of the unit are the responsibility of the coordinator. A Regional Advisory Committee, consisting of a senior economist from each of the ASEAN countries, guides the work of the unit.

Contents

Contributors

JOHN FUH-SHENG HSIEH is associate professor of political science at the National Chengchi University, Taipei. He is also secretary general of the Institute of International Relations. Mr. Hsieh has written widely on political methodology, foreign policy and political conflict. Mr. Hsieh received his Ph.D. from the University of Rochester, in New York.

ALBERT KEIDEL is president of Rock Creek Research, which specializes in China's economy, and editor of the *China Letter*. He has also served as the project mission economist for the UN Development Programme, Office of Project Execution, and the UN Food and Agriculture Organization. From 1981 to 1984 Mr. Keidel was the senior economist for China Wharton Econometric Forecasting Associates.

CATHERINE H. KEYSER is the research assistant for China Policy Studies at the American Enterprise Institute for Public Policy Research. She received her bachelor's degree from the University of the South, Sewanee, Tennessee. Currently Ms. Keyser is working toward her doctorate in the political science department at Columbia University, New York City.

DAVID M. LAMPTON is associate professor of political science at Ohio State University and director of China Policy Studies at the American Enterprise Institute. In addition, he is president-elect of the National Committee on U.S.-China Relations. Mr. Lampton is the author of numerous articles on foreign and domestic policy in China. His three most recent books are *Paths to Power: Elite Mobility in Contemporary China; A Relationship Restored: Trends in U.S.-China Educational Exchanges, 1978–1984*, and *Policy Implementation in Post-Mao China*, ed.

ADAM M. PILARSKI is the chief economist and manager of economic research, Douglas Aircraft Company, McDonnell Douglas Corporation. Mr. Pilarski is responsible for all economic analysis for the company. In addition, Mr. Pilarski is the project manager for a joint marketing feasibility study with the People's Republic of China to coproduce an airplane. He is a frequent traveler to China and has contributed to the *Review of Economics in Statistics, American Journal of Sociology, Economic Inquiry,* and the *Journal of Travel Research.*

DENIS FRED SIMON is an associate professor of international business at the Fletcher School of Law and Diplomacy at Tufts University. Mr. Simon has written widely on the issues of international technology transfer and science and technology policy, especially in East Asia. He is a consultant for the Department of Defense as well as several industries. He is the author of *Taiwan, Technology Transfer and Transnationalism: The Political Management of Dependency.* In addition, Mr. Simon has published articles in *Technology Review, Bulletin of Atomic Scientists,* and *Studies in Comparative Communism.*

ROGER W. SULLIVAN is president of the National Council for United States–China Trade. He was formerly a senior staff member of the National Security Council and a career Foreign Service officer. In 1978 he was appointed deputy assistant secretary of state with responsibility for managing and coordinating relations with Japan, Korea, China, Mongolia, Hong Kong, and Taiwan.

ROBERT G. SUTTER is the assistant chief, Foreign Affairs and National Defense Division, Congressional Research Service. Previously he headed the Asia–Latin American Section. Mr. Sutter has worked with the Foreign Broadcast Information Service, and the Central Intelligence Agency, Office of Current Intelligence. His most recent book is *Chinese Foreign Policy: Developments after Mao,* published in 1985.

WILLIAM T. Tow is assistant professor of international relations at the University of Southern California, specializing in Asian security affairs and U.S. foreign policy interests in alliance systems. Mr. Tow is co-editor of three books dealing with Asian security affairs, specializing in China: *China, U.S.S.R. and the West, U.S. Foreign Policy in Asia-Pacific,* and *China's Defense Policy,* with Gerald Segal.

CHUNG-LIH WU is an associate research fellow at the Institute of Economics, Academia Sinica, Taipei, and adjunct associate research fellow and chairman, Economics Division, Institute of International Relations. In addition, Mr. Wu teaches in the Department of Public Health, College of Medicine, National Taiwan University, and the Institute of Business Administration, at Chung-yuan Christian University. Mr. Wu's research focuses on the economics of health issues, price expectations, and trade.

Preface

This volume, comprising eight provocative chapters by leading analysts of China, assesses the economic and security implications of the modernization of the People's Republic of China (PRC) and Taiwan as we approach the twenty-first century. The first drafts of this book's chapters were presented at two March 1987 conferences that the American Enterprise Institute (AEI) jointly convened in Singapore with the Institute of Southeast Asian Studies and in Seoul, Korea, with the Ilhae Institute. The views expressed and the vocabulary used reflect those of each author, not necessarily those of the sponsoring institutions or the other contributors to this volume.

The revised chapters (and accompanying discussion) reflect the probing interchanges that occurred in Asia. AEI would like to express its gratitude to the director of the Institute of Southeast Asian Studies, Dr. K. S. Sandhu, and to the president of the Ilhae Institute, Dr. Kim Kihwan. Both institutes were full intellectual partners in this endeavor, and this volume benefited greatly from the collaboration and exchange. In Singapore, the superb staff led by Y. L. Lee, executive secretary, was most responsive. In Seoul, AEI would like to thank Mr. Taehyun Ha, coordinator, international programs, for his consideration and excellent arrangements.

Individually, the chapters address the following topics: the prospects for reform in the PRC amid the politics of succession; economic and political change on the island of Taiwan; the potential for Sino-American trade and economic relations; the growth outlook for the PRC's economy; the likely configurations and global significance of China's electronics and aircraft industries in the next dozen years; China's strategic role as a middle-range nuclear power; and the implications of the growth of the PRC's power for Asia and the Pacific.

Taken as a whole, the research presented in this volume leads to several important conclusions. First, Taiwan's remarkable record of growth, though perhaps it will be somewhat slower in the future than in the past, will continue. The prospects for increased internationalization of the island's economy are good, and the political system will likely be able to maintain reasonable stability as the polity moves into the post–Chiang Ching-kuo era. U.S. trade policies that put too much pressure on Taiwan's economy and polity would not serve these important objectives. It is essential that the pluralization of Taiwan's polity not exacerbate secessionist tendencies. Were this to occur, the PRC might undertake military or other initiatives that would prove contrary to the interests of the people on Taiwan and put the American polity in a quandary, with unpredictable consequences for all three.

Second, in the PRC, economic and political reform are somewhat precarious, as the Beijing elite seeks to deal with the dislocations and disequilibriums caused by previous reform efforts, all the while trying to ensure a smooth transition to the post–Deng Xiaoping era. While there is ample reason for caution in predictions about the future, recent reform efforts have improved Chinese living standards considerably, although there is a very long way to go: it is these improvements, and the widespread desire among members of the elite and citizenry alike to avoid social instability, that make continuation of economic reform policies probable.

Third, with respect to Sino-American trade, the prospects for significant future expansion are good, although total commerce between China and the United States will still remain a modest component of total U.S. trade in the year 2000. To ensure that American business shares in the growth of the China market and the significant anticipated expansion of the Chinese economy, Washington needs to avoid protectionist measures that would reduce the PRC's ability to earn the hard currency needed to import American goods. In addition, technology transfer procedures need to be further simplified, and consideration should be given to financing arrangements that would help make American exports more attractive to China; more active Export-Import Bank activity would be helpful, for example. For its part, Beijing needs to make further and effective efforts to improve the investment climate, open the domestic market, and reduce the excessive costs of doing business in the PRC.

Fourth, in the areas of advanced electronics and aircraft, China's huge domestic market ensures its own enterprises of large internal sales. By the year 2000, however, the PRC is unlikely to become a major solo producer of advanced systems that are competitive on the global market. The most feasible way for China to participate in international high technology manufacturing and trade is to develop cooperative arrangements with foreign firms and raise the domestic technological and managerial level gradually. Beijing's political and economic leaders should recognize that most complex items are no longer single-country products. China must find and nurture its niche in the international division of labor.

Fifth, turning to China as a global military actor, the expansion of the PRC's nuclear forces will likely exceed current publicly available projections, although Beijing's strategic nuclear forces will remain much behind the superpower arsenals, both qualitatively and quantitatively. Of increasing concern to Chinese leaders will be how to ensure a retaliatory capability as the superpowers forge ahead with their respective strategic defense initiatives. This worry, and the financial and opportunity costs of trying to compete in a world in which strategic defense plays an increasing role, should give China's leadership growing incentives to play a role in arms control. If China seeks security through continued expansion of its nuclear forces, this could well have consequences for American efforts to halt proliferation, particularly in Asia. Nonetheless, China's exercise of conventional and nuclear muscle will probably be quite circumspect because of the priority that Beijing attaches to internal economic objectives.

This latter point brings us back to reform and domestic politics in China. Whether the issue be stability in the Taiwan Strait, security on the Korean Peninsula, Sino-American trade, cultural, scientific, and educational exchanges, or arms control and strategic stability, the keys to managing them will be the maintenance of internal order in China and the continued presence in Beijing of leaders who believe that they have a stake in a China with a multiplicity of economic, political, and cultural ties, in all directions. A truly independent foreign policy in which economic and cultural ties dominate, as this volume indicates, would best serve American interests and the interests of a developing China.

David M. Lampton
Washington, D.C.

1
Driving beyond the Headlights: The Politics of Reform in China

David M. Lampton

The January 1987 demotion of Hu Yaobang from his post as general secretary of the Chinese Communist party, the curtailment of the freewheeling discussion of political change in the fall of 1986, the placement of older and more orthodox leaders in the propaganda, cultural, and security systems, the thrust against "bourgeois liberalization," the moves against China's most outspoken intellectuals, and the closure of several magazines and tabloids raise two fundamental questions: What accounts for these shifts? Where are reforms in China headed?

Any projections concerning China's economic and military impact in the year 2000 must be premised on certain assumptions about the political trajectory of the People's Republic of China (PRC) between then and now. This paper argues that dramatic *political system* change (beyond the limited goals of reducing the average age of cadres, promoting more competent personnel, streamlining the bureaucracy, and trying to define more clearly the respective roles of the Party and state) is unlikely, for the foreseeable future. Moreover, without change in the political system beyond those contemplated, rapid progress in economic reform will be difficult to sustain.

Nonetheless, one should also not underestimate the difficulties facing those who would seek to impede further economic reform, much less reverse China's course. The material welfare of most Chinese has risen considerably over the past decade, and the policies associated with Mao Zedong in his Cultural Revolution incarnation have virtually no popular support. And, while those who criticize current economic reform efforts have identified many defects, they have little to offer by way of practical alternatives that could provide a

I would like to thank Christopher Clarke, John Fuh-sheng Hsieh, Albert Keidel, Arthur H. Rosen, Roger W. Sullivan, and Friedrich Wu for their helpful comments on an earlier draft of this paper. I am responsible for any errors of fact or interpretation which may remain.

focus for either elite or popular consensus. Finally, in the past decade many younger and more educated leaders have been promoted throughout the central and local hierarchies—they presumably would resist wholesale abandonment of the reform effort. In a nutshell, while we identify social and leadership groups below whose values and interests have been offended in some ways by specific reform initiatives, no cohesive opposition to reform per se has yet emerged. The prognosis for the immediate future is, therefore, for continued debate and political positioning, as all eyes are turned upward to see how the leadership issue will be resolved. This will remain so until at least the Thirteenth Party Congress now scheduled for fall 1987. Even after that, the prognosis is that muddling through will be the order of the day.

Recent events have their origins in three fundamental processes. First, political *control* has been one of two major internal goals of all Chinese regimes in the twentieth century. China (indeed any system) has only four broad alternative means by which to achieve control, each of which has specific liabilities in the Chinese setting. "Socialism with Chinese characteristics" will be a mixed control system in which *the bureaucracy will always loom very large.*

Second, this resultant bureaucracy conflicts with the second enduring Chinese objective—to achieve economic efficiency and high rates of material growth. To overcome bureaucratic inertia and spur economic expansion, Chinese leaders periodically have been, and will continue to be, driven to decentralize financial resources and managerial authority; sometimes they have also sought to introduce market forces. These measures inevitably produce inequalities, social mobilization, demands for further economic and political change, and extensive corruption.

Finally, this social mobilization, the demands for further social and economic reform, the dissatisfactions resulting from inequalities, and the corruption generate opposition in three quarters. First are those, in both the leadership *and* the public at large, who simply fear that political order will break down in the absence of clear patterns of authority. Second, the decentralization efforts and attempts to introduce market forces have distributional consequences and breed corruption, which offend the tangible economic interests of large groups in the populace and offend traditional cultural norms. Third, the interests of the large bureaucracies, territorial jurisdictions, and the Communist party are jeopardized.

The problems reform faces, therefore, are not merely that the state and Party structures impede it, although that is true enough.

The deeper problem is that the mass itself desires a set of goals among which are sharp internal contradictions: political order, high rates of growth, economic security and well-being, distributional fairness, and the maintenance of traditional social and cultural patterns. Consequently, *every* policy gyration meets *some* of the deeply felt needs of at least some segments of the Chinese populace at the same time that those very shifts make unlikely the attainment of others. There is no fulcrum of enduring stability.

These basic features of the Chinese system have the following implications: China is likely to have an ever-bigger bureaucracy as time progresses; the expanded use of market forces will proceed slowly; policy oscillations will be frequent, sometimes abrupt;[1] and the PRC will remain a leadership-dependent system in the sense that who the leader is will remain of critical importance—a stable succession process will be most difficult to institutionalize. And reform could easily become synonymous with corruption in the eyes of many in both the elite and the populace at large.

In the following pages, we shall look at the dilemmas of control facing the Chinese, the social forces that question reform, and the specific considerations that provided the impetus to the December 1986 and January 1987 events.

Dilemmas of Control

In attempting to rule, *every* political system has only four broad ways in which to exert control and acquire necessary information: hierarchical (bureaucratic) command systems; bargaining systems in which large-scale organizations (groups and bureaucracies) make deals among themselves; voting systems in which expressions of popular preferences provide information and resolve issues; and market systems in which economic preferences expressed in the marketplace provide information and "automatically" make decisions.[2] Although all societies use each of these mechanisms to greater or lesser extents, China, both traditionally and in its post-1949 incarnation, has placed overwhelming reliance upon bureaucratic and bargaining mechanisms.

Chinese leaders have eschewed popular voting because the cultural and educational basis for such a system has not existed and because of the fear that expressed mass preferences would diverge greatly from elite desires.[3] Consequently, all mainland Chinese political regimes have looked with apprehension upon popular voting as a solution to the control problem. Even liberals in China today are deeply distrustful of what popular sovereignty would mean given the fact that 80 percent of the population is rural and that illiteracy is very substantial. One PRC intellectual recently confided to me that if the peasants were asked to vote they would probably choose autocracy— perhaps Mao Zedong!

Market mechanisms have been eschewed because to increase the role of the market is to weaken central political and planning control. China is still sufficiently close to the subsistence line that many in both the leadership and the society are risk averse. The costs of mistakes can be very high, and many Chinese simply do not trust Adam Smith's "invisible hand" to make the "right" choice every time. Moreover, there has been an enduring fear (before and after 1949) that market mechanisms invite foreign penetration of the Chinese economy and polity in ways that work to China's disadvantage. Too, there is the widespread recognition that to decentralize economic control is to give rise to political demands among the new groups that acquire economic leverage. Finally, there is the pervasive concern that market mechanisms do not necessarily produce "fair" distributional results.

These deeply ingrained fears, inhibitions, and sociocultural proclivities concerning voting and market mechanisms mean that *any* mainland Chinese regime would place relatively heavy emphasis on hierarchical or command mechanisms—the fact that the PRC is a Marxist-Leninist-Stalinist institutional system and a centrally planned economy serves only to exacerbate this fear and to give the institutional and political forces in favor of bureaucratic command still greater weight. It is no accident that even though the reform drive has repeatedly called for a reduction in the size of the bureaucracy, the institutional apparatus has relentlessly expanded. The Party's theoretical journal, *Red Flag*, recently acknowledged that "for many years we have carried out the work of streamlining the administrative structure, but the number of organs has not reduced but increased."[4] The number of official personnel has predictably expanded as well. When the campaign to reduce the size of the state bureaucracy was launched in 1982, there were 19 million state cadres; at last count this number had jumped to 24 million. Similarly, in 1980 there were about 38 million members of the Chinese Communist party—that number now is reportedly 44 million.[5]

This brings us to bargaining, that is, mutual accommodation among large organizations, bureaucracies, and territorial administrations. Bureaucracy, with all the ills well known both to us and to the Chinese, inevitably leads organizations to bargain with each other to introduce speed and flexibility into the system. Because of the inherent rigidities of a centrally planned economy, units and localities at all levels must bargain to overcome endemic material scarcities and blockages.

Because of the great profusion of state and Party organizations, the bargaining process is of great complexity—a veritable treadmill.[6] The most eloquent description I have seen of the Chinese bureaucratic system was provided by an official of the Shenyang Branch of the Chinese People's Construction Bank in August 1986:

> Assuming that the current procedure of assessing and approving construction projects consists of two lines (in effect there are definitely more than two) and eight examination and approval departments (in reality there are more than eight departments) such as planning, finance, banking, materials and resources, construction, land control, assembling, and the department in charge, and also assuming that under each department there are two bureaus and under each bureau there are two relevant offices and under these offices there are two people responsible for making relevant comments (in reality, generally speaking, there are more than this number of relevant departments and people), then each procedure on a project has to go through the hands of eight times two plus two to the second power plus two to the third power equals 112 people and two procedures mean 224 people are involved. If the documents stay in the hands of each person for only 1 day, a total of 224 days will be required for clearance. During this period, each person has a veto power but nobody can make a final decision. If one person casts a veto, then the turnover will have to be repeated.[7]

Any official trying to expedite "his" project through this maze finds himself being forced to strike bargains with a variety of horizontal equals over whom he has little or no direct control.

Moreover, given the absence of an effective legal system, few decisions are permanent, few outcomes are final. This, then, is the origin of many of the frustrations that foreigners encounter in China. It is unclear who can speak definitively, who can commit the many relevant actors to a fixed course of action. One never has certainty that today's negotiating outcome will be a guide to tomorrow's behavior or demands. Capitalist foreigners long for a command system that is more predictable and less arduous to deal with.

This bargaining aspect of the Chinese system has several implications. Most important, when bargaining facilitates cooperation, it is in the public interest, and this is essential, proper, and good; when it promotes the interests of those involved, it quickly becomes corruption. The line between legitimate behavior and corruption is a thin one. Since financial and many material resources have been shifted to the lower levels of the system since 1978, this line frequently has been crossed. This corruption, in turn, can erode *both* mass and elite support for continued reform.

The second important implication of a bargaining system is that those with leverage will do best. In the Chinese case, these will be bureaucratic and territorial (Party) officials,[8] those with "connections" *(guanxi)*, those who have access to scarce commodities (iron, steel, hotels, services, and automobiles, for example), and those with comparatively high education levels. As *People's Daily* explained,

> Within "connection networks," the law of exchange generally works. In other words, today you abuse your power to help me seek private gains. Tomorrow, I will "give you a plum in return for a peach." I will also abuse my power to help you seek private gains. The practice of exchanging power for goods, exchanging goods for power, and exchanging power for power and goods for goods is extensively pursued and injures the public interest to profit the private interest, and lines one's pockets with public funds.[9]

In a bargaining system in an authoritarian setting, therefore, prevalent perceptions that outcomes reflect power distributions rather than equity or fairness are inevitable. In a twist of fate, reform can easily be seen as unfair if the central authorities are unable to maintain sufficient control of distributional outcomes and if middle and lower-level officials are not disciplined.

To summarize, severe cultural, institutional, and political inhibitions work against the large-scale introduction of voting and market mechanisms. Second, because of the rigidities of the centralized, hierarchical command mode of control, the central elite has been periodically driven to allow, if not encourage, a substantial amount of bargaining among bureaucracies and territories, particularly in the economic realm. Third, this bargaining can easily produce widespread corruption, particularly when the control over significant economic resources is shifted downward in the system as a result of decentralization or the introduction of market forces.

Moreover, permitting territorial and bureaucratic leaders to deal with one another (and foreigners) means that reform in a bargaining system can mislead the foreigner (or Chinese citizen) into believing that a definitive decision is at hand when, in reality, closure will never be reached. Finally, loss of central control and corruption provide the pretext that central authorities (particularly the Party) can use to reassert their dominance.

The Fallout from Reform

The events of January 1987 not only reflect the above-mentioned generalized dilemmas of control, but also are a consequence of the specific economic, social, and political repercussions from the economic and political reforms.

When reform focused on changes in the agricultural system in the late 1970s and early 1980s, the lot of enormous numbers of persons improved while the interests of comparatively few were damaged. Peasants were asked simply to do what they always had wanted to do—be left alone. Farmers were to be paid more for their goods, and food prices for urbanites were to remain low and stable. Even rural cadres could adapt to their reduced control because the loosened economic structure afforded them opportunities to use their connections to enrich themselves. The only loser in the arrangement was the state that became saddled with budget-busting subsidies.

When reform moved from the countryside to the urban areas (at the Third Plenum of the Twelfth Central Committee in late 1984), some of the immediate interests of large numbers of managers, workers, urbanites in general, and Party cadres were threatened. When the state was driven to relieve itself of tremendous subsidy burdens by raising food and other prices, still more people (both consumers and managers) became alarmed. When (in the summer of 1986) some reformers, students, and intellectuals began to assert that fundamental changes in the political system (beyond the limited ones that Deng had sanctioned in the early 1980s) were preconditions for further change in the urban economic system, the privileged positions of many of the tens of millions of state and Party cadres were threatened. Particularly alarming to many Party cadres and senior officials were reformist calls for a diminution of Party control over state organs and enterprises and calls for accelerated retirements. Finally, when intellectuals and students used the demands for political change to suggest that the Communist party was part of the problem, the limit had been reached. Hu Yaobang and his associates had committed the cardinal sin of politics by overrunning their political support. They were driving beyond their headlights.

These extremely tough issues must now be resolved in the context of a process in which the major political groupings are posturing themselves in anticipation of Deng Xiaoping's death, the passing of much of the Standing Committee of the Politburo, and the approaching demise of many of the senior leaders in the Central Advisory Commission.

Disquiet with reform comes from two principal directions: elite bureaucratic and territorial interests that have been negatively affected and social strata (particularly in urban areas) that have come to associate reform with diminished economic security. The issues are power and individual security.

Bureaucratic and Territorial Interests. *Agricultural systems.* Agriculture is widely viewed in China and abroad as one of the bright spots in China's reform effort, and overall a stunning increase in the gross value of agricultural output has occurred since 1978. Nonetheless, diversifying China's agriculture and giving peasants considerable discretion in determining what to grow and where to devote their efforts have resulted in several negative consequences, most notable of which are the increasing difficulty of inducing peasants to grow grain and insufficient investments in land and agricultural infrastructure. Moreover, using higher prices to solicit desired behavior translates either into higher government subsidies or urban inflation, which could produce instability.[10]

Not surprisingly, the bureaucratic interests that have always been concerned with "balance" and predictability look with considerable anxiety at present agricultural policies. Grain production figures for 1984, 1985, and 1986 (407.3 million tons, about 380 million tons, and about 390 million tons, respectively) provide a convenient club that the bureaucrats and skeptics of reform can use to beat the reformers. The "drastic" reduction in grain acreage between 1978 and 1985 provides additional ammunition for those arguing for more planning.[11]

In a revealing article entitled "A Latent Danger Not to Be Ignored," *Liaoning Daily* said,

> Some peasants without high enthusiasm for engaging in agricultural production have made fewer investments in farmlands. . . . The pace of agricultural modernization slows down. Major indicators are that agricultural production is not steady and the province lacks sufficient reserve strength to promote agricultural production. The total grain output [in Liaoning] in 1985 showed a drop of 31.5 percent from that of 1984. All this indicates that the argument in which a latent danger exists in our province's agricultural production is not alarmist talk. . . . Of course it is a dangerous situation. . . . Some comrades [the reformists?] hold that the only way to stabilize and develop agricultural production is to ask the state to make more investment . . . and to raise the prices of agricultural products. This situation must be changed. . . .

In order to eliminate the danger hidden in agricultural production . . . the Party committees and governments [the
bureaucrats] at all levels should . . . change the blind situation in which "we think of agriculture when we are hungry
but forget it when we eat our fill." We must . . . eliminate
lopsidedness in our ideologies and working methods. . . .[12]

In June 1986 Deng Xiaoping pointed out that, "in agriculture, the
main problem is grain. If agriculture suffers a setback, the problem
cannot be solved in 3–5 years."[13] In speaking to the November 1986
Central Rural Work Conference, Vice-Premier and reformer Tian
Jiyun said that "in agriculture, because of weak material and technical
foundations, excessive tapping of certain resources, and the aging of
existing facilities, the ability to withstand natural disasters is deplor-
able."[14] In short, many persons, particularly the planners and agricultural bureaucrats, see great dangers in the degree to which the
production of key commodities reflects market forces over which they
have little influence. Moreover, they argue that the state treasury
cannot withstand added burdens and that more bureaucratic controls
are needed. Finally, many central officials are worried by what they
see as peasant proclivities to spend on "frivolous" consumer items
rather than to invest in future production.[15]

Financial and industrial systems. These comments bring us to the
worries of central financial authorities. Rising enterprise deficits have
slowed the rate of increase in budgetary revenues,[16] precisely at the
time when political pressures require greater expenditures. The 1986
budget was in deficit more than seven billion *yuan:*[17]

The national economy grew steadily in 1986, but more and
more enterprises fell behind in delivering tax payments and
profits to the state while increasing their expenditures. These
have affected state revenues. Given the fact that high expenditures, rooted in 1985's excessively rapid economic
growth rate, still linger, China's budget will be in the red for
1986.[18]

Also alarming is the fact that China's trade was in deficit in 1984
and 1985; 1986 witnessed a further erosion in China's hard currency
holdings. The deficit in "ordinary trade" during the first eleven
months of 1986 was US $8.6 billion. According to the *Beijing Review,*
"China's import payments exceeded export revenues in both 1984 and
1985. This resulted in a sharp drop in foreign exchange reserves. This
unfavorable situation grew worse in 1986."[19]

These financial deficits were, of course, not all attributable to reform. To some extent they reflected declining world oil prices and devaluation of the Chinese *yuan* in comparison to major currencies. These deficits, however, also reflect a disquieting inability to improve labor productivity, "declining product quality," and an environment not adequately conducive to foreign investment.[20] Regarding the latter problem, the central authorities issued a twenty-two–point document in the fall of 1986 in the hope of improving the climate for foreign investment.

The political effect of these deficits is to make cautious central financial officials exceedingly worried. Their immediate response is to tighten up on expenditures, to recentralize authority over investments and imports, and to pull in the reins. They believe the central financial system has been placed in double jeopardy by the economic reforms—the rate of revenue increase is declining while lower-level authorities and individuals are not choosing to make the investment that the central planners believe is essential for future stability and sustained growth. Moreover, local authorities and other individuals call for *more* central investment.

Military systems. China's military is not entirely happy either, seeing its ranks in the process of being reduced by about 1 million troops, many officers retired, and its budget suffering a succession of cuts. Indeed, so persistent have been the rumors of military dissatisfaction with aspects of the reform that Deputy Chief of Staff Xu Xin met foreign correspondents on April 4, 1987, specifically to deny such assertions. Absolute *yuan* expenditures for the military dropped by 25 percent from 1979 to 1981, and from 1979 to 1985 the proportion of government expenditure devoted to the military dropped by one-third, from 17.5 percent to 10.5 percent.[21] The low esteem in which the reformers are held by at least some in the military is reflected in the fact that the Military Affairs Commission continues to be headed by the aged Deng Xiaoping because none of the younger reformist leaders appear acceptable to the top brass.

Predictably enough, in January 1987 the People's Liberation Army (PLA) was quick to say that it would become a forerunner "in the struggle to oppose bourgeois liberalization."[22] The military has taken to speaking on behalf of social groups that fear price rises and unemployment and has assumed the role of grand protector of the Party under assault from hostile "bourgeois" elements.[23] The Nanjing Military Region recently issued a circular asserting that "the Communist Party of China's image is never tarnished in the eyes of the people, as some people have asserted."[24] Finally, the PLA icon of the 1960s and Cultural Revolution era, Lei Feng, is once again being praised in the mass media.[25]

Regional inequalities. As for localities and the effects of reform policies on them, the situation is unclear. Nonetheless, given the rapidity with which some inland provinces (such as Hunan, Henan, Shanxi, and Anhui)[26] appear to have adopted "antibourgeois liberalization" rhetoric, some cleavage between inland and coastal areas seems to be apparent, a division that has been of tremendous political significance throughout the Communist era. One deputy to the spring 1987 National People's Congress (NPC) from Gansu province observed that "there seems to have been a tendency for the gap between the region [Gansu] and the developed coastal areas to become wider."[27]

Recently released data reveal that the 1985 per capita money income of urban dwellers in east China averaged 810 *yuan,* the incomes of those in the central provinces averaged 655 *yuan,* and those in the west 708 *yuan.*[28] If one were to consider the public services and fringe benefits provided eastern urban dwellers, the "real" income differential would be considerably greater, although inflation has been higher in the east than elsewhere, thereby offsetting some of these disparities. The pattern of peasant incomes among regions looks much the same, although 1985 Chinese data indicate a very small narrowing of the gap in regional percentages—the gap in absolute *yuan* narrowed less.[29] The diet (particularly of highly prized items such as meat, poultry, fish, and dairy products) of those living in east China is considerably better than that of their urban counterparts in the central and western provinces. As for consumer items such as refrigerators, televisions, and music systems, easterners (per household) have more of these items than do residents of the central and western provinces.[30] Finally, between one-half and two-thirds of those students and scholars now enjoying the prized opportunity of studying in the United States have current addresses in Beijing, Shanghai, and Guangdong.[31]

These data suggest that regional inequalities may be providing some of the impetus for a reassertion of central control, because disadvantaged provinces can hope that the central authorities will protect their interests in a way that market forces and the logic of international comparative advantage will not. More research is needed on this point.

This brings us to the Chinese Communist party. In trying to overhaul China's economy, at least some of the reformers (Hu Yaobang, for example) concluded that fundamental changes in the political system were required if economic growth was to be sustained, changes beyond Deng's initiatives to promote younger and more competent cadres and efforts to delineate and separate the functions of state and Party organs. To propose such expanded political reform is to call for diminished Party power; this logic was lost on neither China's intellectuals nor on much of the Party apparatus. Throughout the last quarter of 1986, *People's Daily* was paraphrasing Lord Acton, saying that "power corrupts; and absolute power corrupts absolutely. . . . The history of our Party has also furnished us with distinct examples in this regard. To stop the possible emergence of corruption resulting from an overconcentration of power, we must adopt practical and effective measures."[32] In another major *People's Daily* piece, one historian said,

> Marxism is a set of guiding principles for the country's political activities, but it is not the conductor's baton in academic studies. Marxism is a science, not a branch of theology that can dominate and lord it over science. The disputes between Marxism and non-Marxist ideologies can be settled only through free discussion.[33]

Not only was *People's Daily* carrying what heretofore would have been considered heterodox ideas, a multitude of widely read publications were printing daring discussions of topics such as the utility of multiparty systems, the need for checks and balances and separation of political powers, the need to recognize the pluralism of interests in society, the lessons of the Watergate affair for political leaders, the need to divide power to prevent its abuse, the importance of constitutional limits, the need for humanist values, the appropriateness of Maslow's theory of the hierarchy of human needs ("self-realization"), and the need for media to be independent of the regime. Media "run by trade unions, the Youth League, women's federations, government departments, or other organizations should consider the interests of their own readerships. . . . Editors or editorial boards should have the right to decide what to publish."[34]

One other demand threatened the Party—intellectual calls for "democracy." To an indeterminant extent, intellectual calls for democracy in December 1986 and early January 1987 reflected both the power of democratic ideals *and* a historic sense of mission among Chinese intellectuals, a sense that their power or influence should be commensurate with their learning. In the finest Confucian tradition, knowledge and virtue should confer on their possessor the right to rule and an obligation to bring his knowledge to bear in the service of the state and society. Intellectual demands for democracy were becoming a demand for intellectual rule, an obvious challenge to a Communist party with a far different social basis.

Fang Lizhi, a well-known astrophysicist, now former vice-president of the Science and Technology University in Anhui province and one of the most prominent victims of the January 1987 crackdown, was the most articulate spokesman for the proposition that intellectuals have a duty to stand up to political authority and shape public policy in light of their knowledge. After a trip to Italy, Fang gave an interview in mid-November 1986 in which he said that the pay and conditions of Chinese intellectuals were second lowest in the world, ahead of only Cambodia. He went on to argue that "in the present-day society, knowledge and information represent the most advanced productive forces. Since these forces are mastered by intellectuals, it is natural that intellectuals are the leading force of the society."[35] A Communist might well ask, What then is to be the leading role of the vanguard party? Fang said,

> Chinese intellectuals should straighten up their bent backs. They should not be completely obedient to the higher level, or wait for orders from "above" when dealing with things, still less place their fate on the favor bestowed by certain officials. Fang Lizhi maintained that once intellectuals show their independent character, they will demonstrate their strength immediately. This is because "knowledge means strength."[36]

To summarize, economic reform had alarmed many bureaucrats and central leaders in the agricultural, financial, industrial, and military systems. Inland provinces, which, in general, have benefited less from the open policy than the coastal areas, have reason to be dissatisfied. When, in the last quarter of 1986, the reformers and intellectuals took on the Party, they had truly overreached themselves. The words uttered by Liu Zaifu, director of the Institute of Literature of the Chinese Academy of Social Sciences, in a July 1986 interview, were a straw in the wind: "I expect that in a certain period to come, the cultural concept of 'taking class struggle as the key link' and socialist humanitarianism will be the fundamental cultural clashes in our nation's life."[37]

The policy and personnel changes of early 1987 not only represent the outcome of elite, territorial, and bureaucratic politics, but also reflect the anxieties of broad sections of the populace. It is to their apprehensions that we now turn.

The Concerns of Society about Individual Security. The basic desires of many urban Chinese in the PRC are fundamentally incongruous with the needs of an economy that is efficient by Western standards. For the urban Chinese, economic security is the overriding priority.

13

Mass social values in the PRC are, in considerable measure, risk averse. The findings of a recent poll of young persons in twenty-three cities throughout the country support this view. This poll revealed that 65.6 percent of those surveyed agreed with the following statement: "The government should take care of everything in people's lives"; 84.1 percent agreed that "it's better to let the state cover our pension and medical care than to have to worry about it ourselves."[38] The results of another poll, this one taken in Fujian province in April 1986, summed up the findings as follows: "The poll questionnaires also reflect that the masses in Fujian bitterly hate the practice of 'eating from one big pot,' but they are not well prepared mentally for the risks that reform may bring about."[39] In speaking of popular fears concerning an economy in which supply and demand determine price, one PRC report said of the Chinese people, "They are psychologically unprepared to accept normal price changes. This is one of the important reasons for the difficulties faced by the current price reform."[40]

This cultural milieu, however, clashes with the premise of the reformers, which is that a certain degree of personal insecurity is essential to spur economic performance—to provide incentives. As the *Beijing Review* observes, "Some worry that once job competition is encouraged, there will be an unemployment problem. This is not a bad thing. Once a worker feels a sense of crisis, he will be forced to study and to work hard."[41] This incongruity between the needs of the economy and the apprehensions of the urban mass is part of the reason why the discussion over a "bankruptcy law" in China has been so heated and protracted. In the end, it is not only managers that have a vested interest in keeping "inefficient" industrial and commercial enterprises running (indeed in the first eleven months of 1986, the profits of commercial enterprises *declined* 54.4 percent),[42] but also workers themselves resist change.

In one heated discussion of the bankruptcy law, *Gongren Ribao* reported that "a small number of people hold the view" that the law will lead to unemployment and that older and unskilled workers "will remain jobless for a period of time, being unable to find new employment."[43] Because factories and enterprises do not yet actually possess independent decision-making authority, many managers and workers felt that to hold them accountable for economic performance over which they had little control was like using the "stick" on a powerless "daughter-in-law." "If issuing orders and commands can be an excuse for immunity from responsibility for bankruptcy, while the workers of a failed enterprise suffer the consequences, then it is really unfair."[44]

Not only were workers concerned about preserving their job

security, but since 1980 a revived subgroup among workers has been growing—"contract laborers." These laborers have no permanent employment rights with enterprises, frequently they are seasonal workers from the countryside, and they have few of the fringe benefits reserved for permanent employees. During the Cultural Revolution this subset of workers was one of the most antiestablishment groups among red rebel factions.[45] Resurrection of the contract labor system reintroduces this element of instability into labor-management relations; some people oppose the system on ideological grounds: "Some comrades equated labor contracts under socialism with those under capitalism, or considered that the labor contract system would weaken the status of laborers as masters of the country."[46]

Another important cleavage is developing within the urban laboring community; some workers in state-run enterprises perceive that "owners of private enterprises" have rapidly growing incomes while their own enterprises are in difficulty and their income potential is limited, if not precarious. An interview with a ship fitter in Wenzhou is particularly revealing. He said, "Owners of private enterprises in Wenzhou are getting rich while we workers [in state enterprises] can only lead a life on the margins with just enough to eat and wear. Our fate is closely linked to the fate of the enterprise. I have no capital nor any social connections to help me start a new career. Anyway, I don't dare give up my job."[47]

It is these working class fears and divisions, and the elite's apprehension that they could develop into a worker-student alliance under the banner of "democracy," that accounts for the immediate arrest of workers who expressed support for (or "incited")[48] the student demonstrations. One man who had been dismissed by his factory in Guizhou province was arrested after allegedly having incited students in Guangzhou, Shanghai, and Beijing.[49] One Chinese told me that the students missed a large opportunity to gain support by not joining with workers; this is the nightmare of the Party leadership. It was this spectre that helps account for the speed with which Hu Yaobang was replaced and the power that antireform elements of the leadership were able to exert in the first half of 1987.

Experiments in insecurity, such as the bankruptcy law and contract labor systems, are a result not only of reformist zeal but also of Western influence. State Councilor Gu Mu said,

> As for some new conditions of the current economic structural reform such as the implementation of the "lease system" . . . and the enforcement of the "Bankruptcy Law" within some enterprises that produced poor returns, they all

15

have something to do with new concepts resulting from China's opening to the outside world.[50]

In the minds of many there is a close connection between opposing reform and opposing Western influence. Attacks against "spiritual pollution" and "bourgeois liberalization" may be little more than acceptable covers for jabs at foreign concepts that threaten the tangible economic interests of vast sectors of the society. It is in this context that one must assess the regime's crackdown statement that "wholesale westernization advocates capitalism and is against socialism."[51]

Workers are not the only urban social group to have anxieties: consumers fear future price rises and resent those that have already occurred, despite regime attempts to soften the impact of these increases by providing cushioning subsidies. In 1985, the overall price index rose 8.8 percent, and in 1986 it rose a further 6 percent. It is important to note that this inflation did not result simply from price reform. In late 1984 and 1985, decisions to peg future wage bonus and bank lending levels to current spending rates encouraged sudden jumps in bonus payments and bank lending. This put an enormous volume of extra money into circulation, money that a consumption-starved public used to compete for a constrained supply of goods.

While the rate of inflation dropped somewhat in 1986 and although these rates seem tolerable to Westerners who have experienced higher rates of increase, such price rises alarm conservative Chinese leaders who climbed to power in the wake of a hyperinflation that the Kuomintang was unable to tame. Moreover, the reformers have repeatedly called for *further* upward adjustments in the prices of food, fuel, housing, and basic industrial and consumer items in order to cut government subsidy burdens and to ensure that prices more accurately reflect scarcity values:

> Experience has shown it is unrealistic to expect there to be no price increases in the course of the reform. Without them there could be no reform, which is aimed at boosting the prices of some important commodities that have been kept artificially low in the past. . . . This being so there will inevitably be an increase in the general level of commodity prices.[52]

One Beijing lady summed up her view: "Prices keep going up and up. I wonder when it will end."[53] Among some of the students involved in the December 1986 and January 1987 demonstrations, tuition hikes and rising fees were a concern. Predictably, in late December, amid the student demonstrations and fear of a worker-student alliance, the central government announced that prices would remain stable throughout 1987.[54]

One other aspect of the reforms needs to be underscored: their *deregulatory* character. Allowing individuals and cooperative groups to engage in new forms of economic activity caused an explosion of new entrants into industries that had previously been monopolized by state enterprises. This influx had many consequences, including unwelcomed competition for the state sector. Because this entrepreneurial activity was released without precautions having been taken to establish an adequate regulatory apparatus to replace the former direct central control, there was a marked increase in fraudulent products and a decline in worker safety.[55] These consequences did not add to the public luster of reform.

Concisely, reform, particularly the speed with which it was being implemented, not only threatened the power interests of the Communist party, important bureaucratic systems, and major localities, but also offended the perceived interests of an indeterminant share of China's urban populace. To attribute the early 1987 policy and personnel changes solely to bureaucratic self-interest is to make the problem of change in China simpler than it, in fact, is. In reality, much of the populace has now developed an interest in the security that "inefficiency" can confer. At the same time, there is virtually no social support for the policies of restriction, closure, and autarky characteristic of the late Maoist period.

It is against the backdrop of these elite and mass forces that we now turn to a brief analysis of the December demonstrations and the January 1987 policy and personnel changes. What are the implications of these events?

Positioning for the post-Deng Era

Above I have analyzed recent events in the dispassionate terms of political science: dilemmas of control and the ebb and flow of social forces. No less important, however, what we see unfolding in China today is a struggle over who, and what line, will dominate in the post-Deng Xiaoping era. One Chinese acquaintance described the process now under way as like *nei gong,* a form of kung fu in which the combatants look as though they are moving in slow motion, no contact is made, but each participant's placid exterior masks subsurface volcanic forces.

The student demonstrations of December 1986 and January 1987 provided opponents of reform with the immediate rationale to oust Hu Yaobang and squelch talk of fundamental political change. The

17

demonstrations alone did not cause his ouster, however; this had been in the works for the previous six months. The reformers had sustained an important series of setbacks throughout the summer and fall of 1986, and those had their origins in the forces analyzed in the preceding sections.

Every summer, China's elite takes a respite from the heat, dust, and noise of Beijing and moves to Beidaihe, which in effect becomes the summer capital. In the summer of 1986, the period in Beidaihe was used to prepare for the upcoming Sixth Plenum of the Twelfth Central Committee, which was to meet in late September. Four items were on the agenda, and each was important given the constellation of political forces and problems analyzed above: (1) reform of the political structure; (2) the retirement of senior leaders and discussion of their possible replacements in anticipation of the upcoming Thirteenth Party Congress; (3) review of the economic reform and "open" policies; and (4) "the building of spiritual civilization" (ideology).[56]

No consensus could be reached on the first three issues without first agreeing on the political "line," that is, ideology. Consequently, the "draft resolution regarding the building of spiritual civilization" became the dominant agenda item. Throughout the Beidaihe meetings, those with concerns about market-oriented economic reform, political reform, and extensive Westernization called for the focus of attention at the Sixth Plenum and thereafter to be on "opposing bourgeois liberalization."

Hu Yaobang played a lead role in trying to divert the focus from "bourgeois liberalization." In the end, those (Chen Yun, Bo Yibo, Hu Qiaomu, Deng Liqun, and Deng Xiaoping, for example) promoting the concept that "bourgeois liberalization" was the principal problem prevailed.[57] In breaking with this group of senior leaders (particularly Deng Xiaoping), Hu Yaobang had overrun his support base in the key area of ideology. Zhao Ziyang, according to the available *Cheng Ming* report, did not choose to buck the Party elders on this decisive issue.[58] Although the "Resolution of the Central Committee of the Communist Party of China on the Guiding Principles for Building a Socialist Society with Advanced Culture and Ideology," adopted on September 28, 1986, was comparatively moderate, it did mark a reassertion of Leninist ideological values, the primacy of the Party, and the importance of Communist ideals.

This, then, is the context in which the December 1986 and January 1987 student demonstrations erupted—a weakened reformist leadership, a Hu Yaobang that was already in serious trouble with his patron, a Hu Yaobang that had already made several foreign policy missteps on previous occasions, a summer of strident intra-elite debate, increasingly fundamental critiques of the economic and political system by both Party and non-Party intellectuals, and mixed year-end economic performance indicators.

Those who opposed aspects of reform found the student demonstrations made to order to launch an attack not only on Hu Yaobang, but also against reform efforts more broadly. For those concerned about public security, the student disturbances, crime, and the potential for a worker-student alliance were alarming symptoms that pointed to the danger of further political liberalization and the risks inherent in economic reform. For those concerned about the explosive impact of price rises, the calls for lower inflation among students and urbanites strongly argued against further change in the price system, at least for a while. For the Party propaganda agencies, calls for multiparty systems were indicative of what lay in store for the Communist party if it failed to step in.[59] And those who opposed wholesale Westernization saw in the student demonstrations a concrete manifestation of the corrosive implications of extensive foreign penetration of Chinese society.

Concisely, the student demonstrations did not cause the January changes; they simply provided the powerful compelling political rationale for them. The demonstrations became a mirror in which each group that was worried about reform saw a different frightening visage.

The dismissal of Hu Yaobang from his position as Party general secretary (mid-January 1987), the dropping of three prominent intellectuals from the Party (Fang Lizhi, Wang Ruowang, and Liu Binyan), the replacement of Zhu Houze by Wang Renzhi in the Propaganda Department, the closure of several periodicals, and the media's reemphasis on the need for central planning in the economy all shook the confidence of both foreigners and intellectuals in China, not to mention Chinese students studying in the United States and pondering whether this was the time to return to their homeland.

In an attempt to reassure these audiences, Premier and Acting General Secretary General Zhao Ziyang told senior Party and military leaders on January 29, 1987, that "the current work of opposing bourgeois liberalization will be strictly limited to the Chinese Communist Party and will be conducted mainly in the political ideological field." "The work will not be conducted in rural areas," he added, and "in enterprises and institutions only positive education will be carried out."[60] Because Party fractions are in all major units and because intellectuals know well that their work is in the political and ideological fields, if the Party so wishes to consider that to be the case, Zhao's statement did little to dispel anxieties. In a further bid to

19

reduce the apprehensions of domestic and foreign groups, a broad array of China's officials answered foreign press questions in open forums during the spring 1987 session of the National People's Congress.

Conclusion

Reform in China now is at a crossroads, with an eighty-two–year old man at the wheel. Power among groups on the ruling Politburo is divided, and the delicate balance that existed prior to Hu's ouster is more precarious after his demotion. A hopeful interpretation is that the reformers, led by Hu Yaobang, had moved too rapidly and that a more circumspect central leadership could create a more enduring and sustainable basis for reform in the long run. Nonetheless, a January 3, 1987, *Guangming Ribao* column sums up the dilemma:

> We can choose between two risks in the pace of reform: One consists of speeding up the pace of reform, and the other consists of slowing it down. The former indeed carries relatively great risks, but the risks involved in the latter may be even greater. . . . This is because, first, the simultaneous existence of the new and old systems will inevitably cause chaos in the economic operational mechanism and will also provide opportunities for all kinds of unhealthy trends. Second, like a boat moving against the current, the reforms can only retreat if they do not advance, and the inertia role of habitual forces and traditional methods, together with old concepts and lines of thought that have formed over a long time, will unwittingly send the reforms into reverse. Third, if the new systems are unable to play the dominant role for a long time, this will have a psychological effect on society and cause people to lose enthusiasm and confidence for reform, and may even make people sick and tired of reform.[61]

Power over policy direction is concentrated in the Standing Committee of the Politburo, a body of five persons (four discounting Hu Yaobang). Two of the individuals (Chen Yun and Li Xiannian) are skeptical of market-style reform (much less fundamental change in the political order), and two others (Deng and Zhao Ziyang) appear more zealous in this regard. This precarious balance among a few old men, in turn, has created a situation in which those in the Politburo and other important organs (the Secretariat, the Central Advisory Commission, and the Military Affairs Commission, for instance) are positioning themselves and trying to exert influence. In such a carefully balanced situation, a single death or removal can make an enormous difference. Talk of Deng's complete retirement is not in fashion, and recently Peng Zhen, chairman of the NPC, publicly opposed Deng's retirement and was lukewarm about promoting too many young persons.[62] It is in this situation that one must interpret persistent rumors that the upcoming Thirteenth Party Congress may well be unable to resolve the succession issue fully.

In his March 3, 1987, conversation with visiting American Secretary of State George Shultz, Deng Xiaoping perhaps best summed up the current situation in China: "As far as the troubles here, they're almost finished, but maybe it will take years. They existed for a long time."[63]

Notes

1. Lucian W. Pye, "On Chinese Pragmatism in the 1980s," *China Quarterly,* no. 106 (1986), pp. 207–34.

2. Robert A. Dahl and Charles E. Lindblom, *Politics, Economics, and Welfare* (New York: Harper Torchbooks, 1963).

3. Andrew J. Nathan, *Chinese Democracy* (Berkeley: University of California Press, 1985).

4. Foreign Broadcast Information Service (hereafter *FBIS*), August 13, 1986, p. K3.

5. Beijing, *Xinhua*, in English, September 25, 1986; in *FBIS*, September 26, 1986, p. K14.

6. David M. Lampton, "Chinese Politics: The Bargaining Treadmill," *Issues and Studies*, vol. 23, no. 3 (1987), pp. 11–41.

7. *Jingji Yanjiu* [Economic Research], in Chinese, no. 11 (November 20, 1986), pp. 46–49; in *FBIS*, January 9, 1987, p. K33.

8. David Zweig, "Prosperity and Conflict in post-Mao Rural China," *China Quarterly*, no. 106 (1986), pp. 1–18, especially p. 4; see also Thomas B. Gold, "After Comradeship: Personal Relations in China since the Cultural Revolution," *China Quarterly*, no. 104 (1985), pp. 657–75.

9. *Renmin Ribao* [People's Daily], December 10, 1986, p. 1; in *FBIS*, December 18, 1986, p. K17.

10. "Food Grains Remain Important," *Beijing Review* (hereafter *BR*), no. 49 (1986), p. 4.

11. Ibid.

12. *Liaoning Ribao*, November 11, 1986, p. 1; in *FBIS*, November 28, 1986, pp. S4–5.

13. *Xinhua* Domestic Service, in Chinese, November 25, 1986; speech by Tian Jiyun, *FBIS*, November 28, 1986, p. K7.

14. Ibid., p. K5.

15. *Nongmin Ribao*, in Chinese, March 5, 1987, p. 1; in *FBIS*, March 17, 1987, p. K15.

16. Beijing, *Xinhua*, in English, December 23, 1986; in *FBIS*, December 23, 1986, p. K12.

17. Beijing, *Xinhua*, in Chinese, March 26, 1987; in *FBIS*, March 27, 1987, p. K4.

18. "China's Economic Development in 1986," *BR*, January 5, 1987, pp. 20–21.

19. Ibid., p. 21.

20. *Xinhua* Domestic Service, in Chinese, November 25, 1986; in *FBIS*, November 28, 1986, p. K5. For one highly critical appraisal of China's environment for foreign business and investment activity see, "Report on the Visit to China of the Senate Delegation led by Senator John Heinz," October 18, 1986, (Washington, D.C.: United States Government Printing Office), pp. 9–12.

21. "PLA Priorities," *BR*, no. 43 (1986), p. 16; see also *FBIS*, April 20, 1987, p. K1.

22. Hefei, Anhui Provincial Service, January 11, 1987; in *FBIS*, January 14, 1987, p. O1.

23. Ibid., O1–2.

24. Ibid., p. O2; see also speech by Yu Qiuli, *FBIS*, September 11, 1986, p. K3.

25. *Zhongguo Qingnian Bao* in Chinese, March 5, 1987, p. 1; in *FBIS*, March 19, 1987, p. K6.

26. *FBIS*, December 22, 1986, pp. K22–23; also *FBIS*, January 12, 1987, pp. R2–3.

27. Beijing, *Xinhua*, in English, March 31, 1987; in *FBIS*, April 1, 1987, p. K10.

28. "Differences in Urban Living Standards," *BR*, no. 50 (1986), pp. 21–22.

29. Beijing, *Liaowang*, in Chinese, no. 32, August 11, 1986, p. 26; in *FBIS*, August 26, 1986, pp. K18–19.

30. *BR*, no. 50 (1986), pp. 22–23.

31. David M. Lampton, with the assistance of Joyce A. Madancy and Kristen M. Williams, *A Relationship Restored: Trends in U.S.-Chinese Educational Exchanges, 1978–1984* (Washington, D.C.: National Academy Press, 1986), pp. 40–42.

32. *Renmin Ribao*, December 8, 1986, p. 5; in *FBIS*, December 17, 1986, p. K4.

33. *Renmin Ribao*, November 6, 1986, p. 3; in *FBIS*, November 13, 1986, p. K1.

34. *China Daily*, in English, September 29, 1986, p. 4; in *FBIS*, October 1, 1986, p. K13.

35. *Shijie Jingji Daobao*, in Chinese, November 24, 1986, p. 3; in *FBIS*, December 19, 1986, p. K13; for more, see also *BR*, December 15, 1986, pp. 16–17.

36. Ibid., p. K16.

37. *Zhongguo Xinwen She*, in Chinese, July 17, 1986; in *FBIS*, July 21, 1986, p. K13.

38. Beijing, *Xinhua*, in English, August 27, 1986; in *FBIS*, August 28, 1986, p. K24.

39. *Zhongguo Xinwen She*, in Chinese, November 5, 1986; in *FBIS*, November 10, 1986, p. O2.

40. Beijing, *Xinhua*, in English, April 1, 1987; in *FBIS*, April 1, 1987, p. K15.

41. *BR*, no. 35 (1986), p. 27.

42. "China's Economic Development in 1986," *BR*, no. 1 (1987), p. 20.

43. *Gongren Ribao*, in Chinese, November 15, 1986, p. 3; in *FBIS*, December 2, 1986, p. K10.

44. Ibid., p. K11.

45. John W. Lewis, "Commerce, Education, and Political Development in Tangshan, 1956–1969," in John W. Lewis, ed., *The City in Communist China* (Stanford, Calif.: Stanford University Press, 1971), pp. 153–79.

46. *Renmin Ribao*, October 24, 1986, p. 5; in *FBIS*, October 30, 1986, p. K19.

47. "Rural Changes Promote Urban Reform," *BR*, October 27, 1986, p. 21.

48. *FBIS*, January 5, 1987, p. R1; see also *FBIS*, January 2, 1987, pp. O5–6.

49. *Xinhua* Domestic Service, in Chinese, December 30, 1986; in *FBIS*, December 31, 1986, p. R3.

50. Gu Mu, in *Liaowang* Overseas Edition, in Chinese, no. 50, December 15, 1986, pp. 3–6; in *FBIS*, December 24, 1986, p. K10.

51. "The Slogan Wholesale Westernization Is Entirely Wrong," *Gongren Ribao*, December 30, 1986, p. 1; in *FBIS*, January 5, 1987, p. K14.

52. "Price Reform Essential to Growth," *BR*, August 18, 1986, p. 17.

53. "Milk Price Goes Up in Beijing," *BR*, November 3, 1986, p. 11.

54. *New York Times*, December 31, 1986.

55. *FBIS*, August 12, 1985, p. 6 and O2; August 12, 1985, pp. K18–19; August 14, 1985, pp. K13–14; January 31, 1986, p. K15; April 1, 1986, pp. K27–28; and *BR*, February 3, 1986, p. 27.

56. *Cheng Ming*, in Chinese, no. 109, November 1, 1986, pp. 6–10; in *FBIS*, November 18, 1986, p. K1.

57. Ibid., pp. K1–5.

58. Ibid., p. K3. It needs to be pointed out that opposition to Hu Yaobang also centered on issues beyond those that one associates with reform. There was considerable resentment that Hu Yaobang had favored long-time associates in promotions (for instance, Qiao Shi, Wu Xueqian, Hu Qili, Wang Zhaoguo, and others). Also, Hu had a penchant for making remarks in public (particularly on foreign policy) that then created difficulties and necessitated an exhaustive round of "clarifications." Finally, there was a sense that Hu had failed to develop an integrative ideology that would provide a stable basis for future reform efforts.

59. See, for example, *Renmin Ribao*, November 17, 1986, p. 5; in *FBIS*, November 20, 1986, p. K15. This article argues that Chinese Marxism has been "tainted" by militarism and feudalism and needs to be "modernized" in light of the advanced experiences of capitalism and progress in science and technology.

60. *New York Times*, January 30, 1987.

61. Hong Kong, *Zhongguo Tongxun She*, in Chinese, January 3, 1987; in *FBIS*, January 9, 1987, p. K30. This is a report of an article appearing in *Guangming Ribao*. Sounding the same theme is an article by Wu Jinglian entitled, "Some Views on the Choice of a Strategy for Reform," in *Jingji Yanjiu*, in Chinese, no. 2, February 20, 1987, pp. 3–14; in *FBIS*, April 22, 1987, pp. K15–33.

62. *Ta Kung Pao*, April 9, 1987, pp. 2–3; in *FBIS*, April 10, 1987, pp. K6–8.

63. *New York Times*, March 4, 1987.

Commentary

John Fuh-sheng Hsieh

I think it is very important to distinguish between political and economic reforms as we talk about opposition to the reforms, since the opposition may not come from the same sources for different types of reforms. I think Dr. Lampton talks mainly about economic rationality, such as the concern with job security, as the source of opposition. True, it is very important; however, some other sources should also be dealt with, for instance, ideological and cultural considerations. Some people may dislike the reform programs because they contradict what they believe. In addition, some people may be opposed to the reforms for fear of instability or chaos in the society.

This source of opposition is probably more relevant for political than for economic reform. Besides, the retirement policy advocated by some reformists may have contributed to opposition to the two reforms as well. This refers mainly to the job security of the senior leaders, not job security of the general public as mentioned in Mr. Lampton's paper. Only when we examine those factors we can assess the likelihood that political reform will follow in the wake of economic reform.

Finally, I agree with Mr. Lampton that the PRC will remain a leadership-dependent system.

Arthur H. Rosen

One question I might ask is, Who really understands China? Americans have faced this lack of understanding for generations, but I have concluded, however, that the Chinese themselves don't always understand what goes on in their own country. Those who visit China frequently can come up with as many answers to a single question as there are people to talk with.

Nonetheless, in discussing current issues in China with a broad range of people, I found repeatedly a kind of consensus on the impact of what has been happening to the individual: essentially there is wide agreement that what has been happening for the past six or seven years in China has been for the good, and the overwhelming mass of those who have been affected by the changes in the past several years have been affected favorably. This conclusion applies both in the rural and in the urban areas. I sense a strong bedrock of support for the new economic policies and the more liberal atmosphere, which I think the Party conservatives would be taking a serious risk to oppose.

There are many shades of gray, and what appear to be conflicts of black and white to outsiders may possibly be issues over which the pragmatists in Beijing may be unwilling to risk the political instability and chaos that affected them all just over a decade ago. After all, people like Peng Zhen were themselves victims of the cultural revolution. They are not about to stop the whole process and go in reverse, risking instability themselves.

Perhaps all of them, whether it be Deng Xiaoping, Peng, or any of the others, have been very seriously concerned to ensure the gains made in the past several years without risking the instability that can come by rocking the boat.

I believe they feared that the student demonstrations had the potential for creating instability. I question, however, whether the leaders really seriously feared that the working masses would join the students: the cleavage is just too great. The three cases of worker participation reported apparently were three rather highly disgruntled individuals, nothing like mass representation of the workers. The students marched down the streets of Shanghai, but only a couple of workers joined in and not masses of people.

Some workers may have been sympathetic, Shanghai being a far more sophisticated environment in which to operate than most of China. What we saw, however, in large measure, was a rather inert group of people who were themselves annoyed by the fact that the students were in the way. But the students themselves have also developed a stake in the status quo, and they do recognize that many improvements have been made. The problem there is that they have rising hopes, if not rising expectations, and democracy and a democratic government, which they do not quite understand, are what they want very much for China. At the same time, they are concerned about the risk of upsetting the social order.

Moreover, in the set of goals desired by the masses there are

25

sharp internal contradictions. Although Dr. Lampton mentions the importance of political order, distributional fairness, and maintenance of traditional social and cultural patterns, I suggest that these goals have never been met in China. It is not that these goals are suddenly being overturned: in fact, I argue that perhaps they are as close to realization today as they have been in the past.

To that list of goals, I would add economic well-being, which is today certainly higher among the vast majority of Chinese, especially in the rural areas, than it has been in the recent past. I think even the conservatives are very much aware of that but are worried about the cost in the future. And this fear may motivate them to slow down the engine of change.

Perhaps there is no fulcrum for enduring stability, but then that doesn't necessarily indicate ominous implications for the future. Perhaps no fulcrum for enduring stability has been present in China in this century.

I found it rather significant and perhaps troubling to note the rapid growth of the Chinese bureaucracy mentioned in the paper. Can this be true after the many stringent efforts to cut back on the bureaucracy? Do those figures included in the bureaucracy and in the increasing Party membership comprise those who have been retired from positions, for example?

In that context, mention was made earlier of the reluctance to retire as a factor in the growth of bureaucracy, but in any case my impression is that those senior members of the Party who have retired have lost none of the basic perks that might have worried them or delayed their retirement—their houses, their cars, their access to privilege because of their positions. Perhaps it may trouble them that they are not able to guarantee these same perks for their children. I would argue that *no* leaders want to risk instability in China, the potential for which exists in the student demonstrations. But one might question whether the masses would have supported the students; and it can be argued that they do have a stake in the status quo—not just the masses but just about everybody in the Party hierarchy.

The suggestion that the Party has lost—to use that old term—the hearts and minds of the intellectuals and students in China has very serious implications for the Party and for the future. Very few young people or those considered intellectuals even by the loosest Chinese definition have any respect today for the Party, the bureaucracy, for many Party leaders, or for the ideology itself. That lack will be the real problem for the departing leadership.

Another element that unites the young and the intellectuals is a widespread revulsion against corruption, which is becoming an extraordinarily serious problem and preoccupation. This complaint is not well voiced, but it does trouble the leadership today. And certainly some of the leaders associate this increase in corruption with the opening of the doors to the West and with political liberalization.

Dr. Lampton speaks of the struggle between who and what line will dominate in China after Deng Xiaoping. I believe it is probably less "who" than "what," because the ambitions of individuals are probably now outweighed by prudence. After all, Chinese history suggests that those who have been ambitious and hopeful, expecting to take over the leadership of the country, those who are "as close as lips and teeth," "close comrades in arms," and so on, never seem to have made it. In fact, the desire is not necessarily to see who will dominate but to see who will not dominate. It may be more obstructive than constructive.

Finally, I believe that while Deng may not have institutionalized the succession process, he and others have institutionalized the basic reforms of the urban and the rural sectors and that while there may be interruptions in fits and starts, the great mass of Chinese people (the workers, peasants, students, and intellectuals) have already developed too large a stake to risk abandoning them. And thus who comes in may not be all important since without the kind of mandate that Chairman Mao enjoyed the new order must satisfy public aspirations and popular demands.

Friedrich Wu

To accept completely Dr. Lampton's delineations of recent political developments in China, one would have to draw some fairly pessimistic conclusions regarding China's economic and political future. According to Dr. Lampton's description, the conservative coalition is so overwhelmingly formidable across such a wide spectrum that the reformists in China today would seem to have no chance to turn the political tide in their favor. It seems to me, however, that his analysis is somewhat conservatively biased.

With the benefit of hindsight, the paper concentrates on highlighting the various disruptive and unpopular aspects of the reformers' programs and the multitude of political and social groups that these programs have alienated. These political and social groups include, according to Dr. Lampton, not only veteran Politburo and Central Committee members but also a large number of military leaders and mid-level state and party cadres, as well as a sizable number of urban workers and even consumers. What is conspicuously absent in the paper is a systematic assessment of the strength of the reformers, as well as those social and economic groups that have benefited from the reformers' programs. For all we know, these could be as numerous as those who have joined the conservative coalition.

Here I am referring to the new managerial and bureaucratic elite, the intelligentsia, the scientists, the administrators of the maritime provinces as well as the special economic zones, the officials who handle China's foreign economic relations, and finally the urban entrepreneurs whose numbers are growing every day. These are the people who have developed a vested interest in China's reform programs over the years. They are also the people who possess the knowledge and the skills required to guide China into the modern world.

How do these beneficiaries of reforms react to the conservative backlash? More important, how do they weigh in the power equation in the current political struggle between conservatives and reformers in China? And with their vested interests now being directly threatened, will the beneficiaries of reforms converge to form a unified and powerful countervailing force against the conservative coalition? If so, what is the likelihood of success for the reformers' coalition to shape the eventual outcome of the current political conflict in China?

My last point addresses the problems of forecasting China's political trends. After reading Dr. Lampton's paper, and for that matter other recently published analyses of the current political scene in China, I get the distinct impression that, with the benefit of hindsight, all the major signals pointing to the eruption of a conservative backlash were well in place by mid-1986 or perhaps even earlier.

Yet I am hard pressed to find a single piece of analysis published during the second half of 1986 that warned us of an imminent conservative backlash in China. Let me just cite one example. Even a veteran China watcher like A. Doak Barnett of Johns Hopkins University wrote in *Foreign Affairs* in October 1986 that the chance for a conservative backlash in China would be highly unlikely in the near future, given the popularity of the reformers' program and the continuous consolidation of power by the reformers based on this popularity.

The question does arise how China specialists could have misread the political situation so miserably. In analyzing the Chinese political scene, must we always depend on hindsight to make sense of Chinese politics? If this were the case, then the profession of China studies has not made much progress since the 1950s despite the proliferation of so-called new concepts, theories, approaches, and methodology in political science.

Discussion

ALBERT KEIDEL: I am concerned at the casual acceptance of the notion that there has been an across-the-board conservative backlash. Can a backlash against so-called moral or ethical imports from the West, on the one hand, be separated from a backlash against technical transfers from the West, on the other?

I do not believe that a backlash in the moral dimension necessitates a backlash in the economic dimension.

ROGER W. SULLIVAN: We have focused on this backlash issue because it happens to be in the news.

At a similar seminar a few years ago someone also raised the question, Why were we wrong about China? He was referring to the conventional wisdom among government analysts and academics that in the 1978–1980 period the reforms could not possibly be adopted—and that even if they were, they could not go very far. The reason given was an entrepreneurial observation that a lot of people in the Party and in the bureaucracy would be hurt by reforms and that people do not do things that are contrary to their self-interest. Moreover, the Party and the bureaucracy, this reasoning goes, are so huge that it is impossible for the reforms to go anywhere.

The reforms did in fact go somewhere. And now I am a little distressed that Dr. Lampton argues that because the economic reform involved such change and affects people's interests that there are bound to be a lot of difficulties with it.

I think that we went wrong because we overlooked the fact that reform was seen to serve a greater interest.

When I went to China for the first time in 1973, people actually in the Party said to me that they had now concluded that the people of China would judge the Party solely by its economic performance and that they had no respect for the party in any other regard. That was one reason why the party leaders were interested in improving relations with the outside world. All Chinese leaders have been aware of this single criterion for some time, and they have been operating accordingly. They became convinced that if they could not do some-thing about the economy and were unable to raise living standards, they would lose everything. And to improve living standards and to improve the economy, they had to reform the economy. Fear was what prompted these people to cooperate, however reluctantly, in the progress of economic reform.

In the process of cooperating in economic reform, however, they were assured, and Deng Xiaoping really believes, that economic re-forms could be conducted without compromising the position of the Party. They were convinced that Deng Xiaoping would honor the commitment that economic reform would proceed without significant political reform, but then when Hu Yaobang began to look as if he were departing from that understanding, the reaction not only of the so-called conservatives, but also of Deng Xiaoping himself was strong and sudden.

COMMENT: Mike Lampton very lucidly explained who constitutes the conservative forces. But one of the weaknesses of these forces, as evident in the progression of the reform movement against consider-able opposition over the past eight or nine years, has been the appar-ent inability to coalesce around a group of leaders that they can support.

In other words, there are a lot of complainers in China, but they really do not have an alternative program that is acceptable over the long term.

DENIS FRED SIMON: I think that we've drawn the impression that somehow the conservatives are people who seek instability in China's society, resist economic growth, and want a system antithetical to the interests of Chinese progress: I think just the opposite is the case.

These conservatives want stability. They want security. In fact, I would argue that their desire to impose more control is an exact reflection of their desire to grip this whole system. They feel that things are getting out of control, that the market is really not a good model for the Chinese economy, and that political freedoms will lead to anarchy. Some in Chinese society are very much afraid of the loss of control.

Someone has made the excellent point that in China today there still continue to be two definitions of reform. One kind of reform is the one that we are most familiar with and tend to view positively: that is, the introduction of market forces and greater autonomy to decision makers and the like. Others in the decision-making structure in China, however, look at improvements in the planning structure as also part of reform: that is, how to plan better and whether to rely on centralized or decentralized planning. Nonetheless, they want to have planning. While there is not, then, a broad-based commitment to reform only in a market sense, there is a broad-based commitment to improve the planning structure.

COMMENT: I would like to address the question of reforms as opposed to insecurity. In my understanding, reforms are intended to speed up the economic growth, and economic growth introduces many inequalities. My question is whether within the social structure it is possible to deal with those inequalities. If the government cannot deliver and we are then facing great unfulfilled expectations, what are the alternatives?

COMMENT: As for inequalities in a socialist structure, I don't think the impact of the present inequalities, and they are certainly very obvious, is quite as serious as many of us may believe they are. First of all, as the old story goes, as the water rises, all ships rise with it. Some perhaps are going up faster than others. But their opportunities seem to be greater now than they have been in the past. And people are rewarded for work.

Many inequalities existed beforehand, which are often unacknowledged or overlooked. Even during the time of the Cultural Revolution, privileges were given to and protected for those people in positions of authority throughout society. A Party secretary, wherever he was in the factory, had a car, a chauffeur, and other privileges for himself. The wives of the army officers used to go shopping in the friendship store in Beijing, with their chauffeurs out in front dusting off the car, when the masses had nothing like that.

These privileges are accepted almost traditionally in China, whether they belong to the Communists or the new capitalist class. If the socialist structure had been more pure in the past, then equalities would be more striking than perhaps they are today.

MR. LAMPTON: I found the questions and points of contention very helpful. I will consolidate them into several themes as best I can.

I find Mr. Wu's comments on the issue of forecasting interesting. China watchers have failed to forecast almost every landmark. We see a good bit of post-hoc analysis so that, once we see a shift, we go back into the previous printed record to try to extract how that was the logical and foreseeable outcome. I don't know how to get around it.

This problem of forecasting is treated in a very interesting book about why the United States did not see the Iran problem coming. The author, Gary Sick, was troubled by this very issue: why we did not see that crisis coming early enough, after all the investments and comparatively good access to Iranian society, or at least to the top levels there. His analysis may shed some light on the China studies community. For people who begin to build close relationships in a society, as we have begun to do with China and as certainly the United States had with the shah in the period before his fall, it becomes too terrible for them to contemplate any substantial change that would affect the fabric of that relationship. I say this as a person who is trying to develop these relationships in China. Sometimes we become captive to them and resist many of the signs that are there.

As for the need to distinguish between reform as technological modernization and reform as cultural change, the Chinese themselves are trying to separate them, but when I consider them in tandem, I come to a somewhat more sober conclusion about reform.

As I see it, in a longer historical perspective, an argument has continued in China between *t'i* (essence) and *yong* (use) for at least a hundred years. Not long ago, Vice-Premier Li Peng, when asked about reform, said, "We want your technology, but we don't want your democracy." In other words, "Give us the things of the West— the technology—but we don't want to change culturally or politically."

In a nutshell, I don't think that's possible. I am certainly *not* one that believes that to have technological change China has to become like the United States. And yet, to attempt to insulate a culture from the logic of change, which technology requires, is futile. So I think this historical perspective is the origin of my willingness to put technological and cultural change together. I may be wrong about that. But I think one of the key questions we have to ask is, Can Chinese society introduce technology and new economic management and resist cultural and political change? And if that society will inevitably have cultural change, then the question to me is, In what direction will it change, and what are the implications of that change for political cohesion? Concerning that, I am probably as uncertain as everybody else. But I do think that the desire to insulate the culture from the effects of economic reform is the core of China's problem with modernization.

In response to the point about overreacting to rhetoric, I agree that reality is frequently much calmer than the rhetoric generated in China. Perhaps I have overreacted a bit, but I have a good reason for it. A number of my graduate students from the People's Republic of China are very worried, even alarmed, by what is occurring there.

33

Concerning the charge that reform has created inequalities, it is true that some inequalities in fact have been *reduced* by reform, one of which is the urban-rural dichotomy. With respect to Mao's commitment to overcoming urban-rural income differences, for example, reform has done more for that particular cleavage than, I would say, most of Mao's efforts. There have been other inequalities, though, that have been made worse. Within villages, for instance, the level of income inequality has frequently gone up. When we talk about the effects of reform on equality and the like, then, I think we really need to know more than we do. What we do know, however, indicates that reform is going in several directions at the same time depending on the particular aspect.

My concluding point is simply this: I do not think the evidence will unambiguously support what has been up to now a fairly optimistic scenario about stability and growth in China. In other words, if this paper pulls us back toward the center, it will have served its purpose.

2

Economic and Political Development in the Republic of China

John Fuh-sheng Hsieh and Chung-lih Wu

Economic Development

The Locus of Past Development. When Taiwan was handed back to China at the end of World War II, severe war damage had ruined almost two-thirds of the infrastructure and economy, and there was widespread distress among the population.[1] The government of the Republic of China (ROC) was faced with the task of recovering from the chaos and devastation of warfare and transforming a ravaged and backward Taiwan.

From 1949 until the end of 1952, economic efforts were chiefly concentrated on maintaining stability. Stabilizing the economy and halting inflation had become prerequisites for all financial and economic policy. In the meantime restoration of damaged productive capacity was also carried out under difficult circumstances. In 1953, when the program for stabilizing and restoring the economy had achieved satisfactory results and hyperinflation had been greatly eased, the government launched its first Four-Year Economic Development Plan. The idea behind the economic development plan was to use resources (both at home and abroad) more efficiently and rationally and to reach the stage of self-sustaining economic growth.

Table 2–1 compares plan targets and actual performance for the past eight plans. It shows that development commenced in the agricultural sector, ensuring a firm foundation for subsequent industrial

We would like to express our gratitude to the participants in the conference on China's Modernization and the Seminar on China in the Year 2000 for their useful comments and suggestions. Special thanks must go to Dr. Yu-ming Shaw, Dr. David M. Lampton, and Ms. Andra Leonard for their invaluable help.

TABLE 2-1

TARGETS AND ACTUAL PERFORMANCE, FIRST THROUGH EIGHTH ECONOMIC DEVELOPMENT PLANS, REPUBLIC OF CHINA, 1953–1985

	First Plan 1953–1956	Second Plan 1957–1960	Third Plan 1961–1964	Fourth Plan 1965–1968	Fifth Plan 1969–1972	Sixth Plan[a] 1973–1975	Seventh Plan 1976–1981	Eighth Plan 1982–1985
Plan targets	Promote agriculture and industrial production	Promote industrial and mining development	Maintain economic stability	Modernize the economy	Maintain price stability	Accelerate industrial modernization	Improve living standards	Maintain reasonable price stability
	Foster economic stability	Promote exports	Accelerate economic growth	Maintain economic stability	Promote exports	Expand infrastructure	Upgrade industrial structure	Sustain economic growth
	Improve balance of payments	Increase employment	Expand industrial base and upgrade economic structure	Promote development of advanced industries	Develop export infrastructure	Upgrade quality of manpower	Strengthen manpower development	Balance the growth of various sectors
		Improve balance of payments	Improve investment climate		Upgrade industrial structure	Promote exports	Promote balanced economic and social development	Ensure adequate job opportunities
					Modernize agriculture		Complete the ten major development projects	Promote equitable income distribution
								Balance regional development

								Promote harmonious social life
Annual economic growth rate (%)								
Target	—	7.5	8.0	7.0	7.0	7.0	7.5	8.0
Performance	8.1	7.0	9.1	9.9	11.6	6.0	9.7	6.6
Annual rate of increase of wholesale prices (%)								
Target	—	—	—	—	2.0–3.0	3.0	7.5	5.0
Performance	9.5	8.3	3.8	0.6	1.7	19.5	−0.9	8.4
Annual trade balance (US$ millions)								
Target	−54.1	−53.5	−84.5	−10.9	−137.1	349.0	−12.8	6,810.0
Performance	−84.0	−85.3	−59.5	−117.8	120.8	−426.3	982.5	

a. The sixth four-year plan was terminated one year ahead of schedule.

SOURCES: K. T. Li and W. A. Yeh, "Economic Planning in the Republic of China," in K. T. Li and T. S. Yu, eds., *Experiences and Lessons of Economic Development in Taiwan* (Taipei, Taiwan: Academia Sinica, 1982), pp. 103–29; "Ninth Medium Term Economic Development Plan for Taiwan (1986–1989)—Targets and Basic Policies," *Industry of Free China*, vol. 65, no. 1 (January 1986), pp. 13–30; and Tzong-Shian Yu, "The Relationship between the Government and the Private Sector in the Process of Economic Development in Taiwan, R.O.C.," *Industry of Free China*, vol. 64, no. 4 (October 1985), p. 13.

development. This strategy of balance between agriculture and industry was known as "fostering industry with agriculture and promoting agriculture with industry."[2]

During the 1950s agricultural development was given first priority in development policies. The first of a series of land reform programs was the 37.5 Percent Rent Reduction. Then came the Sale of Public Land and finally the Land to the Tiller programs. Once they had their own land, farmers became much more interested in increasing production and promoting further development. As a result agricultural productivity and farmers' incomes increased significantly. The distribution of income also became substantially more even. The ratio of the income share of the richest 20 percent to that of the poorest 20 percent came down from 20.5 in 1953 to 5.3 in 1964 and 4.4 in 1984.[3]

In the 1960s the development of light industry became the first priority. Small-scale, labor-intensive, import-substituting industries that needed little capital and few skilled workers and could be set up in a short time were chosen. In addition to continuing to improve the agricultural structure and expand exports, a Statute for the Encouragement of Investment was promulgated to enhance the investment climate. Industrial parks and export processing zones were set up to develop export industries, acquire technology from abroad, and expand foreign trade.

During the 1970s the construction of heavy industry and the enhancement of welfare nationwide became the dominant considerations. The main measures taken were the mechanization and modernization of agriculture to increase farmers' incomes and well-being; the construction of the ten major development projects to speed up the comprehensive development of infrastructure; the inauguration of the twelve new development projects to strengthen the foundations of the economy and maintain balanced social-economic development; and the launching of massive grass-roots development programs, such as construction of public housing and new towns to benefit low-income people so that they could enjoy the fruits of economic development directly.

In short, the economic goals during the 1950s and 1960s were to improve living standards and to strengthen the nation. Since the 1970s the target has shifted to the establishment of a self-reliant economic system. In addition to the continued pursuit of the previous goals, development has focused on strengthening the foundations of the economy, reducing dependence on foreign aid, and improving international economic relations (see table 2–2).

One question often asked is, How has a nation with a small

TABLE 2–2
CHARACTERISTICS OF THE TAIWAN ECONOMY, 1953–1984
(percent)

	1953–61	1961–71	1971–81	1981–84
Growth rate of GNP	7.5	9.9	9.2	6.8
Growth rate of per capita GNP	4.0	7.1	7.3	5.2
Population growth rate	3.6	3.0	1.9	1.7
Inflation rate				
Wholesale price index	8.3	1.8	10.4	1.7
Consumer price index	9.6	3.3	11.6	5.4
GNP deflator	6.7	3.7	10.4	4.7
Unemployment rate				
Broad definition	5.9	4.6	2.7	3.0[a]
Narrow definition	3.9	2.5[b]	1.6	2.1[a]
Primary industry employment as percentage of total employment	52.3	44.0	27.3	18.5
Income distribution: Gini coefficient (ratio)	n.a.	0.372	0.311	0.311[a]
Growth rate of exports (in real terms)	23.0	23.3	16.2	11.6[a]
Export surplus as percentage of GNP	n.a.	1.1[c]	1.3	5.2
Current account surplus as percent of GNP	n.a.	1.3[c]	1.3	5.0[a]
Balance of payments as percent of GNP	n.a.	3.1[c]	3.4	7.3[a]
External trade as percent of GNP	26.6	45.6	92.6	102.5
Debt service ratio	n.a.	n.a.	3.8[d]	4.3[a]
Exchange rate (N.T. $ = U.S. $1)	28.7	40.0	37.8	38.9
Saving as percent of GNP	10.1	21.9	32.1	31.7
Investment as percent of GNP	16.6	22.4	30.7	24.6
Direct foreign investment as percent of domestic investment	1.3	7.3	4.8	3.5
Tax revenue as percent of GNP	12.5[e]	15.2	18.6	18.3

(Table continues)

TABLE 2–2 (continued)

	1953–61	1961–71	1971–81	1981–84
Government revenue as percent of GNP	21.1[e]	23.7	24.4	26.3
Government expenditure as percent of GNP	12.9[e]	23.7	24.4	26.3
Bonds outstanding at year end to the year's GNP	0.2[e]	3.1	2.0	2.1
Increase in manufacturing real wages				
Staff	3.1[f]	1.3[g]	5.6	6.9[a]
Worker	3.6	11.9[g]	9.7	3.3[a]

n.a. = not available.
a. 1981–1983.
b. 1964–1971.
c. 1970–1971.
d. 1974–1981.
e. Except 1959.
f. Average of staff and worker.
g. 1969–1971.
Sources: Shirley W. Y. Kuo, "The Taiwan Economy in Transition" (Paper presented at "Conference on Prospects for the Economy of Taiwan, Republic of China, in the 1980s," Taipei, June 1985), p. 3; and Council for Economic Planning and Development, *Taiwan Statistical Data Book, 1985*, June 1985.

territory and virtually no natural resources managed to develop its economy so rapidly? In her book *The Taiwan Economy in Transition*, Shirley Kuo indicates several internal and external factors that greatly helped the ROC's growth during the 1950s and 1960s.[4] They were the availability of cheap energy, the rapidly expanding and receptive world economy, a sound international finance system, abundant reserves of low-cost labor, and speedy technological progress.

L. R. Klein, the 1980 Nobel Prize winner in economics, also points out some quantitative and qualitative factors that have contributed to the ROC's impressive economic performance.[5] The quantitative factors include agricultural land reform, high savings and investment rates, strong export-led growth, and anti-inflationary discipline. The qualitative factors are devotion to a work ethic, excellent educational attainment, thriftiness, population growth restraint, and the acceptance of equalizing tendencies (that is, equalized income distribution and balanced industrial development).[6]

C. K. Yen, former president of the ROC, in a speech delivered at the "Conference on Experiences and Lessons of Economic Development in Taiwan," attributed the successful transition of Taiwan's economy to the following factors and offered them as a valuable guide to other developing countries: correct guiding principles, strong leadership, stable social conditions, widespread popular education, the diligent attitude of the people, flexible economic policies, and a free economy.

The question whether the so-called guided free economy depresses the market mechanism is still being debated and may not be easily resolved. One of the pioneers of the ROC's economic planning, Kwoh-ting Li, advocated the merits of economic planning in these words: "Among the various factors contributing to Taiwan's rapid industrial development and steadily improving industrial structure, the government's strategy of promoting rational, stage-by-stage development is certainly one of the most important."[7]

Over the years the arguments for and against government planning have never ceased. The noted newspaper debate between two prominent economists, Sho-chieh Tsiang and Tso-yung Wang, over the problem of regulated interest rates almost became a confrontation between a "monetarist" and a "Keynesian." The main dispute between them was, What is the proper role of government in the process of economic development? Another well-known theme strongly advocated by Mu-huan Hsing, a distinguished economist and fellow of the Academia Sinica, is that of the gymnasium instead of the oxygen mask for industry, focused mainly on the incorrectness of government's overprotection of industry. Although these arguments reflect the diverse views held by established scholars, a gradually less important role for the government in the process of development seems more widely accepted.

How can the ROC continue to pursue an appropriate rate of growth while at the same time maintaining stable prices and full employment and improving welfare? Arguments for striving to achieve these multiple objectives are persuasive:

• Economic stability is as important as rapid economic growth. In the short run stability comes first; in the long run we need growth. To achieve both ends, each must be carefully fostered.
• Balanced growth in agriculture and industry is a prerequisite for further development. Large agricultural and industrial imbalances will only generate social, political, and economic confrontations.
• Solid foundations of general development are much more important than a few prestige projects. The scope and speed of develop-

ment will be bound by resource endowments. Therefore, across-the-board or massive development must be preceded by feasibility studies.[8]

These are lessons that the People's Republic of China (PRC) has learned through its unbalanced development experience of the past thirty-eight years.

The Current Situation and Future Prospects. For the ROC economy 1973 was a turning point, because pressures for change were coming from both inside and outside the society. As a trade-oriented economy with close ties to the international market, the ROC has since experienced two great periods of inflation, both succeeded by economic stagnation. These harsh blows not only forced economic growth down to an unprecedentedly low level (1.1 percent in 1974) but also made us realize that we were entering a new era, which would be characterized *internationally* by expensive oil, the threat of inflation, sluggish demand, prevailing unemployment, budget deficits, expanding protectionism, high interest rates, financial disorder, and keen competition from newcomers. *Domestically*, the stage of labor surplus had passed, wages had gone up, the speed of technological progress had decelerated, and people started to desire a better quality of life.[9]

For an area with a trade dependency ratio as high as Taiwan's (see table 2–3), any minor change in the world market will eventually reverberate throughout the domestic economy. The trade sector therefore reflects our economy. In that sector our problems basically lie in a weakness of structure.

- Manufactured goods for export are still mostly labor-intensive, low-technology, low-value-added light consumer goods that are easily restricted by quotas or competition.
- Cheap labor has gradually been canceled out by higher wages and low productivity.
- The growth rate of imports of capital goods has lagged far behind that of general exports, making it impossible for us to upgrade our industry.
- The markets for exports and sources of imports are still not very diversified.
- The ROC-United States trade surplus and the ROC-Japan trade deficit are getting worse.
- The marketing system is weak.

Another troublesome area is our industrial structure. A mentality of protectionism still prevails. Industries are accustomed to being

TABLE 2–3
TRADE DEPENDENCY RATIO OF TAIWAN, ROC, 1952–1985
(percentage of GNP)

	Exports	Imports	Trade Dependency Ratio
1952	8.1	14.2	22.3
1953	8.7	13.8	22.5
1954	6.5	14.9	21.4
1955	8.3	12.6	20.9
1956	9.1	16.0	25.0
1957	9.6	14.7	24.3
1958	10.3	16.8	27.1
1959	12.5	20.8	33.3
1960	11.3	18.9	30.2
1961	13.8	21.0	34.8
1962	13.5	18.9	32.3
1963	17.8	19.0	36.8
1964	19.5	18.7	38.1
1965	18.7	21.8	40.5
1966	21.2	20.9	42.2
1967	21.8	23.8	45.6
1968	23.9	26.8	50.7
1969	26.3	27.1	53.4
1970	29.7	29.8	59.5
1971	35.0	32.5	67.5
1972	41.8	35.5	77.3
1973	46.8	41.5	88.3
1974	43.7	51.5	95.2
1975	39.5	42.8	82.3
1976	47.6	45.4	93.1
1977	49.5	44.5	94.0
1978	53.2	46.5	99.6
1979	53.9	53.0	106.9
1980	53.8	55.2	109.0
1981	53.7	51.4	105.1
1982	52.2	46.4	98.6
1983	54.9	46.3	101.2
1984	58.8	46.4	105.2
1985	54.5	41.9	96.5

NOTE: Trade dependency ratio is sum of two other columns, that is, exports plus imports as a percentage of GNP.
SOURCE: Council for Economic Planning and Development, *Taiwan Statistical Data Book, 1985,* June 1985.

shielded from external competition. Most of them lack the interest or the funds to undertake research and development and therefore either imitate or counterfeit products developed by others. All these factors indicate that the technology they control is not very deeply rooted.

Moreover, private sector investment has been low for the past decade, because of the high risk attached to such investment, the short life cycle of products, and uncertainty about the market. As a result, the technological content of products has remained low, and the upgrading process in industry has been halted.

In addition to difficulties in foreign trade and the industrial structure, we have other problems.

- The difference between the investment rate (the ratio of gross fixed capital formation to GNP) and the savings rate (gross savings to GNP) in 1985 was 12.6 percentage points, which clearly indicates a lack of economic activity. In addition, the increase of foreign exchange reserves to over U.S. $58 billion has had the direct effect of pushing prices up.
- Because the traditional focus on production has not been replaced by the more modern idea of market orientation, management skills and operational strategies have lagged behind.
- Moreover, existing economic legislation and old-fashioned social norms are not suited to the dramatically changed society. As a result, economic crime is common, moral standards in business have deteriorated, tax evasion and illegal operations have become common practice, and a highly disordered, competitive situation seems to prevail.
- Finally, the public's concern for the environment, health, and consumer rights has recently become a leading social-economic issue. Economic development at the expense of the environment is finding no base of support.

With a view to dealing with these problems, an Economic Reform Committee (ERC) was established under the Executive Yuan in May 1985. Its main task was to diagnose the ills of the economic system and offer some prescriptions. Composed of scholars, business leaders, and government officials, the ERC faced high expectations and was under tremendous pressure to come up with substantive suggestions. This reflected the general desire for change and the widely held belief that the ERC could accomplish this goal. People seem to forget, however, that one condition for a successful transformation is that every aspect of society—economic, social, and political—must move along in step. Given a pluralistic system like that of the ROC today, there is no immediate cure or remedy for all (or even for most) problems. Besides, because the ERC had no power to execute or carry out policies, it is difficult to judge its accomplishments, especially since it had only a relatively short life (from May to November 1985). One thing is certain, however: the process of economic policy formation should be improved in the future.

Although some short-term measures and policies have been implemented since then, a far-sighted, long-term economic policy is also being pursued—that is, an economic policy of liberalization, internationalization, and systemization. Liberalization means complete freedom within the law for every worker to choose a job and for every businessman to make an investment or start a business, such decisions being governed only by the profit motive. Internationalization means opening up the economy as much as possible and permitting the free flow of factors of production across national borders so that efficiency can be raised and productivity increased. Systemization consists of formulating sound rules and comprehensive guidelines that are the foundation for liberalization and internationalization.[10]

In other words, the function of liberalization and internationalization is to uphold the market mechanism so as to give full play to market forces in allocating resources. But since the market mechanism is sometimes imperfect, a reasonable amount of intervention from the government in the form of rules and guidelines is called for, which is the very essence of systemization.

What is the outlook for the ROC economy? Will the ROC be able to enter the ranks of the developed countries at the turn of the century?

Table 2–4 shows the targets for the Ninth Economic Development Plan (1986–1989) and the Ten-Year Perspective Plan (1980–1989). The plans include clear and specific goals for future development.

In table 2–5 every indicator, apart from population, seems to show that by the year 2000 the ROC will rate as a developed country. Per capita GNP will be five times as great as it was in 1984; manpower quality, measured as the percentage of the population aged fifteen and over with upper secondary education or above, will be doubled; everyone will be covered by a social insurance program; and there will be one telephone for every two people and one automobile for every five.

Furthermore, table 2–5 reveals a very important trend, that is, that the composition of foreign trade will be completely changed. In 1984 the trade dependency ratio was 105.2; by the year 2000, it should be 206.6, which means that we will be twice as dependent on foreign

TABLE 2-4

NINTH ECONOMIC DEVELOPMENT PLAN, 1986–1989,
AND TEN-YEAR PERSPECTIVE PLAN, REPUBLIC OF CHINA, 1980–1989

	Ninth Economic Development Plan, 1986–1989	Ten-Year Perspective Plan, 1980–1989
Goals	Promote the fourteen important development projects and other public investments	Enhance energy efficiency
		Improve industrial structure
	Expand private investment and maintain steady growth of the domestic economy	Improve administrative efficiency and promote foreign trade
	Promote trade liberalization	Coordinate industrial and export development
	Strengthen the role of fiscal operations	Enhance efficient use of human capital and promote full employment
	Streamline the financial system	
	Restructure the economy	
	Strengthen manpower and science and technology development and the programming and managing of energy resources	
	Improve national welfare	
Targets		
Annual economic growth rate (percent)	6.5	7.9
Annual rate of increase of wholesale prices (percent)	2.5	6.0

TABLE 2–4 (continued)

	Ninth Economic Development Plan, 1986–1989	Ten-Year Perspective Plan, 1980–1989
Annual trade balance (US$ million)	6,440.0	n.a.

n.a. = not available.
SOURCES: Council for Economic Planning and Development, "Ninth Medium Term Economic Development Plan for Taiwan (1986–1989)—Targets and Basic Policies," *Industry of Free China*, vol. 65, no. 1 (January 1986), pp. 13–30; and K. T. Li and W. A. Yeh, "Economic Planning in the Republic of China" (Paper presented at the "Conference on Experiences and Lessons of Economic Development in Taiwan," December 18–20, 1981, Institute of Economics, Academia Sinica, Taipei, Taiwan, ROC, pp. 169–95.

trade as we are now. The trade surplus, as a percentage of GNP, however, will have dropped from 12.2 percent in 1984 to 1.2 percent; that is, the ROC will no longer enjoy a huge trade surplus. Although services will probably constitute the same percentage of total trade (12 percent), the trade balance (excluding services) as a percentage of GNP will also decrease from 14.6 percent in 1984 to 1.6 percent by the year 2000. All these data simply reflect the fact that we will be more dependent on the rest of the world. Because of a great increase in imports, however, our trade surplus will not be as high as it is today.

One general conclusion seems appropriate at this point: as long as the advanced industrial countries continue to enjoy a healthy rate of growth, the ROC can undoubtedly realize its goal of continued rapid economic development. As L. R. Klein has pointed out: "Given no unforeseen international breakdown, the expected world economic environment should propel Taiwan into advanced status, i.e. developed."[11]

Political Development

The Political Experience of the Republic of China. What has been the political performance of the ROC since 1949? Normally, the word "development" implies the achievement of certain goals. We usually take economic growth, for instance, as one of the goals of economic

TABLE 2–5

MAJOR ECONOMIC INDICATORS, REPUBLIC OF CHINA, 1984 AND 2000

Indicator	Unit	1984	2000[a]
Total population (midyear)	1,000 persons	18,877	22,685
Manpower quality (population aged 15 and over with upper secondary education or above)	Percent	37.6	79.9
GNP	NT$ billion at 1984 prices	2,291	6,224
Per capita GNP	NT$ at current prices	121,467	590,305
	(US$ at current prices)	(3,067)	(15,136)
Goods and services exports	NT$ billion at current prices	1,319.3	6,467.6
Goods and services imports	NT$ billion at current prices	1,039.4	6,392.1
Goods exports	NT$ billion at current prices	1,205	5,723
Goods imports	NT$ billion at current prices	871	5,625
Agricultural product self-sufficiency (ratio of domestic agricultural supply to total supply)	Percent	79.8	83.5
Welfare spending	Percentage of GNP	6.1	8.3
Population covered under social insurance program (health insurance)	Percent	24.8	100
Living space	Square meters per person	17.9	25.0
Hospital beds	Per 10,000 persons	31.0	40
Physicians	Per 10,000 persons	8.0	10
Telephones	Per 100 persons	27.7	49.5
Automobiles	Per 100 persons	6.4	20
Private noncommercial consumption of electric power	Kilowatt-hours per month	53.0	118.3

a. Target.
SOURCE: T. K. Tsui and C. C. Chao, "Perspectives of the Taiwan Economy up to the Year 2000" (Paper presented at "Conference on Prospects for the Economy of Taiwan, Republic of China, in the 1980s," June 17–18, 1985, Taiwan, ROC), p. 51.

development. There is more controversy, however, about the goals of political development. Even so, we find certain political goals mentioned more frequently than others by political scientists in the non-Communist world. In the following discussion, we single out two particularly interesting and important goals, political stability and democracy, which we designate the "minimum" and the "maximum" goals, respectively.[12]

We use two indicators to measure political stability: military coups and political riots. To examine the degree of democracy, we adopt Robert A. Dahl's definition of polyarchy, which is equivalent to democracy. In *Polyarchy: Participation and Opposition*, Dahl defines polyarchy as a regime that achieves both high participation and high public contestation.[13] We employ these two concepts to measure the extent of democracy in the ROC.

First, let us consider the minimum goal, political stability. The ROC has been very stable politically since 1949. As Ralph N. Clough, an American observer of Taiwan politics, has stated, "The ROC has been exceptional among developing countries for its political stability."[14] No real coups in the ROC have occurred in the past several decades, in sharp contrast to many other developing countries. The ROC's record of political riots has also been remarkably clean. There have been only a few riots since 1949, such as the Liu Tzu-jan incident in May 1957, the Chungli incident in November 1977, and the Kaohsiung incident in December 1979. The small scale of these riots indicates the high degree of stability that the ROC has maintained over the past thirty-eight years.

What factors have fostered such an achievement? Of primary importance has been Taiwan's success in developing its economy. Indeed, the ROC's almost constant economic growth has successfully reduced people's "relative deprivation"—the perceived discrepancy between expectations and achievements[15]—and has thus minimized social frustration and contributed to political stability.[16]

Second, opportunities for mobility may also contribute to the ROC's political stability. There have been ample opportunities not only for mobility from rural to urban areas but also for occupational and income mobility through education and hard work.[17] Indeed, such opportunities are generally open to every segment of the society, no matter whether they are mainlanders or native Taiwanese whose ancestors came from the mainland and have been settled in Taiwan for generations. Taiwan is becoming more urbanized. Only 51 percent of the total population lived in urban areas in 1961 but 73 percent in 1986.[18] As for occupational and income mobility, table 2–6 shows that

TABLE 2–6
EMPLOYMENT STRUCTURE BY INDUSTRY, REPUBLIC OF CHINA,
1956–1980
(percent)

	Agriculture	Industry	Service
1956	55.5	16.7	27.8
1966	38.2	17.2	44.6
1970	38.4	20.7	40.9
1975	30.8	28.6	40.6
1980	20.4	37.2	42.4

SOURCE: Census Office, *General Report: The 1980 Census of Population and Housing, Taiwan-Fukin Area, Republic of China*, vol. I (Taipei, ROC: Census Office of the Executive Yuan, June 1982), p. 246.

a great number of people have moved from agricultural to other sectors. That is to say, many people have found different, perhaps higher-income jobs.

Third, the ROC has achieved a high level of political institutionalization, which also contributes to political stability.[19] The ruling party, the Kuomintang (KMT), is well organized, penetrating almost every level of society. The government, combining efforts with the military forces and the police, has effectively maintained political and social order, surpassing the achievements of other developing countries in this regard. In addition, because of the tenure system and the system of checks and balances between commanders and political officers in the military, the ROC military forces have generally been submissive to the civilian leadership. This largely explains the absence of military coups.

Fourth, the ROC has faced the constant threat of the Chinese Communists across the Taiwan Strait. This threat is perceived as real by many people on the island and serves as an important restraint on behavior—even that of the opposition—reminding them not to rock the boat. That is to say, a grand coalition has been formed as a result of the perception of such a threat.[20]

Because of these factors the ROC has been remarkably stable politically in the past several decades. Nonetheless, stability is not the sole end of political development. The maximum goal is democracy, characterized by high levels of popular participation and public contestation.

Since 1950 the ROC government has held regular local elections for county magistrates and city mayors, provincial assemblymen, county and city councilmen, and so forth. Since 1969 supplementary elections have also been regularly held for the tricameral national legislature—the National Assembly, the Legislative Yuan, and the Control Yuan—with the exception of late 1978, when Washington announced its intention to sever diplomatic relations with Taipei. In all these elections ROC citizens above the age of twenty are generally entitled to vote. As more offices are filled through popular election, political participation continues to expand.

As for public contestation, politics in the ROC has undoubtedly grown increasingly competitive, especially since the mid-1970s with the emergence of the Tangwai (literally, "outside the party"). In the beginning the Tangwai was only an informal coalition of independent political activists. As time has passed, however, they have become more and more organized and formed the Democratic Progressive party (DPP) in September 1986. Although the party has not yet been officially recognized as legal, the government has tacitly accepted its existence. In addition to the Tangwai and DPP, there are two small opposition parties, the Young China party and the China Democratic Socialist party, both of which accompanied the KMT in the move from the mainland to Taiwan in 1949. These two parties have not been very active for a long time.

In the early days after 1949, the government was often accused by the opposition of perpetrating irregularities in the elections. The reduced frequency of such accusations indicates that elections in Taiwan have become freer and fairer. This does not mean that there are no disputes whatsoever about the government's handling of elections. The opposition still argues with the government about official restrictions on campaigning, for example. Nevertheless, the vote-counting procedure is no longer a major issue.

Although elections are a very important part of the democratic way of life, their existence is certainly not equivalent to democracy. In the West democracy in practice also means freedom of speech, freedom of assembly, and the like. The ROC has made important progress in these areas, as the publication of numerous Tangwai magazines, for example, indicates. Moreover, consideration is being given to allowing the publication of more newspapers.

While not yet fully democratic, the ROC has clearly become significantly more democratic over the past few decades. Probably the most important factor in this process has been economic progress. As Dahl has pointed out, economic development brings about democracy not directly but through such intervening variables as a pluralistic social order. An advanced economy, he says,

> not only makes possible but at the same time requires a multiplicity of durable and highly specialized organizations manned by strongly motivated staffs who are loyal to the goals of the organization. . . .
>
> As a pluralistic social order evolves, . . . some of its members make demands for participating in decisions by means [such as bargaining and negotiation] more appropriate to a competitive than to a hegemonic political system.[21]

In the ROC economic progress has brought about a multiplicity of organizations, such as factories, stores, the press, and schools. These organizations exert pressures on the government, compelling it to bargain and negotiate with them. Democracy develops as a natural result.

Some people suggest that economic progress fosters the growth of a large middle class that makes democracy possible. The term "middle class," though fashionable, is not very clear, but the existence of a large middle class does mean that the society is relatively equal, with only a small number of people clustered at either the top or the bottom, a situation that favors democracy.[22] Clearly, Taiwan's society is relatively egalitarian, a fact that is surely helpful to democratization of the island.

In addition, the impact of cultural change over the past several decades cannot be underestimated. A strong dose of democracy contained in Sun Yat-sen's teachings and Western culture has had an enduring influence on the political attitude of both the masses and the elites, incessantly promoting the value of democracy. From 1950 to 1985, 91,428 students went abroad for study, and 13,219 of them returned, finding jobs in the universities, public and private companies, various governmental agencies, and so on.[23] They have played a very important role in transforming the political attitude of the public.

Some would argue that pressures from the international community, particularly from the United States, may play an important role in democratization on the island. While the influence of such pressures cannot be neglected, they should not be exaggerated. If pushed too far, they may in fact evoke public resentment and have a negative effect on democratization.

Recent Developments and Future Prospects. In recent months tensions between the ruling party and the opposition have heightened somewhat, partly as a consequence of a number of judicial cases involving opposition figures. Such tensions did not erupt into serious riots, however, although a few minor confrontations occurred at the Chiang Kai-shek Airport in Taoyuan during the elections of December 1986. Basically, the political situation remains stable.

In March 1986 the KMT held the Third Plenum of the Twelfth Central Committee, which introduced a series of political reforms for further liberalization. A special task force was formed in the party after the meeting to review such matters as lifting martial law, lifting the ban on the formation of new political parties, and reorganizing the national legislature. In September the DPP was formed. A few days later, President Chiang Ching-kuo, in a discussion with Katherine Graham of the *Washington Post*, announced: "Now, we've decided to institutionalize and legalize other political groups. A 12-man group was established . . . to study proposals for the termination of emergency decrees as well as the possible formation of new political parties."[24] Thus the proposals for further liberalization were confirmed, and it is expected that they will soon be put into practice.

What about the future? It seems to us that since the factors that contribute to political stability and democratization in the ROC will, for the most part, persist, there is no reason to fear that the course of political development will be reversed. Certainly, there are risks, such as the issue of "self-determination" advocated by some opposition figures, meaning, possibly, permanent independence from the mainland. If this highly emotional issue ever becomes a major point of contention, political stability, democracy, and even national security may be damaged.[25] Nonetheless, judging from the fact that in almost all elections in the past several decades, the KMT has obtained about 70 percent of the valid votes, it is safe to assume that the majority of the people on the island favor the status quo and do not want to risk change that may result in chaos. That is to say, this issue will not, in the foreseeable future, become so critical as to endanger political development in Taiwan.

Some people have worried about the problem of succession. Since, however, the military forces are generally submissive to the civilian leadership and democracy is becoming more and more an accepted way of life, it can be expected that the succession process will be relatively smooth in Taiwan compared with that in many other developing countries. We are generally optimistic about the political future of the ROC.

A final note: On the eve of lifting the ban on the formation of political parties, it is interesting to consider what kind of party system will eventually emerge in the ROC. Since the system used in the elections for the national and various local legislatures is that of the single nontransferable vote, where each voter has only one vote in a multimember district, it is likely that more than two significant parties will emerge.[26] But since in the elections for administrative heads a different system is employed—the single-member district with plurality, which favors a two-party system—the number of significant parties will remain somewhat limited.[27] On balance, while there may be more than two significant parties, there will not be very many. If the KMT maintains the same popular support as it has enjoyed thus far, the party system that eventually emerges will be one in which a giant party dominates the scene, surrounded by several opposition parties. If the KMT's vote total should decline to, say, 45–50 percent, the party system would resemble that of Japan, with the KMT remaining in the governing position but facing more vigorous competition from the opposition parties.

Conclusion

Chinese people on Taiwan have created a strategy of development that may serve as a valuable example. While Taiwan has indeed been extremely fortunate in the past four decades, the word "miracle" does not really describe our experience, for it does not acknowledge the hardships and difficulties we have struggled to overcome along the path of development. We believe that the ROC's success was not and will never be a "windfall" but is due to our creativity, energy, and persistent effort.

Today the ROC's economy and society are in transition. Whether we can become a developed nation by the year 2000 depends on a revision of concepts. Government officials and the public alike should realize that time is no longer on our side. Without an immediate and thorough reform of the system and of policies, prospects will not be rosy.

In summary, history will give credit to all those who have devoted themselves to the construction and development of the ROC since 1949, but proud memories will not bring us a better tomorrow. We must be conscious of the results of past development and use them as guides to future events. For the ROC to be reclassified as a developed country, economic, political, social, and cultural achievements must advance hand in hand.

Notes

1. C. K. Yen, "The Fundamentals and Conditions of Postwar Economic Development in Taiwan," in *Proceedings of the Conference on Experiences and*

Lessons of Economic Development in Taiwan, Institute of Economics, Academia Sinica, Taipei, Taiwan, ROC, December 1981, pp. 35–42.

2. K. T. Li and W. A. Yeh, "Economic Planning in the Republic of China," ibid., p. 176.

3. Shirley W. Y. Kuo, *The Taiwan Economy in Transition* (Boulder, Colo.: Westview Press, 1983), pp. 96–97; and Council for Economic Planning and Development, *Taiwan Statistical Data Book, 1986,* June 1986, p. 60.

4. Kuo, *Taiwan Economy in Transition,* chap. 15.

5. L. R. Klein, "Economic Strategies for Taiwan in the Remainder of this Century" (Paper presented at the Conference on Prospects for the Economy of Taiwan, Republic of China, in the 1980s, National Central University, Chung-li, Taiwan, ROC, June 17–18, 1985), p. 1.

6. This phrase is added by the author for clarification.

7. Li and Yeh, "Economic Planning," p. 178.

8. Yen, "Postwar Economic Development," p. 40.

9. Shirley W. Y. Kuo, "The Taiwan Economy in Transition" (Paper presented at the Conference on Prospects for the Economy of Taiwan, Republic of China, in the 1980s, National Central University, Chung-li, Taiwan, ROC, June 17–18, 1985), p. 9.

10. Y. T. Chao, "Liberalization, Internationalization, and Systemization: New Currents in Taiwan's Economic Development," *Industry of Free China,* vol. 63, no. 3 (March 1985), pp. 1–7.

11. Klein, "Economic Strategies," p. 16.

12. These two goals are certainly not the only goals that political scientists have stressed. Gabriel A. Almond and G. Bingham Powell, Jr., for instance, suggested cultural secularization and structural differentiation as two characteristics of political development. See their *Comparative Politics: System, Process, and Policy,* 2d ed. (Boston: Little, Brown, and Co., 1978), pp. 19–20.

13. Robert A. Dahl, *Polyarchy: Participation and Opposition* (New Haven, Conn.: Yale University Press, 1971), pp. 5–8.

14. Ralph N. Clough, *Island China* (Cambridge, Mass.: Harvard University Press, 1978), p. 33.

15. For a general treatment of the concept of "relative deprivation," see Ted Robert Gurr, *Why Men Rebel* (Princeton, N.J.: Princeton University Press, 1970), esp. p. 24.

16. See Samuel P. Huntington's argument in his *Political Order in Changing Societies* (New Haven, Conn.: Yale University Press, 1968), pp. 49–55.

17. Ibid.

18. The figure for 1961 is obtained from unpublished materials prepared by the Urban and Housing Development Department, Council for Economic Planning and Development, Executive Yuan, ROC; the other is from *Urban and Regional Development Statistics, Republic of China, 1986* (Taipei, Taiwan, ROC, 1986), pp. 12–13. It should be noted that the former figure refers to nonagricultural population, the latter to the population living in planned districts.

19. Ibid.

20. One of us has used the notion of the core in game theory to develop a

theory of the formation of grand coalitions. See John Fuh-sheng Hsieh, "The Formation of Grand Coalitions in Politics" (Ph.D. dissertation, University of Rochester, 1981), esp. chap. 3.

21. Dahl, *Polyarchy*, pp. 76, 78.

22. Ibid., chap. 6.

23. See Ministry of Education, *Educational Statistics of the Republic of China* (Taipei, Taiwan, ROC, 1975), pp. 50–55.

24. "Saying Goodbye to Martial Law," *Newsweek*, October 20, 1986, p. 23.

25. For a discussion of the relationship between such highly emotional issues and political instability, see Alvin Rabushka and Kenneth A. Shepsle, *Politics in Plural Societies: A Theory of Democratic Instability* (Columbus, Ohio: Charles E. Merrill, 1972), pp. 74–88.

26. See John Fuh-sheng Hsieh, "The Political Consequences of the Limited Vote System: The Case of the Republic of China on Taiwan" (Paper presented at the Inaugural Meeting of the Asian-Pacific Political Science Association, Pattaya, Thailand, July 1984), pp. 4–5.

27. That the single-member-district-with-plurality system may lead to a two-party system is sometimes called Duverger's law. See William H. Riker, "The Two-Party System and Duverger's Law: An Essay on the History of Political Science," *American Political Science Review*, vol. 76, no. 4 (December 1982), pp. 753–66.

Commentary

Albert Keidel

I want to say how pleased I have been to have a chance to read this paper and to have in one place a pulling together of Taiwan's entire forty-year development experience and a consideration of what might lie ahead both economically and politically. The authors are to be congratulated for undertaking this review and for condensing it into such an accessible form.

I lived in Taiwan for several years in the 1960s, and I have a strong personal and professional interest in this paper. As an economist who works heavily with statistical materials, I am especially interested in the many nonstatistical factors it brings to our attention for explaining Taiwan's growth record.

First, the authors stress the importance of Taiwan's successful land reform and link it to the emergence of a strong middle class and its importance for political stability. Second, the authors document the many successful official plan periods and the focus of the plans on a range of central projects, building infrastructure, and encouraging investment. Third, the authors stress cultural and social factors, high literacy rates, thriftiness and high savings rates, strong leadership, population restraint, and discipline in resisting inflation.

The paper's discussion of Taiwan's future is a good starting point for us to consider the problems of maturing economies that have already industrialized, the generalizations that we now need to face for a range of countries. But my recommendation for the paper is on a different tack. I have some marginal notes that I will pass on to the authors, but I want to mention just a few factors that are not in the paper and can be added without adding much to its length. Although some of my suggestions may be difficult to carry out, in an international meeting such as this where the East Asian and Southeast Asian economies are so relevant and business interests are also taken into consideration, we need to raise two points in particular.

First, we should consider that many of the patterns in Taiwan's forty-year domestic development strategy, particularly those beginning in the 1950s, offer some parallels with what mainland China is now setting out to accomplish. My second point is that the paper should make some reference to the role of mainland China's economic and political development and its influence on Taiwan's past development experience and its future strategies.

My reason for raising these issues is to clear the air. They are important topics. Although I realize they are complex and uncharted areas, they should not be ignored. It is comfortable to think that Taiwan's economic environment will stay roughly the same: there will be some oil price fluctuations, world economic slowdowns and speed-ups, and debt crises. But those shifts are minor for Taiwan compared with the emergence of post-Mao China.

I hope we will have some discussion about this today. Perhaps one way to do this would be for the authors to say why they think that the mainland Chinese evolution is not going to be important for the future of Taiwan. By ticking off some of the factors that they think may not be relevant, they will have addressed the issue and opened it up for others to offer their disagreement or agreement. Without that there is an uncomfortable feeling that this paper, valuable as it is in pulling together very important problems and discussions, has left something out. I want to run down a few points in each of those two major dimensions.

First, on the domestic parallels between, say, Taiwan's economic position in the 1950s and China's now, both Taiwan and mainland China have had rather radical land reform. The Chinese land reform took thirty years to accomplish, and it was finished only in this decade.

For both Taiwan and mainland China the major emphasis on infrastructure investments is important—transportation, communications, energy development. All of those, of course, are now the highest priority for central investment projects, those that have not been decentralized under the reforms on the mainland. A number of characteristics of the mainland economy are paralleled by those of Taiwan described in this paper: the high savings rate, extremely high investment rates, high literacy by third world standards, strong central party control, and considerable political stability—although I imagine we will be arguing about that for the next couple of days.

We can also discuss the introduction of market forces. Certainly, a free enterprise system was one of the early descriptions of Taiwan. How far and how fast are the market forces in China beginning to set up a situation similar to Taiwan's in the 1950s? Taiwan's economy was mixed in the 1950s and 1960s, and we are now seeing the emergence of a mixed economy on the mainland. I would like to have that issue addressed, the domestic parallels.

My second point is the relationship between the Taiwanese economy—past, present, and future—and the mainland Chinese economy. It is important to recognize the important role played by the confrontation with a nearby Communist power in Taiwan's economic development. There were trade preferences. There were war booms, particularly associated with Korea and Vietnam. I do not mean to disparage the very hard work and good planning that were essential parts of Taiwan's economic development. Those have to be part of the equation. But there were other factors as well, and I would like to see some discussion or integration of them.

More interesting, of course, is the question of the 1970s and the 1980s. The oil shocks in the 1970s were concurrent with the early changes as China emerged. The cancellation of the Yoshida letter, the normalization of relations with both Japan and the United States—these events, although they may not have had such a dramatic effect in the 1970s on Taiwan's economic development, portend some of the problems Taiwan may be facing now and in the future.

Can we really expect that Taiwan's future economic development will be isolated from the economic development of mainland China? I question that assumption. There are many opportunities for investment, marketing, joint ventures, and transfers of technology; and cheap labor, which is no longer easy to find on Taiwan, is available on the mainland.

In Isaac Asimov's *Foundation Trilogy*, as the galactic empire is collapsing into a period of dark ages and turmoil that social scientists predict will last for tens of thousands of years, an isolated outpost of intelligence and order establishes itself on the fringes of the galaxy and develops new methods that will eventually shorten the period of chaos and speed the evolution of the galaxy into one of order, discipline, and law. Perhaps Taiwan can play that role to some degree as the galactic center now comes out of its dark ages.

In conclusion, I would like to see some discussion in this paper of these two issues relating to mainland China. Can Taiwan stay independent without fear of economic blackmail? Does it threaten itself if it ties itself too closely to the mainland economy? What is "too closely"?

Robert G. Sutter

This well-argued and well-documented paper acknowledges many of the current and potential problems faced by Taiwan's economy and its polity to the year 2000. I think the conclusion is justified in looking at the future in an optimistic way. I would like to talk about the potential role of the United States, which could affect the generally optimistic projection in this paper.

We can argue perhaps about the PRC's role vis-à-vis Taiwan today. We can argue about its extent and about what it will be like in the future, but we don't need to argue about the U.S. role in Taiwan. I think that is quite clear. The United States absorbs many of Taiwan's exports. It is a major supplier of military equipment to Taiwan, and it seems to be very important for the security of Taiwan.

Managing this relationship will be very important for Taiwan as it moves nearer to the year 2000. Managing it is becoming more complex. The United States is not going to change its policy toward Taiwan—and I am speaking only for myself in this regard; this is not a prognostication of what the U.S. Congress is going to do. But we see the discussion in the United States over issues relating to Taiwan becoming more complex, and the ability of the government in Taiwan to manage this relationship will be increasingly challenged on a broad range of questions.

In the 1950s and 1960s the U.S. discussion over ties to Taiwan focused on security issues, on how much aid to give to Taiwan. Military aid and particularly economic aid were designed to promote stability and enhance the security of Taiwan vis-à-vis the mainland. As the United States shifted its policy toward the PRC in the late 1960s and the early 1970s, the issue for the United States became one of striking a proper balance between its emerging ties with the PRC and its relationship with its old friends, as many of our leaders have put it, on Taiwan.

In the current situation, the issues are not quite so simple. A range of questions now pose problems for the government on Taiwan. The authorities there will have to deal with three clusters of issues in managing their relationship with the United States, complex issues that are worth watching.

First, Taiwan's authorities have a continuing need to work in a situation where the United States is trying to find a proper balance between its relationship with the PRC on the one hand and Taiwan on the other. This relationship is now stable, but it is subject to competing influences. Some people in the United States are very much inclined to push the country toward a policy of more support for the government on Taiwan. At the same time others are very much inclined to push the United States toward a more accommodating approach toward the PRC in ways that the authorities in Taiwan would see as detrimental. This is an old issue, but it continues to be important.

Two new issues have emerged in the 1980s that I think are equally important in the policy discussions in Washington and will be equally difficult for the authorities in Taiwan to manage. The first relates to economic issues and economic relations with Taiwan. Here we see the U.S. Congress taking the lead in promoting various pieces of trade legislation. This is not directed explicitly against Taiwan, but if some of these provisions become law, they may have a very serious effect on U.S.-Taiwanese economic relations. I am referring in particular to the Gephardt provisions; variations of those are still in House Resolution 3, which is working its way through the U.S. House, particularly the Ways and Means Committee. It is something that must be considered in managing this relationship. Of course, the countervailing view in the United States is the so-called free trade view and the concern that free trade, free access to U.S. markets, is important for the stability and prosperity of Taiwan.

From a political point of view, Taiwan's authorities face some difficulties in the United States that may be as serious in some respects as some of the economic issues and U.S. relations with the PRC and Taiwan. That is, Taiwan is in the position of having a leader who is old and ill, but who is essential to the stability of Taiwan. At the same time forces in Taiwan—the Democratic Progressive party and others—are pushing for a more pluralistic society. This kind of push enjoys a good deal of support in the United States, in the Congress and in the Democratic party. That support is backed by a fairly vocal group of Taiwanese Americans who are very active in lobbying the U.S. Congress in the interests of the opposition forces in Taiwan. This too is a difficult issue to manage.

In conclusion, I am optimistic about economic and political developments in Taiwan, but I think the paper should address not only the variables involving the PRC but the potential variables involving U.S. policy toward Taiwan. The United States exerts perhaps more influence on Taiwan than any other large entity in East Asia, and the complexities of U.S. policy in dealing with Taiwan today are greater than they have been in recent years. We now have a three-pronged problem as opposed to what in the past has been viewed as more of a one-dimensional issue in our dealings with Taiwan.

Discussion

DAVID M. LAMPTON: What has impressed me in my travels to Taiwan has been recruitment into the Kuomintang, what one might call the renewal of that party. In thinking about the revisions of your paper, you might talk about recruitment both within the bureaucracy and within the party and what some of the trends there are.

I think particularly of the trends in a couple of regards. Recruitment of people who were in Taiwan before 1949 is one. In addition, how have people studying in the United States been recruited into the party and the bureaucracy more generally? What role have these people been playing?

There is a larger question that goes back to 1950. That is, what was it about the Kuomintang that allowed it to put this pattern of recruitment into effect, and why and how was it able to make decisions to let so much of the economy out of its hands so rapidly in the early 1950s?

COMMENT: When mainland China made overtures to discuss the issues of unification with Taiwan some two or three years ago, the ROC on Taiwan chose to refuse even to make contact. My belief is that this had something to do with the Kuomintang's perception of its mandate to rule. We will go into the refinements later if necessary.

With the recent trend toward liberalization, with greater participation, with the greater consensus that has been achieved in the past year or two, the question arises whether Taiwan has developed sufficient confidence to be able to respond positively to any future proposal to unify. As I see it, remote though the possibility may be, the Kuomintang is the only viable option to any steps toward the pluralization of politics in China.

ARTHUR H. ROSEN: The paper makes the point that the pressures on Taiwan may be counterproductive. In particular, pressures by the United States for further democratization in Taiwan may evoke public resentment and have a negative effect on the democratization. I am concerned about that statement because I have heard it for forty years or more in China. I was on the mainland of China after World War II and know that the United States and powerful influences in the United States were deterred from pressing for democratic reforms, deterred from pressing with sufficient force, by that argument.

The argument was used in Taiwan in the early 1950s. But we were not deterred, and at that time it was the weakness of the government, the dependency on American economic support, the Seventh Fleet, and the Strait of Taiwan, that made it possible for the United States to exert effective pressures that brought about the land reform so vital to Taiwan's economic development.

I would argue here that the logic of this is not as valid in today's situation as it might appear to be. Let me say, first, that we are very quick to make carping comments to our friends. We refrain from making such comments to those who are not our friends and who may deserve them even more. There are internal pressures for further democratization that will become stronger because Taiwan is becoming more worldly. Its population is very well educated today, and this argument is more counterproductive than the pressures themselves.

DENIS FRED SIMON: I wonder if one could push the argument against closer links with the PRC on economic as well as political terms. One could argue that it is good economic policy for Taiwan not to become too closely linked to the PRC, for a number of reasons. One is that the pendulum-like swings in economic policy on the mainland with respect to tightening up the open door on technology and imports would hurt Taiwan. It may be safer to stay away for a while until China's policy gets straightened out. I am not much of an advocate of that argument because it could be extended to all foreign businessmen, but from Taiwan's vantage point, that kind of argument could be made; that is, to get too closely linked with the mainland economy promotes not only dependence but also vulnerability.

In the PRC today exactly the opposite argument is being made: that as Taiwan is getting pushed out of the markets of the industrialized countries, it will inevitably be driven to the PRC market to sell its goods. Given the desire of Taiwan to go through a technological transition and to rearrange the kinds of products it offers on the international market, what kinds of links should it develop with the mainland economy, and what kinds should it stay away from? Clearly there are some that it should stay away from.

ALBERT KEIDEL: I am very interested in the issue of national identity that was raised in the review of the paper and is now brought up again as probably one of the major stumbling blocks for relationships

63

with the PRC. That is an issue that can be tiptoed around or addressed straightforwardly, and I would like to see it addressed straightforwardly. We are now in a situation where Taiwan and the PRC have both matured in certain ways, and that issue is something about which a new generation can begin to talk soberly. I would like to see something of that in the paper. Finally, I want to return to the questions about what kinds of economic interrelationships to introduce first between Taiwan and the PRC. I have come up with three kinds.

One kind, which will help the PRC earn foreign exchange, is to produce pieces that are assembled in Taiwan in more sophisticated facilities—something that links the PRC's earning of foreign exchange to a relationship that it would want to continue in that form.

A second is one that transfers to the PRC technology that is suited to its labor skills—the kinds of things that Taiwan may no longer be experimenting with or that may no longer be on the frontier of what is used on Taiwan but that may be very useful in the PRC and could be produced there. A transfer of appropriate technology from Taiwan to the PRC would be an economic link that the PRC would not quickly want to break.

A third is to speed up the product life cycle development of Taiwan's exports to the rest of the world. Taiwan may speed up the ability at which it can move to more sophisticated products—by taking advantage of the larger market on the mainland. By having runs large enough, Taiwan can experiment with mass production of sophisticated commodities that cannot be produced in small enough numbers for a domestic market the size of Taiwan's and for which the world market is too unstable to justify the needed investment in mass production facilities. By taking advantage of a mass market that is not as critical of quality and perhaps is more willing to absorb some products that cannot be produced in the PRC, Taiwan can produce sophisticated products that it could not otherwise develop as fast and can thereby strengthen its export position in the rest of the world.

CHUNG-LIH WU: The economic and political reform of the PRC certainly will continue to affect Taiwan. The competition from the PRC in the world market for labor-intensive manufactured products, such as textiles, and the advocacy of the idea "one country, two systems" to the Western world are two examples. In trying to find some theoretical foundations for the economic reform, the PRC government has found nothing yet in either Marxism or Leninism. Government leaders have openly acknowledged, however, that the economic reforms have had something to do with Sun Yat-sen's Industrial Plan, which was formulated as early as 1921.

According to data we collected, ideas like the science park in Hsinchu, the industrial parks all around Taiwan, and the export processing zones constructed since the late 1950s have been widely adopted by the PRC in attempts at economic reform and development. I agree with Professor Simon, however, that we had better maintain a certain distance from the PRC. We do not want to depend too much on it, because it is huge. Even though the PRC's total trade is not as large as Taiwan's today, once we become involved with heavy trade with that huge market, we will be sunk by the PRC economy.

The argument in Taiwan now is how to separate politics from economics if we allow indirect trade to go forward. That trade is now about $1 billion per year, about 2 percent of our total foreign trade. How can we stop the figure from rising to, say, over 5 percent or even 10 percent? At some time, if the PRC should suddenly cancel a large order, Taiwan might lack any way to secure itself and might be totally absorbed by the PRC. Since we have experienced this sort of thing before, we do not want to stress the link between the ROC and the PRC.

Of course, many issues are now being raised in Taiwan. For example, Why shouldn't we pay more attention to this market and make good use of it? For the benefit of the Chinese people as a whole, why shouldn't we help them? What do we lose in helping the PRC move forward in its development?

In conclusion, I should say something about reunification. Every Chinese is looking for the reunification of China; the only problem is, reunification on what terms? That question includes what system and what life style, as well as what institutions. The Chinese people will continue to search until an ideal system, which can be accepted by most of the Chinese, is found. During the trial of dissidents involved in the Kaohsiung incident in December 1979, the judge asked one leader why he had undertaken such activities. He replied that he was worried that the Kuomintang would eventually sell out Taiwan, because the Kuomintang, as manager, would have contact with the PRC sooner or later. The government has a hard time maintaining its stubborn, "three no's" policy, but the claim made earlier clearly pointed out the other side of the story. Although I am not speaking for the government, I do see that it is very difficult to make everyone happy. As time goes by, I believe there will be more arguments and that the government will probably be more flexible as well.

JOHN FUH-SHENG HSIEH: One comment was that we should discuss the recruitment process in Taiwan. That point is well taken. We will take this into consideration as we rewrite the paper.

The other questions were all related to either the PRC or the United States—the external environment of Taiwan.

The role of the PRC in influencing the political process in Taiwan is mostly indirect, and somewhat contradictory. On the one hand, the existence of the PRC has made people on Taiwan united, thus contributing to the stability and progress on the island. On the other hand, the very existence of the other side may cause serious concern among some policy makers or certain elements in society that we should not go too fast or too far in the democratization process so as to disrupt the stability or even the democratization process itself.

As for the role of the United States in Taiwan's political development, we certainly recognize it, and undoubtedly, it is very important. On the question whether the pressures from the United States go too far and cause public resentment, I remember that, on many occasions, when the government decides to do something and the newspaper reports that an American congressman is asking the government to do it, then the government decides to drop the idea for the moment because it does not want to give the impression that it makes compromises under foreign pressures. I do not underestimate the importance of pressure from the United States, but I also do not want to overestimate it.

The last question concerns the unification problem which we did not talk about much in our paper. As a Chinese, I do believe that the existence of the Republic of China on Taiwan is the key to the future of China. The success of Taiwan will force the Communist leaders on the mainland to do something to improve the lot of our Chinese compatriots on the mainland. I have talked with some students from the mainland, and many of them have told me that they desire the success of Taiwan to exert a pressure on the Communist leaders. Taiwan is the hope of all Chinese.

3
China's Economy in the Year 2000
Albert Keidel

A Potential Economic Giant

Although some observers, both inside and outside China, question the political viability of China's economic reform program, I argue here that China's experience in the past ten years indicates that by the end of the century all of China will have joined the process of East Asian "miracle growth" already so well documented for Japan, South Korea, Taiwan, Hong Kong, and Singapore. When that occurs—as it almost certainly will to some degree—China's economy will be larger than most current projections suggest. Furthermore, current trends imply that China's international trade and investment activities will be surprisingly sophisticated and offer increasingly important benefits for the world economy and particularly for Pacific Basin economies.

Many signs indicate that the entire reform program, in all its complexity, is in a stage of disequilibrium. If the forward momentum of reform were halted, it would be impossible for the different stages of partial reform in China's many economic sectors and dimensions to stagnate. Either stronger central planning and bureaucratic control—including political management of the rural economy—would have to be reinstated, or reforms would have to resume.

The overwhelming likelihood is that China's economic reforms will continue until some more balanced and stable reform combination is complete. There may be temporary delays, speed-ups, or periods of political turmoil. Even with the current campaigns against "bourgeois liberalism" and "consumerism," however, the sweep of economic reform has already been so broad that no existing or likely leadership coalition could rebuild the old order.

There are very few conditions under which reforms could fail. Apart from events with unforeseeable consequences, such as a successful Taiwan independence movement or a worldwide financial crisis, the major threats to China's economic reforms are related to domestic unrest: public reactions to urban inflation and opposition from midlevel government and Communist party bureaucrats. But these events would have to threaten civil order and party authority badly enough to inspire a totally new leadership consensus for a return to central planning, quantitative output targets, compulsory grain procurements, and a host of other policies that would implicitly abandon China's long-term goals of rapid acquisition of foreign technology and economic development. The chances that such a new leadership coalition will arise seem extremely small at this time. Without a complete about-face, reforms will have to go on.

As a result Chinese policies strengthening domestic market institutions and aggressively expanding foreign trade will by the next century make China a formidable economic power that will present the global economy with a challenge to manage its finance and trade policies in ways that promote growth and economic stability throughout the world. The need to face this challenge in the form of one country's emergence may encourage new solutions.

Prospects for the Year 2000

China's economy in the year 2000 will easily have surpassed official targets to quadruple the output of industry and agriculture. In world trade China will have become an important actor in markets not only for garments and toys but also for consumer electronics and even for more sophisticated heavy industrial products, such as automotive parts.

Formal attempts to predict China's economic future, such as those by the World Bank, have in the past been linked to China's official slogans and targets. But these guidelines are now out of date, and more realistic projections indicate that the quadrupling target could be reached as early as 1995.

Conservative Official Targets. Evidence on Chinese economic performance by the mid-1980s shows that China's targets for quadrupling the gross value of output of agriculture and industry between 1980 and 2000 will be rather easy to accomplish. Growth in 1986, supposedly a year of consolidation, further confirms this conclusion. Table 3–1 compares recent performance with various targets and shows the relatively low growth pace needed to meet the quadrupling target.

Low Economic Projections. The best-known China projections, by the World Bank and Stanford University, have relied on the official quadrupling target as a benchmark.[1] As a result, many of their projections for other economic variables are also conservative. Summaries of the results of these two studies are presented in table 3–2 and are

TABLE 3-1

GROWTH OF GROSS VALUE OF INDUSTRIAL AND AGRICULTURAL
OUTPUT, PEOPLE'S REPUBLIC OF CHINA, 1952–2000
(percent)

Time Period	Category	Annual Average Growth
1952–1976[a]	Actual growth	7.8
1980–2000	Official target	7.2
1980–1985	Actual growth	11.3
1986–2000	Required growth[b]	5.8
1986	Actual growth	9.3
1986–1990	Plan growth	6.7
1991–2000	Required growth[b]	5.4

a. 1952–1976 growth is calculated from five-year averages centered on 1954 and 1974, to avoid start-year and end-year distortions.
b. "Required" refers to the average annual growth required to reach quadrupling targets for the year 2000.
SOURCES: Adapted from "Year 2000 Targets Appear Conservative," *China Economic Letter*, June 30, 1986; 1952–1976, 1980–1985 data from State Statistical Bureau (SSB), *1986 Statistical Yearbook;* plan data from *Xinhua*, "The Seventh Five-Year Plan of the People's Republic of China for Economic and Social Development (1986–90), Excerpts," in a special 23-page insert of the *Beijing Review*, April 28, 1986; and 1986 data from SSB, *Communiqué on 1986 Plan Fulfillment*, reported in *Jingji Ribao* (in Chinese), February 22, 1987.

compared with more recent alternative projections based on the Rock Creek Research eleven-sector model.

Because both the Stanford and the World Bank projections are tied to the official quadrupling targets, their projections for total average annual gross domestic product (GDP) growth are also very similar: 6.6 percent. The structure of output projected in the World Bank study, however, foresees lower growth for industry and somewhat higher growth for agriculture and other sectors (mostly services) than the Stanford model.

Because the results were forced to conform to the quadrupling gross output targets, both the World Bank and the Stanford estimates are too low. Updating the projections requires higher overall growth rates for the twenty-year period. The Rock Creek Research estimates present likely growth patterns. The higher agricultural growth rate reflects the remarkable achievement of the early 1980s, while the higher industrial and service growth rates indicate likely sources of future expansion. By coincidence, the Rock Creek Research GDP

TABLE 3–2

GDP GROWTH PROJECTIONS, PEOPLE'S REPUBLIC OF CHINA, 1980–2000
(annual average percent)

	World Bank	Stanford University	Rock Creek Research
Agriculture	4.9	3.4	5.5
Industry	7.1	7.8	9.9
Other	7.6	6.6	9.8
Total GDP	6.6	6.6	8.0
Per capita GDP	5.5	5.5	6.8

NOTE: Growth rates refer to gross domestic product (GDP) valued in constant 1980 yuan, except for Rock Creek Research estimates, which are based on constant 1980 dollars converted at shadow exchange rates.
SOURCES: World Bank and Stanford University estimates adapted from Rock Creek Research, "The Role of Technology Transfer for China's Economic Future" (Prepared for the Office of Technology Assessment, United States Congress, Contract No. 633-2730.0), May 1986. Original data in World Bank, *China: Long-Term Issues and Options;* and Lau, "An Econometric Model of China". Rock Creek Research estimates from Rock Creek Research, *China Economic Trends, Spring 1986* (Washington, D.C., June 1986).

estimates in table 3–2 are consistent with the gross value of output, which more than quintuples over the twenty-year period.

Coastal Economic Preeminence. Even the Rock Creek Research projections shown in table 3–2 are conservative for the large part of China along its long coastline. This coastal region, or belt, as Chinese officially refer to it, already has a strong lead in industrial growth and in production of GDP per capita. Part of the Seventh Five-Year Plan (1986–1990) singles out the coastal belt as privileged in receiving investment funds and foreign technology. Interior provinces have in effect been told they must wait for regional "trickle through" while the coastal regions are allowed to advance.

For the dynamic coastal provinces, projections of per capita GDP that leave it below U.S. $1,000 by the year 2000 are clearly insufficient. Given that the coastal provinces have nearly half China's population (425 million in 1984, excluding the three northeastern provinces), estimates of growth for the whole economy significantly understate the impact of China's economic future on the rest of the world.

China's Increasingly Sophisticated World Trade. Predicting actual levels of trade for China is understandably tricky. Recent experience emphasizes, however, that China's trade and other external economic relations will be more sophisticated than is usually thought, as China's ability to accelerate the "product-life-cycle" evolution of its export lines makes many exports competitive with those of other East Asian economies.

Most foreign businesses are particularly interested in China's potential for imports; but because of the strong control over foreign exchange China is likely to continue to exert for some time, interest in its imports almost immediately translates into an investigation of its export potential. Although China will undoubtedly continue its program of modest foreign borrowing, the major limitation on its ability to import will be its ability to earn foreign exchange through exports.

Highly Uncertain Prospects for Trade Growth. There are no official slogans about the scale of international trade in the year 2000, but the likely structure of trade, especially of exports, depends on how well China disciplines domestic consumption of grain, how successful coal exports are, whether offshore oil is eventually found in large quantities, and how rapidly China can acquire technology for large-scale production of high-quality manufactured exports. Because of these and other factors—including the general state of world trade markets—estimates of future trade are more uncertain than projections for the domestic economy (see table 3–3).

The World Bank and Stanford projections reflect both ends of the trade projection spectrum. Average growth rates projected by the World Bank are more than triple those of the Stanford model. This difference occurs because the World Bank expects farm exports to grow rapidly and also makes extremely high projections for machinery exports, which are not shown but are part of the "other" category. The high machinery exports result from the assumption in the World Bank model that high anticipated investment in machinery capacity will create an output surplus in need of world markets.

The Stanford trade projections are low because they are based partly on econometric regressions using China's trade record in the Maoist period.

Both World Bank and Stanford estimates foresee a decline in fuel exports over the period, apparently because domestic demand for petroleum products will command domestic production. Recent trends show, however, that China not only is willing to squeeze domestic petroleum consumption to conserve foreign exchange but also is implementing ambitious plans to export coal. As for many of China's export products, the quality of coal will be most critical for its export success, and investments for screening and washing coal are receiving high priority. Modeled projections of energy demand and supply indicate that China will become a major importer of refined

TABLE 3–3

EXPORT GROWTH PROJECTIONS, PEOPLE'S REPUBLIC OF CHINA, 1980–
2000

(annual average percent)

	World Bank	Stanford University	Rock Creek Research
Foods	5.7	3.0	2.8
Crude products	7.5	3.1	7.2
Fuels	−7.0	−0.3	4.0
Other	9.7	3.3	7.6
Total exports	9.0	2.8	6.2

NOTE: Growth rates refer to exports in current U.S. dollars.
SOURCES: See table 3–2.

petroleum products in the twenty-first century but that its coal exports may grow even more, leaving China with a net long-term growth in energy exports.[2]

Climbing the Product Life Cycle. The promise of China's export future, however, lies not in primary products but in manufactured goods. Because of the many uncertainties about world markets in the twenty-first century, the most useful trade estimates investigate China's likely pace as it moves up the product sophistication scale, from historically older export products such as textiles to newer products such as automotive parts and consumer electronics. There are many indications that this maturing process is well under way.

Three categories of export products reflect the range of product sophistication through which China will develop in the coming fifteen years: garments, consumer electronics, and automotive vehicles. China is already a formidable exporter of clothing, and consumer electronic exports in significant volume will come by the early or middle 1990s. China will be a credible exporter of vehicles not long after the year 2000, and export of automotive parts could become important well before that time.[3]

The major reasons that China will be able to increase its exports so rapidly are its national leadership's focus on technology transfer and trade expansion, the literacy and skill of its labor force, the large size of its domestic market, the focus of its imports on capital goods, and its already significant base in virtually every major industrial sector. China's challenge is to transform what are often laboratory or very small-scale production setups into enterprises for large-scale production of products of acceptable quality.

China's pattern of export success in 1986 is a clear example of the shift in trade strategy from relying more on crude oil exports to emphasizing manufactured products. Total export revenues grew more than 10 percent in 1986 in spite of a sharp decline in earnings from petroleum sales.[4] Much of the revenue growth was due to the improved quality as well as the increased quantity of textile and garment exports.

Economic Institutions in the Year 2000: Markets and Central Guidance. Both rapid domestic growth and increased sophistication of foreign trade are nearly certain for China's next fifteen years and indicate the rapid emergence of a new East Asian commercial giant. The likelihood that China's economy at the end of the century will be governed by a blend of market and centrally coordinated forces further strengthens the impression that China is fitting into a pattern of growth common to many of its successful East Asian neighbors.

Relatively free exchange will be allowed to govern consumer goods transactions and a significant segment of the housing market. Labor mobility will be greatly increased, but labor markets will lack effective union advocates for workers' rights, and in labor disputes the central government will play a major role in support of enterprise interests. There will be financial markets in many dimensions, and foreign exchange transactions will be significantly decentralized, but strong central monitoring and control will govern most money matters.

The forces of Chinese central economic guidance in the year 2000 will be most concerned with investment, productivity, and the maintenance of some degree of privilege and social security for members of the Communist party and urban bureaucratic elite. The state budget will still be important in direct support of key development projects, and bank credit will be allocated on the basis not only of profit but also of national development priorities.

Regulations will limit interest earnings and profits on free-market bonds and private bank loans. Even though currency convertibility will become an increasingly attractive alternative for practical reasons, rather strict control of foreign exchange holdings will continue to channel foreign funds into projects with high priority for central economic authorities. Subsidies will continue to support an urban standard of living higher than that warranted by urban productivity, and rural-urban migration will still be administratively disciplined.

In other words, China will evolve a new balance between central planning and decentralized private incentives and market signals. It is difficult to say just how authoritative central planning will be, but it is unlikely that even steel or petroleum will operate from plans de-

73

scribed purely in terms of physical output. At the other end of the spectrum, an extraordinary variety of economic activities will flourish in the service and consumer sectors. The balance between these two economic dimensions—between markets and central control—is impossible to predict, but a balance it most certainly will be.

Prospects for Market Reform and Economic Growth. China's promising prospects for the year 2000 derive largely from its experience, in both economic growth and economic reform, since the death in 1976 of Mao Zedong and Zhou Enlai. For over ten years China has sustained an economic record for which the annual growth of real national income never fell below 4.9 percent and stayed above 6 percent in every year but one. Since 1978 and the onset of major economic reforms, growth has averaged more than 8 percent a year. Added to this post-Mao acceleration of growth has been a structural shift in favor of rapidly growing commercial activities. In other words, growth not only has stepped up, but has shifted in favor of the delivery of goods and services.[5]

The economic reforms responsible for this record, however, more than the record itself, are the major reasons why China in 2000 is likely to be a balanced combination of market forces and central guidance. Economic reforms since 1978 have gone so far in so many dimensions that China's economic institutions are in a state of disequilibrium. The system could not work for long if it were frozen in its current state. It will continue to reform until a new balance between markets and planning is achieved, unless some extremely authoritative new leadership coalition reinstates many of the central planning mechanisms of the Maoist era.

A Critical Phase for Economic Reforms

The economic reform record can most easily be divided into four major dimensions for purposes of reviewing just how much China's economic system had already changed through the end of 1986 and how rapidly it is continuing to change in 1987.

Unraveling the Soviet System: Plans, Finance, and Service Sectors. Physical five-year and annual economic plans are the clearest symbols of the macroeconomic management system China imported from the Soviet Union in the 1950s. The degree to which this planning system has been replaced by market mechanisms in both the rural and the urban economies is one of the most dramatic indicators of how difficult it would be to freeze the system in its current state of transition.

Not only are the plans themselves much weaker, but formerly centralized financial institutions have also evolved very far and very fast away from the monobank system of most centrally planned economies. Even the measurement of economic output and growth by the State Statistical Bureau is shifting from the Soviet system emphasizing physical commodities to the Western system, which also considers output of services an important contribution to national welfare.

In China's rural economy two pillars of the Maoist planning program are gone: communes and compulsory grain procurement. Their demise has brought rapid rural development but also some significant problems. Grain output declined in 1985, the year compulsory procurement was abolished. In the early and middle 1980s, as commune management first weakened and then disappeared, irrigation investment and upkeep suffered. Nevertheless, neither reform has been reversed, and rural economic diversification has accelerated.

In the urban economy most industrial products were taken out of the physical plan in 1984 and 1985. Profits have replaced physical output as the primary measure of enterprise performance. In place of a compulsory physical plan, planning authorities have introduced an "indicative plan," which unlike its French namesake is intended to allow local authorities to use arm-twisting techniques to persuade state, collective, and rural enterprises to tailor investment to state wishes.

When pitted against the economic incentives responsible for much of China's current economic dynamism, arm twisting has had limited effectiveness. As the continuing major financial reforms in 1987 reinforce investment independence, central control over investment will be weakened even further. This loss of control over a significant portion of annual investment is one of the clearest signs of central planning's increasing eclipse.

New Rural Independence: Land, Nonfarm Growth, and Urban Links. China's replacement of communes and compulsory cropping patterns with the equivalent of a rural middle class tilling its own land for monetary gain has triggered an explosion of rural nonfarm growth that some Chinese say, only half in jest, will eventually surround and capture the urban enclaves, just as Maoist guerrilla strategy says it should. Proliferation of rural free markets and small-scale rural industry has put pressure on urban economies to increase their productivity in the manufacture of consumer goods so as to command the increasing supply of rural products available, not through subsidized state stores but for cash in the streets. Stagnation in urban reforms—

maintaining low productivity and high subsidies—will only increase urban-rural economic tension.

In 1985 China's rural industrial labor force grew an astounding 165 percent to make up 33 percent of the national industrial labor force. The rural construction labor force grew nearly 40 percent to more than half the national total. At the same time the rural labor force engaged in agriculture declined in absolute numbers, by 4 percent, for the first time in modern Chinese history.[6]

It is widely acknowledged that a new revolution would be needed to undo these developments in China's rural economy. What is less often realized is that rural reforms cannot stop in their current stage of evolution. Adjustments in the procurement price of grain must continue, and reorganization of fertilizer distribution systems cannot be delayed. The relatively spontaneous generation of jobs and output in rural villages and towns is virtually impossible to repress because it is so far outside the grip of state economic leadership. Rural credit contractions could dampen village growth but only at the political risk of compromising growth in the overall economy, an outcome desired by neither economic conservatives nor liberals.

In short, rural reforms cannot stand still, and reversal is highly unlikely. By the year 2000 some Chinese expect rural industry to employ nearly half China's total industrial labor force.[7] The pressures on the urban economy to respond with goods and markets will be all but impossible to resist.

Urban Enterprise Reform: Investment, Prices, and Management. For 1987 the most sensitive economic reform transition is in urban industrial management. Urban industry is at the heart of Soviet-style central planning, and China's state-owned industrial enterprises have been especially resistant to steps that undermine party cadre control over the operation of factories and the distribution of benefits related to enterprise management. Since 1984, however, after the short-lived but at times viciously conservative "anti–spiritual pollution campaign," party control has gradually given way to management by enterprise directors.

This trend toward "director control" is one of the clearest examples of how current reform disequilibrium compels further reform—in this case toward stronger control by directors. Financial reforms begun in 1984–1985 shifted state budget revenues from dependence on direct remission of all enterprise profits under the Maoist system to the levying of an enterprise income tax. As a result, since 1985 what was a net positive enterprise revenue line in the budget has now become two lines, a positive tax revenue line and a negative enterprise subsidy line. What were once concealed subsidies are now painfully visible to both advocates of reform and doubters.

In a fiscally conservative China the very existence of such obvious deficits argues for their reduction and eventual elimination. This can only be done in one of two ways: by going backward, abolishing the enterprise tax and combining the two budget lines again; or by continuing with "responsibility" reforms that strengthen enterprise management and profitability.

First implemented in experimental units, the so-called factory management responsibility system was instituted nationwide in September 1986. Revisions of the regulations in November transferred complete power for enterprise legal representation from party secretaries to enterprise directors. Under this system of director control party secretaries and worker councils retain important functions and rights, but the wording of the regulations makes it very clear that the enterprise director is legally the boss.[8]

The most important outcome of director control is the strengthened role of profitability in management decisions. Director control makes sure that someone cares about costs and revenues. Without it price reform—perhaps the ultimate goal of urban industrial reform— would accomplish very little. Larger losses would have to be subsidized, and larger profits would be taxed away by the state. Partial reform of some prices contributed to the large enterprise losses reported in 1986.

The important point is that with physical plans greatly weakened, director control makes it difficult to postpone either further price reform or further reform in banking and enterprise finance. Directors will want to buy cheap and sell dear and will do so in black markets and free markets if state markets are inadequate. Investment financing will become increasingly creative, with both retained earnings and decentralized markets growing in importance. This relative investment independence will increase pressure for continued commodity price reform, because without it funds will be attracted by misleading profit rates to sectors of secondary importance.[9]

Just as in the rural economy, urban industrial reforms have proceeded so far and are continuing to evolve so rapidly that stagnation is not an option. Either extremely conservative forces must dramatically reverse current policies and consciously reconstruct bureaucratic planning mechanisms and organizations now abolished, or the reforms must be allowed to continue until they find a new equilibrium in an environment of much-reduced central control. There is no indication that such conservative forces exist at any relevant level of Chinese leadership.

Technology Transfer: Trade, Borrowing, and Foreign Exchange. The fourth dimension of China's reforms that cannot stagnate and would be nearly impossible to reverse is the acquisition of foreign technology. Foreign technology and related productivity gains are at the apex of Deng Xiaoping's reform priorities. Military leaders, political conservatives, and radical reformers all agree that modernization is the fundamental purpose of reform and that foreign technology is the necessary means.

As a result, expansion of foreign trade, financing with foreign borrowing, and channeling of foreign exchange have acquired an independent authority. Importation of production machinery has grown to dominate China's imports, and what importation of consumer goods has occurred has raised consumer tastes and put added pressure on industry to acquire foreign productive capacity. It is as if the more China buys and learns about foreign goods and foreign techniques, the greater the demand for them grows.

The important trend, then, is not the acquisition of foreign technology itself but the acquisition of tastes for foreign technology. Here again stagnation of trade and technology imports would be extremely difficult to enforce, even if any policy maker should wish to do so.

This commitment to importing foreign technology has been underscored by China's response to the foreign exchange crisis of 1984–1985, which was very different from its response to a similar crisis in 1980–1981. In the earlier period China sharply contracted its imports to balance trade and accumulate foreign exchange reserves. But in 1984–1985 a harsh contraction must have been judged too disruptive, and China resorted to borrowing from both subsidized and commercial lenders to maintain import levels.

Trade statistics for the first quarter of 1987 make it clear that as exports are recovering, authorities are also curtailing imports.[10] The policy of restraint has apparently paid off, and prospects for continued acquisition of foreign technology on a significant scale seem certain.

In foreign international economic relations, then, just as in the three other major dimensions of China's economic reforms, the general pattern of policy and behavior is conducive to neither stagnation nor reversal. Continuation of reforms in all dimensions is highly likely, and the results will be a larger economy and more sophisticated trade and domestic institutions than most people imagine.

China's Challenge to the Global Economy

The repercussions of an emerging Chinese economic giant will be felt far beyond China's borders. As more than a fifth of the world's labor force industrializes in a relatively short time, the world's economic leaders will have to address the central issue of how to ensure sufficient world markets for the industrial output of late-industrializing nations.

Because of its size China will air its complaints concerning protectionism and disadvantageous terms of trade. At the same time already industrialized nations will be able to accelerate their transition to an economic stage more heavily based on employment in the service sectors. In short, the economic evolution of the world could be prodded along by China's economic expansion—if economic policies in industrial nations are flexible enough to make the needed adjustments in their domestic economies.

Notes

1. World Bank, *China: Long-Term Issues and Options* (Washington, D.C., 1985), esp. annex D, "Model and Projections"; and Lawrence Lau, Stanford University, "An Econometric Model of China, Final Report, Part II" (Report prepared for the U.S. Department of State, 1985).

2. These energy projections are generated from the Rock Creek Research China energy model and reported in its *China Energy Report* (Washington, D.C., 1987).

3. For a more thorough treatment of the prospects for Chinese exports in these three sectors in particular, see Rock Creek Research, *The Role of Technology Transfer for China's Economic Future*, cited in the sources for table 5–2.

4. See "Exports Healthier," *China Economic Letter*, December 1, 1986; and "Fourth Quarter Imports Curtailed: Buying Shows New Restraint," *China Economic Letter*, February 9, 1987.

5. For a detailed look at both the Maoist and the post-Maoist annual growth record by major national income categories based on very recently released official constant-priced time series, see "The National Income Record," *China Economic Letter*, February 23, 1987.

6. Official Chinese statistics have only recently begun reporting these and other details of the nonagricultural rural economy. For a fuller treatment of these trends, see "Rural Labor Challenges State Sector," *China Economic Letter*, January 26, 1987.

7. Niu Ruofeng, quoted in "Industry Tops Farms in Rural Output Value," *China Daily*, November 14, 1986.

8. See, in particular, "Three Regulations for State-owned Industrial Enterprises," *Jingji Ribao* (in Chinese), January 12, 1987.

9. For actual measurements of very different returns to capital in different state industrial sectors, see "China's Haywire Profits: Sharp Differences Underscore Price Problems," *China Economic Letter*, February 23, 1987.

10. See "Fourth Quarter Imports Curtailed"; and "First Quarter Trade Recovery: Deficit Almost Gone," *China Economic Letter*, May 4, 1987.

Commentary

Adam M. Pilarski

I take issue with Mr. Keidel's point that the high growth rate already achieved will lead to a quadrupling of the Chinese economy in 1994. He compares the numbers with the previous 7.8 average during Mao's time. But historically, the level of 1968 was lower than 1960. High growth rates in China often lead to years of stagnation or very high negative numbers. The fact that the Chinese have done well so far does not mean that they will continue doing it.

One major problem is China's size. It is too big to do what countries like Singapore, Taiwan, or Korea did. In 1960 Korea could enter the market quietly when nobody looked and then suddenly grow, but Korea today is too big to repeat that process. Nobody would allow China that kind of latitude.

Moreover, because of debt problems I foresee generally lower growth in world trade than people expected before—China, and many other countries, will be hurt by it.

The only reason why I believe the reforms will continue is the now-higher standard of living. In reference to earlier discussion: of course some people will lose with the reforms, but many people have gained and will gain a lot. We are not discussing a theoretical argument: millions of people in the past few years got a higher standard of living; they won't give that up.

As economists say, there is no free lunch. A Western economic system that offers freedom to produce cannot exist at the same time with a political system that gives no rights. It does not work.

I am reminded of a story about a country where people drive on the left side of the road. This country decided to switch over to the right side and hired some academic consultants to find out whether the change should be made and how it should be made. The consultants decided to conduct an experiment: 20 percent of the people will switch to one side and the rest will continue the other way. That's a little bit how I feel about the Chinese system: either everybody drives on the right side, or everybody drives on the left side.

Roger W. Sullivan

It's rare to find any analyst who is courageous enough to look at the numbers and come out with the conclusions that the numbers seem to suggest, which is what Mr. Keidel has done.

As Mr. Keidel mentioned, the Chinese journal *Red Flag* very recently commented on the problems with reform. *Red Flag* concluded, however, that the problems with reform can be resolved only by more reform. I think that not only is that point recognized in China but that it's a consensus view there.

There may be a lot of differences about pace and method but, nevertheless, they all know they are riding a tiger and have to keep moving.

It is useful to remember that Chinese numbers, such as target figures and the like, are not really meant to be taken very seriously. I remember when Deng Xiaoping said that per capita income would be $1,000 by the year 2000. The group meeting with Deng asked him where the figure came from; he said, "It's a good number."

This is much like wishing somebody *wan sui*, 10,000 years—we wouldn't wish somebody 8,462 years. I think analysts have to treat these round numbers given by the Chinese very carefully.

It is certainly true that the Chinese are becoming increasingly sophisticated in world trade; we've seen remarkable changes in the past few years. Over 50 percent of their exports are now in manufactured goods, and they've shown surprising sophistication and adaptability in dealing with the problems of selling in the U.S. market. But the Chinese do not see their exports to the world as a means to a development end. They want to earn in order to import. Their principal goal is to give themselves the capability to purchase high-technology products from abroad. They are not embarking on a policy of exporting as an engine of growth.

They have a large domestic market and built-in biases against exporting. I think those built-in biases will continue. In fact, there is an interesting correlation around the world, regardless of level of development, between large developed countries and large underdeveloped countries: they tend to have the same sort of views toward exporting. Exporting is a small part of their GNP.

I think China is unlikely to be very successful in bringing many of its products up to international standards, either in quality or design because their market is largely going to be the domestic market. They will continue to protect against not only foreign competition, but unwittingly against the stimulation effect of foreign example. The World Bank report goes into great detail in a marvelous section where

81

it refers to the open door being more like an airlock of regulation and law that prevents competition in the Chinese economy.

We have consistently underestimated China's ability to generate export earnings, but it will not become a major player in the markets of the world in consumer products like Korea, Taiwan, or Japan.

Let's look at this question of failure again, defined as stagnation. It seems to me that the debate in China is really not so much over ideology as it is over power. I see the struggle not so much as a conflict between planning and market forces, or even between socialism and a market system in the debate, but as a struggle over power and perquisite.

In fact, it is hard to be sure that when a Chinese leader takes a certain position, he seriously advocates that position; he may have just found a good issue to ride. There is some considerable evidence now, for example, that Hu Yaobang did advocate political reform. Hu Yaobang was scheduled to go out no later than the Thirteenth Party Congress; in fact, some were surprised that he was not ousted before he was. He managed not only to survive, but to add to his stature in the campaign fight over spiritual pollution.

The issue, then, is power, not really ideological considerations. When I looked at Mr. Keidel's four dimensions, I saw that the dismantling of the Soviet system was not in itself especially controversial—nobody's perks and power are really endangered. Evidence of this is that Deng has been saying publicly for some time that the Soviet economic model is a dead end. Most people in China would probably agree with that, including the so-called conservatives.

The new independence of rural enterprises is an interesting point because it was an accident. It is not really part of the reform program. Certainly, letting people decide what they will grow was intended as a reform, but the impressive growth of all the rural enterprises was a serendipitous development. It began as essentially a make-work program because the leaders were concerned that making agriculture more efficient would create redundancies on the farms and therefore a rush to the cities for jobs. Therefore, rural workers were allowed to make baskets. As it turned out, they started creating some very successful enterprises. Some Chinese officials worry a lot about this situation but have decided that there is not much they can do about it. It's not very controversial, except that it's worrisome when something like 23 percent of the gross national product is produced by people making baskets out on the farms.

But the heart of the issue over power and perks lies in the urban reforms: is reform a code word for weakening the party structure? When the party cadres in China are convinced that this is what is meant by reform, they will seize all kinds of issues to argue about to defend their position.

It is significant that there was such debate over an eventual postponement of the bankruptcy law. If this law is put in place, there is not much left to the party, because party perks all involve controlling employment and keeping tabs on factories. This is the issue on which reforms in Hungary stumbled, and I think we must reserve judgment on China because this seems to be the litmus test for reform. If the Chinese cannot bite this particular bullet, then I see the possibility of some really extended in-fighting over the question of where China is supposed to go next.

Since reform is not primarily or principally an ideological fight, the Chinese need to evolve a balance, not between planning and market forces, but between confidence in an economy relatively free to respond to market forces and fear that reform equals destruction of the party structure and the power and perquisites that go with it.

It would be interesting to speculate whether Taiwan might not be an example for them. One of the reasons for the great economic success in Taiwan (which went through a similar debate over maintaining the KMT structure, basically a mainland structure, in a Taiwanese-dominated economy) is that the Taiwanese managed to engage in some very impressive economic reform with what was in those days precious little political reform. They isolated the government and party structures from what was going on in the economy and did so very successfully.

I believe that it is not necessary to have democracy along with economic development. There are some very good examples of states that have done quite well economically and have not gone very far in the direction of democracy or human rights.

Chung-lih Wu

This is a very interesting paper, interesting in that it is too optimistic and too good to be true. I particularly like Dr. Keidel's use of this disequilibrium framework, which has been familiar to me ever since I was in graduate school. As a native Chinese currently residing in Taiwan, with the wishful desire for a united China sooner or later, I wholeheartedly hope that what Dr. Keidel says can materialize. But professional training prohibits me from believing those optimistic figures. Therefore, I have a few questions to ask Dr. Keidel.

First, on what grounds do you believe your model is better than the others? The only thing I know about your model is that it is an eleven-sector model, forecasting China's economy. Although I am happy to see that you have included a very modern component such as technology, it is still not clear to me that your model is superior to either Lawrence Lau's or the World Bank's.

Second, you have used something we call "micro foundation" in a macroeconomic analysis. In other words, you used coastal or belt areas as the basis for reference to the whole economy of China. My question is, How representative is this micro foundation?

Third, you mentioned something about inflation, using a figure like 6 percent, but according to my understanding, this is suppressed inflation, not real inflation. The actual inflation in China was somewhere around 18 to 20 percent. Two professors from Colgate University conducted a study a few years ago and came up with the term suppressed inflation. They claimed that official data and earlier estimates of China's inflation are clearly underestimated. And I want to hear your comment on that.

Fourth, it seems that you completely overlooked the common phenomenon in a socialistic system, that is, consumption and investment starvation. And those optimistic results in your paper may just be a reflection of that.

Fifth, as an economist, I think we all, at times, rely too much on the figures, and we have constantly been criticized by other social scientists. But still we believe in figures. Dr. Keidel's problem is believing too much in the figures. When we look at China's economy, some things not quantifiable, like cultural factors or political turmoil, have to be taken into account. That is the bigger problem that we economists do not agree upon.

Furthermore, the structural change or structural problem and the disturbances arising out of the reform process have to be clearly separated, because they can make a tremendous difference in the results. And finally, it remains to be seen exactly how the PRC will manage to fulfill people's expectations and to handle so many different sites like Hong Kong, the special economic zones, the rural areas, and the urban sector.

Discussion

DENIS F. SIMON: What I see here is two discussions. The first discussion is about the quantity of growth, and the other one is about the quality of growth, the qualitative dimensions—the composition and nature—of growth in China will actually be very different from what the figures pure and simple might suggest.

We see that clearly it has not taken much for China's economy to grow fairly fast. The question I raise, however, is that when we extrapolate based on the figures of 1978, are we really extrapolating from a very low base, with low performance and productivity, so that the initial incremental jump seems to be so great? One of my students criticized the comparative figures on Japanese R&D growth versus U.S. R&D growth. Although the Japanese R&D growth figures were higher by a factor of two or three than the U.S. R&D growth, the Japanese were starting from a very low base so that the initial incremental leap was substantial.

I know, of course, that we are talking about a qualitatively different period in Chinese history; the post-1978 period is different from the pre-1978 period. I accept that. How far, however, can we go to carry the initial leaps that have been made from 1978 to 1985 to 1986? Do we carry them to 2000?

DAVID M. LAMPTON: What do we know about changes in labor productivity in the urban-industrial and the state-enterprise sector? In the figures I saw, which are several years out of date, productivity was not responding as some people had hoped to the wage increases and the like. What is the situation now, and what are the implications of the still rather modest increases in labor productivity? How does that fit into Dr. Keidel's model and his assessment for the future?

QUESTION: I want to discuss the relationship of economic development to political reform. The counter-example to the theory that democracy is requisite for economic development is Hong Kong, where, as far as I know, there has not been political democracy, in any sense, for many years.

Another point is that the size of the sector in the economy which is not controlled by the bureaucracy is important. A Big Brother regime can still exist, but some activity must be able to spread outside the control of the bureaucrats. So, what are the prospects of giving tenure to the present bureaucrats over their kingdom, but allowing the economy to spread beyond that particular kingdom and simply allowing an ever-increasing zone that the bureaucrats cannot control? Is there any prospect of that?

ADAM M. PILARSKI: I would like to add something. When I refer to political freedom, I refer to it in sociopolitical terms, and I think the Chinese see it this way also. It's not just the right to vote for a different political party; it's the right to change jobs or to go to another place. The Chinese do not want the problems that we have such as prostitution.

ALBERT KEIDEL: The issue that China is too big to export on the scale of Taiwan is obvious to everybody. The Chinese will not have those export-dependency ratios at all, but some of the export strategies they will try to employ will follow a similar line. They will use export earnings not to create a surplus for the acquisition of assets overseas but to purchase technology to develop the domestic economy.

Adam Pilarski mentioned that the debt problems and a possible world economic contraction, or slowing of growth, in the next decade will hurt China. While that may be the case to a degree, another possibility is that China itself will provide the world with a counter-cyclical economic hot spot where countries will find an economy willing to buy and sell technology and finished products, if they can work out the bilateral arrangements to absorb China's exports. China will work hard to make those relationships a reality, in spite of what may be a collapse in Latin America or elsewhere.

Clearly, the focus is on urban reforms right now, and my notion of a disequilibrium there comes from the change in the legal status of the enterprise director in the past year. This change, among other legal changes, now requires working out. To undo these reforms would require conscious policy decisions and legislative action. If nothing is done, if there is stagnation, the director will be operating in his or her new environment.

The technical point about our model is how it stacks up against the Link model, the DRI model, the World Bank model, or Lawrence Lau's model. For those uninitiated in the voodoo of econometric modeling, it is important to recognize that there are two parts to any modeling: one is the model, and the other is the modeler. If the model is allowed to do whatever it wants to do, predictions will head out the window. What is required, then, is a modeler who examines the results, can recognize something that does not look quite right, and can fine-tune the model until it does look right. This last step is where the skill of the modeler, the "add factoring" as it is called, becomes important.

My philosophy of modeling is that it is very important to build in enough hooks and handles with economic meaning, so that adjustments can be interpreted and the result judged reasonable or not. The Lawrence Lau model, on the other hand, is based on the Cobb-Douglas production function, where each of the elements in the input-output table is an element in the Cobb-Douglas production function and is governed by price.

So the way that Lawrence Lau adjusts his formulas to make them result in quadrupling in the year 2000 is by adjusting prices. There is nothing more difficult to justify adjusting, if we are trying to explain something that controls China's economy, than prices over the past twenty or thirty years, particularly since that model has used a long period of economic history as the basis for its estimated parameters.

As for the short data base of only the past five or eight years on which we base our predictions for China's growth in the future, for China, there has been so much dramatic institutional change over the past eight or ten years that the trends and parameters from the Maoist period are not a very good guide. Instead, parameters and rules from other developing economies make a great deal more sense. What are the kinds of patterns that describe their experiences, particularly if they seem to be two or three decades ahead of China, and to use those as guidelines? That approach strengthens our need to look at Taiwan and its experience in the past thirty years and at South Korea and other Asian economies for lessons we can apply quantitatively to China.

I'm not sure I quite understood the notion that the coastal region is a micro use for a macro analysis. My point is that there are inequalities in China regionally, but they don't necessarily produce political instabilities because the regions are so separated from each other. We will have a gangbuster economy along the coast. It will grow very rapidly, and I have not formally included it into my analysis. Perhaps it is a fair criticism to say that I may be jumping to conclusions based on a micro regional analysis, when, in fact, I really do not have such a sophisticated system.

There is suppressed inflation in China, no question about it. There are two currencies, and I am not referring to foreign exchange certificates and *renminbi*, which I consider one currency. The second currency is the ration coupons that have been in circulation for over thirty years. Of course, there is a scarcity in those. They represent the price of particular goods. So, when the money supply increases, repressed inflation measures what inflation would probably be in the absence of quantitative controls on prices, domestic trade limitations, and monitoring of prices. Actual inflation is not really as relevant for products distributed by ration coupons, but inflation is relevant for goods bought for money without ration coupons. In markets for these goods, with fixed incomes in some urban areas, 6 percent inflation has been important. China has repressed inflation because a lot of money is floating around, it is not necessarily going where it should, and prices are not allowed to meet the level justified by the money supply.

I agree that it is important to use nonstatistical factors in my analysis. I would be happy to leave the rigor of the numbers.

Regarding the notion that the burst of energy in China since 1978 cannot be sustained, it is interesting that the real factors in the high growth in the early 1980s came from agriculture as well as industry. It is difficult to see agricultural growth, farm growth and real growth, going at 6, 7, or 8 percent. It is not growth that China can sustain.

Usually, miracle growth springs from manufacturing industry growth, and here the growth of manufactures has been fueled largely by the less formal, non-state-run sectors. Looking at growth rates by ownership in Chinese industry over the past five years, one sees that the large, modern sectors that are heavily state owned have been the slower growing ones by far. Even in cities like Shanghai and in the heavily industrialized northeast where the metals and some of the truck factories are, growth in the state enterprises has been quite slow. It has been the casual sector that has grown so rapidly.

In response to the question about productivity gains, there has been some growth in productivity based just on labor, but the economy has become more labor intensive. Falling productivity of labor is not necessarily a sign that things are not going ahead well. China may have been too capital intensive in many of its industrial sectors; therefore, the Chinese changed the technology to use more labor where possible, but maybe they paid less and are living with lower labor productivity. This is an adaptation to an Asian environment of what was originally a Soviet solution to industrialization, and it is not necessarily a bad shift. In a breakdown we did several weeks ago between the rural and urban industrial sectors, for example, the average labor productivity in the rural areas dropped from roughly a thousand yuan to about four hundred yuan per person, whereas in the urban industrial sectors it actually grew.

4
China's Evolving Electronics Strategy: The Role of Structural Reform and Technology Modernization

Denis Fred Simon

Since the early 1970s, the global economy has been undergoing a process of basic restructuring. The oil crisis of 1973 engendered the end of a pattern of industrialization that had characterized economic development since the nineteenth century and paved the way for the electronics and information "revolution," a revolution emphasizing the production, storage, and distribution of information as central economic and technological activities. Engendered by the numerous advances and cost reductions in microelectronics, such as large-scale integrated circuits, a new basis for economic and social development has been created.[1]

These changes have not gone unnoticed in China. The Chinese have taken major strides toward creating an infrastructure for electronics research and production that will not only close the technological gap between China and the industrialized nations, but will also eventually allow the country to become a global technological leader in electronics. Accordingly, electronics has been accorded priority status in the recently implemented seventh five-year plan (FYP).

Four factors seem to underlie China's perception that more rapid and sustained modernization of the Chinese electronics sector is imperative. First, electronics, and especially microelectronics, is viewed as a new high-technology industry, one paving the way for China's entry into the so-called new global technological revolution described by Toffler and others. Second, electronics is viewed as an important ingredient in the upgrading of traditional industries such as textiles and food processing. Third, electronics modernization is considered critical for enhancement of China's defense capabilities, especially expanded application of computers and improved communications. And fourth, electronics is believed to be a potentially important export earner. While in the short term Beijing's principal objective is to reduce foreign imports of both components and final products, over time it hopes to play a major selling role in the international electronics marketplace.

Throughout the process of trying to join the electronics and information revolution, however, the Chinese leadership has been confronted with a fundamental dilemma: with the possible exception of its "young" software sector, China's electronics and computer industry over the past thirty years has produced structures that constrain China from following the example of other developing areas such as South Korea and Taiwan. These constraints have much to do with the relationships and contradictions between such things as plan and market, centralization and decentralization, the military and the civilian sectors, R&D and production, and prototype and new product development.

This paper focuses on the development strategies of the People's Republic of China (PRC) for the electronics sector, highlighting the different approaches and perceptions of the Chinese leadership toward electronics. The central argument is that, despite the current high level of commitment in Beijing, China will not become a major player in the international electronics market by the year 2000 and that its main goal should be to meet domestic demand. China remains too far behind technologically (while the pace of technical change abroad is accelerating), and the Chinese remain beset by severe problems of organization, capital, and personnel. China's increased interaction with the international economy and foreign firms still, however, provides an added stimulus for the Chinese system to develop more quickly than it otherwise would.

Historical Dimensions of the Electronics Industry

The beginnings of a systematic approach to the development of an indigenous Chinese electronics industry go back to the mid-1950s. Within the twelve-year plan promulgated for science and technology in 1956, electronics was accorded a priority role.[2] This plan, which was elaborated with the support of Soviet scientists, defined a number of key projects intended to create a solid scientific and technological base. The plan for electronics stressed computer technology, semiconductors, automation technology, and general electronics technology. Through the concentration of critical manpower, material, and financial resources on a few projects, several achievements of national importance were soon realized. As early as 1958, for example, China developed its first computer, only one year after Japan had done the same. The PRC's first transistor was developed in 1960; its technological level lagged about four years behind the Soviet Union, which at that time was still actively supporting the Chinese efforts.[3]

Generally speaking, the development of China's electronics industry before 1978 can be seen in terms of two seemingly contradictory characteristics. On the one hand, the high concentration of overall investment has contributed significantly to R&D and production capabilities. For the most part, these capabilities served the defense sector; the establishment of a dynamic civilian-oriented electronics industry was not a major objective. On the other hand, however, in spite of the appreciable achievements of the electronics sector during its early history, some basic problems emerged, especially in the area of technological innovation, which still remain important today.

Among the most salient characteristics of the electronics industry is the great economic and technological similarity between the Chinese and the Soviet systems. Soviet influence was extensive in all areas, resulting in, for example, the verticalization of the organizational structure and in high barriers between R&D and production, including limited interaction between researchers and end-users. Today, for example, China's computer industry is still widely characterized by the separation of developers, manufacturers, and users. New approaches to developing a more integrated computer industry (the coordinated and interrelated development of hard- and software, peripherals, service and maintenance, personnel training, etc.), although theoretically being implemented, are still far from being realized.

A second feature of the electronics industry has been its orientation toward military uses. Because electronics developed mainly in response to the requirements of the Chinese military, it was nurtured and protected by the military in a number of ways.[4] For example, considerations of cost and efficiency were frequently subordinated to meeting defense requirements and standards. A significant portion of production was highly specialized, customized, and small scale in terms of quantity. Moreover, the electronics industry, as with several of the other "ministries of machine building," was part of a very compartmentalized bureaucratic apparatus, with few incentives or mechanisms for cross-fertilization and interaction.

For many years China's computer industry focused on developing stand-alone machines for the scientific calculations and the processing of large quantities of numbers.[5] Operational speed and memory size came to be regarded as the most important computer parameters, while software and peripheral development lagged far behind. Equally important was the fact that the appropriate incentives for serial computer production did not emerge on their own. Out of over 200 different models of small, medium-sized, and large computers, only ten were produced in quantities of greater than fifty units.[6] The military orientation of the industry also resulted in very limited access to foreign technology. In effect, the modernization of the research and production facilities through external stimuli or the regular upgrading of the equipment through foreign imports was not strongly encouraged.

The military orientation of the electronics industry found its foremost expression in the political squabbles of the 1960s and early 1970s, and the development of the electronics sector suffered at the hands of the political disputes and struggles within the central leadership. The best example of the politicization of the industry is reflected in the steel-versus-electronics debate of 1971–1972.[7] The debate touched on a series of critical political issues as well as economic problems regarding China's overall development policy. Unfortunately for China, electronics became the whipping boy for a number of political groups supporting the steel faction for reasons, in many cases, unrelated to the merits of China's strategy or development capabilities.[8]

Within the broad framework of the political debates taking place at the time, the electronics sector was discussed, for the first time, not only as one industrial sector among others, but as the "core sector" that could potentially have a critical effect on all other areas of the economy and society. That the debate developed as it did and recognized the potential for electronics was somewhat remarkable, especially since the global revolution in electronics and information technology was only beginning to take off in the industrialized nations.

The Structure and Organization of China's Electronics Industry

China's electronics industry can be broken down into six major product areas: (1) television, radio, and recording equipment; (2) computers; (3) radar and communication equipment; (4) electronic components; (5) professional and industrial electronics instrumentation and equipment; and (6) military electronics. Many ministerial-level organizations have an interest in the research, production, and application aspects of electronics technology, components, or equipment; and provincial and municipal authorities control similar research and production units. At times, the mere presence of these numerous organizations has caused intense rivalry and competition as each of the respective ministries and localities has desired to have its own infrastructure for meeting its electronics needs.

Although several ministries are involved in China's electronics industry, the primary one is the Ministry of Electronics Industry (MEI), formerly called the Fourth Ministry of Machine Building. Until late 1985, the MEI was involved both directly and indirectly in the administration of a majority of the 2,600 factories in the country's electronics industry, and over 130 research institutes and six universities focused on electronics technology. At present, the extent of MEI control varies as a result of the recent divestiture decision and the degree to which local authorities are involved in overseeing the operation of specific units.[9] All but two of the 172 enterprises under MEI were placed under "local" control as part of an effort to make their units more responsible for their own profits and losses.[10]

Owing to additional changes in late 1986, MEI is now divided into four main bureaus along with its administrative offices: communication, broadcast, and television; computer and information industry; systems engineering; electronic components and devices; and microelectronics industry. Each bureau under MEI oversees a series of manufacturing and research facilities. The bureau responsible for computers, for example, oversees a fully articulated R&D and industrial structure containing 130 enterprises and 26 research units. Within this structure in the past, there were different management and control amalgams. Several key enterprises were under the direct control of MEI (from a project-budget perspective), including those that are mainly oriented toward military applications. In other cases, the principle of "dual leadership" (shuangzhong lingdao) was followed; that is, enterprises are jointly administered by central and local authorities.[11] According to one Chinese official, there can be as many as ten different organizational forms with different mixtures of local and central control. In spite of recent changes, understanding these organizational principles (tiaotiao kuai kuai) goes a long way toward clarifying why decision making in China can be so complex and why it is so difficult to carry out successful innovation efforts.

Of the major changes in policy and organization that have been introduced to overcome these difficulties since the early 1980s, two stand out. The most prominent has been the creation of the State Council Leading Group for the Revitalization of the Electronics Industry headed by Vice-Premier Li Peng. Sitting on the leading group are high-level representatives from leading government commissions and key ministries. Aside from its broad policy-making powers across a number of important ministries, the group is mandated to resolve many of the coordination difficulties and issues of duplication that have plagued the industry. In 1985 the responsibilities of the leading group were expanded to include communications, thereby giving the leading group supervision of all sectors of strategic importance to the development of China's electronics industry. This is, however, not in contradiction to the strides for decentralization.[12] With respect to the "mass production of quality, inexpensive, and multifunctional products," market competition will be allowed to "eliminate inferior and overpriced products from the market."[13]

The State Economic Commission (SEC) also plays an important role in the electronics industry by providing funds for "technical transformation" and plant renovation. In the sixth five-year plan, for example, the SEC selected 550 projects in the machinery and electronics industries to receive special funds for plant modernization and acquisition of key equipment; 148 of the projects were focused, directly and indirectly, on the electronics industry.[14] In addition, of the 3,000 key technology import projects identified in the sixth FYP, approximately sixty were directly in the electronics industry.

The second important development has to do with what might be called the trend toward corporatization (*ji tuan hua*) in the electronics industry. The process of corporatization is associated with the dismantling of the old administrative structures that managed and oversaw the electronics industry and the creation of new "economic-oriented" structures in which horizontal links predominate over vertical ones. One of the first examples was the creation of the Shenzhen Electronics Group Corporation in January 1986.[15] Through the cooperation of several enterprises, some formerly under the MEI and others affiliated with the Shenzhen authorities, a regional conglomerate composed of over 100 firms was established under the auspices of the Shenzhen municipal government. Membership is voluntary. Moreover, each of the firms will continue to derive its financial revenues from existing sources as well as from developing new sources. A similar type of organization has been created in the computer industry in Beijing (see section on computers). In addition, in cities such as Shanghai, a restructuring of the bureau-company-factory relationship has also been effected with abolition of the company as an administrative unit. It appears that the move toward economic corporatization will continue as part of the effort to reform the existing structure and foster stronger links among functionally relevant units.[16]

Electronics and the Four-Modernizations Drive

The inception of the so-called four-modernizations program in 1978 led to a new attitude toward the role of electronics in China's economic development. At the National Science Conference in March 1978, electronics, especially semiconductor and computer technology, was declared a priority area. The National Development Plan for Science and Technology (1978–1985) set ambitious goals for electronics—for example, the attainment within seven years of the capabilities for the mass production of large-scale integrated (LSI) circuits, the creation of a base for very large-scale integrated circuit (VLSI) research, the building of supercomputers, the establishment of large computer networks, and the widespread application of computers to China's key enterprises to better control and manage the production process.[17] Although there was some disillusionment when the targets of the modernization program had to be adjusted, the strategic outline of the 1978 science and technology plan remained important.

After confronting a plethora of personnel, production, and resource bottlenecks that essentially thwarted attempts to catapult the electronics industry to a position of technological parity with the West, the Chinese leadership realized that the original targets for electronics development were overly ambitious. This awareness led to the search for a new strategy for electronics modernization beginning in 1982. The search was characterized by several factors:

• The new "strategic goal" of the Chinese modernization policy promulgated at the Twelfth Congress of the Chinese Communist party in 1982—the quadrupling of the 1980 agricultural and industrial gross production value by the year 2000—resulted in the "discovery" of the "productive character" of electronics technology. Broad application of electronics in each economic sector promised improvements in labor productivity and product quality. The potential for a substantial increase in revenues to the central and local governments provided the impetus for giving expanded attention to the civilian side of the electronics industry. Consequently, the Chinese leadership shifted its attention to *application* as a priority goal of electronics modernization, particularly in the computer industry.

• The Chinese leadership recognized the need for basic reforms of the structure of the electronics industry in order to realize its short-term and long-term goals. The obstacles identified as major barriers to the development of electronics included: (1) the organizational structure, which, as mentioned, was characterized by its strong vertical nature, functionally (between research and production) and geographically (between central and local institutions), which explains the generally low level of innovation in the electronics sector; (2) the pattern of regional dispersion of the electronics industry, that is, third-line industrial plants, which does not correspond with

95

the requirements of specialization, the division of labor, and economic efficiency; (3) the low technological level of existing enterprises, exemplified by the generally backward state of manufacturing technologies, which helps to explain the low level of competitiveness of electronic products originating from China; and (4) the low skill levels of workers and staff, the inefficient use of qualified personnel, and the absence of institutionalized procedures for regular skills upgrading and enhancement.

For China, 1983 was an important transition year in the development of the electronics industry, marked by the growing attention to the so-called new technological revolution. In addition, faced with a lagging export capability, the Chinese started to consider international standards and quality criteria as requirements for entering the world market. Most important, the Chinese also began to identify electronics as a "pioneer" industry. Because of the pervasiveness of the "microelectronics revolution," the electronics industry came to be regarded as a vital sector responsible for leading the development of all other industrial and economic sectors.

The clearest reflection of Chinese policy goals and intentions for electronics emerged in January 1985 in a document entitled "The Strategy for the Development of China's Electronics and Information Industries."[18] It was formulated and issued by the aforementioned State Council Leading Group and was the first formal effort by this governmental body to coordinate and control activities in the electronics field.

The strategic guidelines elaborated for the electronics industry can be summarized as follows:

• The overall goal of the industry is expanded application of electronics technology in order to better serve the development of the national economy and society. The popularization of microcomputers, for example, is to be stressed along with software, especially Chinese character programs.

• The acquisition and assimilation of foreign technology are to be stressed as a means of closing the prevailing gap between China and the rest of the world. Joint ventures and other forms of cooperation are to be encouraged. The aim of these measures is to complement indigenous R&D and manufacturing programs in order to "speed up the development of China's electronics industry in order to attain advanced world levels sooner and thereby increase our capacity for self-reliance."

• Greater attention should be paid to creating a fully articulated and integrated electronics industry, capable of supplying needed components and manufacturing equipment as well as final products. Within this context, the main goal is "to achieve economical, large-scale mass production with good quality and low cost." Special attention will be given to large-scale integrated circuits; the short-term goal will be "to master selected, suitable, and advanced LSI circuits."

• Efforts should be made to establish an effective balance between centralization and decentralization with respect to the management of the electronics industry. Market regulation, competition and joint production will be used to transform or eliminate inferior yet expensive products. Electronics products that require large investment, long production time, and high technology, such as LSI, must be produced under unified state planning and unified arrangements in order to avoid blind development and waste of time, manpower, and materials.

• There should be close coordination and integration in the development of the electronics, computer, and telecommunications industries.

• The state should adopt a series of policies designed to move away from a system of top-down grants and establish a new system based on competitive bids. While the state should continue to invest money in key projects of national importance, it is not enough to rely on the state alone. Foreign investment should also be more effectively utilized as a channel for acquiring necessary capital to build up the electronics industry.

The guidelines also provide a framework for directing investment, training, and R&D activities. The then new minister of the MEI, Li Tieying, presented similar objectives for electronics in the seventh FYP.[19] With a few minor exceptions, the goals are consistent with those of early 1985.

The 1986 guidelines and development targets are important in a number of areas. First, they refine existing strategy and provide a comprehensive set of goals and measures designed to assist development of an industry that has been slated to play a decisive role in the country's overall modernization. By presenting a detailed set of the guidelines, the State Council Leading Group hoped to gain better control over the rate and locus of activity than in the past. Second, the goals of the major economic categories emphasize consumer electronics. Third, the establishment of a few key regional high-technology centers, mainly in the coastal areas—Shanghai, Jiangsu province (Nanjing and Wuxi), Guangdong province, and Beijing—confirms the departure from the old strategy of establishing self-sufficient regional systems throughout the country. The linking of various regional activities into a comprehensive sectoral policy means that the widening of regional disparities as well as specialization is seen as an acceptable and necessary part of the development process.[20] (See Appendix A.) By 1990, the electronics industry is to attain a 3.7 percent share of the gross value of industrial and agricultural output (GVIAO) with annual growth rates of about 16 percent.

Sectoral Analysis of the Electronics Industry

Integrated Circuits. Among the various subsectors of the electronics industry, integrated circuit (IC) research and production has received the greatest attention for three critical reasons: the importance of integrated circuits to defense-related development, their centrality to a wide range of consumer electronics products, and their critical role in computer design and production. In some respects, the Chinese see ICs as a magic key that will allow them to increase reliability and flexibility as well as to make reductions in the size, cost, and power requirements of various finished products.

China has approximately thirteen key facilities for manufacturing ICs and eight major research institutes. Total workers and staff number about 40,000, of which about 5,000 are engineers and technicians. Because of the significance attached to IC development, ICs have begun to represent a growing, though still small, proportion of total electronics production. The total quantity of IC production in 1985 exceeded 53 million units, an increase of over 100 percent since 1983.[21] Similar gains were made in the production of discrete semiconductor devices, which increased from 734.21 million in 1983 to over 1.30 billion units in 1985. At present, there are thirty different types of ICs in serial production. In most instances, the Chinese state of the art is mid-to-late 1970s vintage, though claims have been made that the manufacturing technologies for ICs in the five-micron, three-inch range were mastered during the sixth FYP.[22] China's IC facilities currently produce linear, small-scale ICs (SSIs), medium-scale ICs (MSIs), and some large-scale ICs, including NMOS, PMOS, and CMOS. Within LSI technology, they have mastered 1K and 4K RAM and are in the process of perfecting their capabilities to manufacture eight-bit microprocessors and 16K RAM microcircuits. They also produce some ECL and microwave semiconductor circuits, both of which approximate prevailing international standards.

Most designs are based on U.S. or Japanese technology.[23] China's CMOS technology appears to have come from RCA's CD4000 and Motorola's MC14000 series, its HTL circuits are derived from Toshiba, and its ECL designs have been based on Motorola's MC10100, MC10500, and MC12000 series. Copies of the INTEL 2114 device have also been produced in China along with copies of the Motorola 6800 and the INTEL 8080A. Although there is some basic design work being conducted in places such as the CAS Institute of Semiconductors in Beijing and in several of the previously mentioned institutes and universities, this is mostly geared to prototype development or specialized R&D for the defense sector.

The demand for high-quality, reliable ICs in China greatly outstrips the supply.[24] According to China's National Semiconductor Physical Chemical Analysis Center, the industry is plagued by a low-yield production rate, unstable quality, resultant high expenses and operating costs, and extreme waste of manpower and materials. Many factories still use manual processes to print circuits in the 10–15 micron range. Western visitors report that Chinese mask-making techniques are fairly satisfactory for the 6–8 micron range but that they experience problems in the 3–5 micron range. Most devices tend to be processed on 1.5–2.0-inch wafers, with only limited use of 3.0-inch wafers.[25] Of the 53 million ICs produced in 1985, medium-scale and large-scale ICs accounted for only 4.0 percent of total IC production.[26] In addition, clean room facilities tend to be inadequate; this, along with other shortcomings in quality control, contributes to reduced yields. The "gap" between the state of the art in the West and what is being done in China has led the Chinese to seek large quantities of IC design and production equipment from abroad, especially from Japan and France. As a result, IC production facilities such as the Japanese imported Jiangnan Plant in Wuxi, Jiangsu (ostensibly to support color television production) are considered of vital importance.

On the R&D side, the State Science and Technology Commission (SSTC) has been mobilizing national resources and stressing greater cooperation in the development and manufacture of large-scale integrated circuits.[27] One major SSTC objective has been to foster greater overall integration in this subsector. The Ministry of Metallurgy, for example, is being encouraged to meet the need for single-crystal, high-quality silicon, while the Ministry of Chemical Industry has been asked to provide super-purity reagents and high-purity air. In addition, the former Ministry of Machine Building Industry and the MEI are attempting to work together in pursuit of more efficient production techniques and equipment—though in the area of automotive electronics, for example, they have yet to work out a well-coordinated plan of action. Relatedly, in December 1982 at the Third National LSI Development Conference, Vice-Premier Wan Li announced that an eight-year program for LSI development would concentrate on a "chain" containing four linking parts: scientific research → technology exploitation → industrial production → wider application of LSI.[28] China's goals are best reflected in what they currently call the "5-3-1" formula: five micron-level production technology, three micron development, and one micron in the laboratory. (See Appendix B.)

Consumer Electronics. One consequence of higher rural and urban incomes has been an increased demand for consumer electronics products. By the end of 1984, for example, there were eighty-two black-and-white televisions and five–six color televisions for every 100 urban households and about seven (mostly black-and-white) televisions for every 100 rural households.[29] By the end of 1985, estimates are that Chinese families possessed close to 60 million television sets, of which 9 million were color.[30] In 1986 14.47 million televisions were produced, 4.14 million of which were color. Other "hot" items range from washing machines to electric fans. In the past, although China's output of such items was significant, it was not able to meet international standards for product reliability. The current stress on improvements in production quality has already begun to yield results. For example, Chinese black-and-white televisions have increased their mean time between failures (MTBF) to over 8,000 hours.[31] In addition, by the end of 1985 only 1 percent of the parts used in the production of China's tape recorders had to be imported—compared with over 40 percent in 1981.[32]

The primary factor holding back more rapid development of the consumer electronics industry has been the poor quality of domestically made components. In addition, many factory managers have eschewed introducing new technologies because demand already exceeds supply for the items being produced at present quality levels. In many cases, China has imported production lines from the West or engaged in joint ventures as a means of acquiring the technical capacity to overcome its shortcomings. The establishment of the Jiangnan Radio Equipment Factory in Wuxi to produce linear ICs (from Toshiba) is an example of this strategy. Some of these efforts have also begun to improve indigenous capabilities. For example, a 850,000 capacity black-and-white television tube production plant was recently set up in Chengdu, Sichuan.[33] This is the first completely domestically built tube production facility in China.

China's desire to significantly expand production of consumer electronics has led Beijing to give high priority to electronics within the "technical transformation of enterprises" effort. Accordingly, the

Chinese have sought foreign technical assistance and have developed close working ties with the Electronics Industry Association of Japan. Through discussions with the various member companies, the Chinese have entered into several agreements to introduce Japanese manufacturing technology and to secure Japanese assistance in improving plant layout, quality control techniques, scheduling, and overall management. The closer links between military and civilian production have enhanced the consumer electronics sector as well. Many civilian units have been able to capitalize on the availability of the better quality and larger quantity of technical and production resources in the defense sector. In some instances military facilities have not only advanced their own revenue-generating opportunities, but have also benefited from access to additional technologies and from pressure by the market to become more efficient.

Computers. China has 130 enterprises under MEI and local governments, among which eighty-three factories produce computers and associated products and forty-seven produce computer peripherals. Ten of the eighty-three factories are considered key computer manufacturing plants. There are also about twenty-six key research institutes and an assortment of subcontractor production facilities. Total employment is more than 89,000 people, with 15,300 engineers and technicians. There are thirty different mainframe and minicomputer models and thirteen different microcomputers produced within the computer industry.

A major organizational reform occurred in late 1986 with the establishment of the Great Wall Computer Group Corporation (GWCGC).[34] Part of the general decentralization of authority in MEI, the GWCGC is composed of fifty-eight existing computer production units, four R&D institutes, and five universities—all of which have been drawn from MEI and the Beijing municipal government. The group will undertake all phases of research, manufacturing, sales and service, and training. Theoretically, it will operate as an integrated entity, fostering horizontal coordination and minimizing administrative interference from the local or the central government.[35] Whether it will be able to achieve this goal remains to be seen. A similar organizational restructuring recently took place in Shanghai with the establishment of the Yangtze River Computer Group Corporation. All together, China will have four major computer conglomerates: (1) Changcheng in Beijing; (2) Changjiang in Shanghai; (3) Changling in Guangzhou; and (4) Changbai in Shenyang.

The evolution of China's computer industry has been heavily influenced by a combination of domestic political, technological, and economic factors. Considerations of self-reliance and technological dependence have played a major role in defining an overall strategy, though it must be acknowledged that an imbalance between foreign imports and indigenous efforts will probably continue well into the future. In early 1982 the Chinese leadership articulated a blueprint for computer development that would catapult China by 1990 to the same technological levels achieved in the advanced developed countries in the early 1980s.[36] This was a very ambitious target given the fact that China's computer design and manufacturing capabilities have been considered by most foreign experts to be seven–ten years behind those of the United States and Japan. Total computer output was designed to triple by 1990, reaching an annual production capacity of 1,800 large and medium-sized computers and 40,000 micro- and single-board computers. According to one former MEI official, "our consistent policy is to rely on ourselves and at the same time learn from the advanced technology of foreign countries. . . . if we blindly import[ed] computers, we would have to spend billions of dollars before widespread use of computers in China was achieved."[37]

At a February 1984 conference, the essential elements of the current strategy for computer development began to take shape. Focusing on the last two years of the sixth FYP, Jiang Zemin, former minister of the MEI (and currently mayor of Shanghai), stated the following objectives:

> . . . we will concentrate our efforts on building a technological basis for the microcomputer industry and raise our ability to produce complete equipment. We will energetically develop the production of 8-bit computers, 16-bit computers, and a general system for microcomputers to form several assembly and adjustment lines for microcomputer sets.
>
> . . . we will energetically raise the percentage of China-made components and parts used for manufacturing microcomputers and focus our attention on making China-made circuit boards.
>
> We will pay close attention to the construction of three computer industrial bases of north China, south China, and east China and to forming combined service bodies for computer research and production to create favorable conditions for rapidly developing the computer industry in the seventh five-year plan period.
>
> To develop the electronics industry, we should centralize financial and material resources, pay special attention to key points, . . . expand foreign economic exchanges, introduce advanced technology, and strive to raise our ability to stand

on our own feet to blaze a new trail in the electronics industry.[38]

For the rest of the decade (1986–1990), China will pursue many, if not all, of the strategies spelled out in 1984 and will focus primarily on linking electronics and the development of information technology.[39] According to Vice-Premier Li Peng, the "emphasis of development of the electronics industry will be shifted onto the course of developing microelectronics technology as the foundation and computer and telecommunications equipment as the main body." Li's statement reflects the realization among the leadership of two key points: (1) that there is an integral link between the electronics, information technology, and communications industries—the latter two of which cannot develop without significant progress in the former; and (2) that there must be a greater degree of synergy between indigenous programs and foreign imports.[40]

Development of micro-computers, which are regarded as the most suitable for prevailing production capabilities and potential applications, will continue to be emphasized. The Chinese have developed and produced 8-bit and single-board computers, many of which have been modeled on existing Western machines. They have also developed and manufactured a limited number of 16-bit microcomputers; again, many of these machines resemble Western equivalents such as the IBM-PC/XT. The Chinese have stopped importing almost all 8-bit machines and many types of 16-bit computers, since they are now able to produce varieties of both machines on their own. By 1990 officials from the MEI anticipate that about 80 percent of China's microcomputer needs will be met by domestic suppliers.[41]

The development of mainframe computers (and super computers), which experienced serious problems in the past, is now entering a recovery stage. This is best exemplified by the attention being given to the 757 computer (10 million operations per second [mips] to be upgraded to 30 mips), designed and produced by the Chinese Academy of Sciences, and the Galaxy (100 mips)—the Chinese answer to the CRAY-1—designed and produced by the National Defense S&T University in Changsha, Hunan. A decision was made in late 1985 to designate Beijing, which was chosen over several other cities, including Shanghai, as a special site for mainframe computer development.[42] The basic designs—which are dictated by considerations of standardization, software compatibility, and networking needs—will be similar to Western models produced by such prominent firms as DEC, IBM, Hitachi, and Control Data Corporation. Nonetheless, although mainframe development will be given additional capital investment and support, it appears likely that the stress on development of microcomputers will continue during the rest of the 1980s, with increasing emphasis on domestic production of components and complete machines. There is also some evidence of a growing interest in minicomputers because of their price–performance ratio compared with that of large mainframes. The driving forces behind the concentration on microcomputers, and more recently minicomputers, are the shift away from stand-alone machines toward networking within and between organizations and the growing application of computers in industrial, management, and office settings. At a national conference on computer application in June 1986, Lü Dong, minister-in-charge of the SEC and vice-chairman of the State Council's Electronics Leading Group, announced that the machine-building and electronics industries were selected to experiment with computer management information systems and computer-assisted production between 1986 and 1990.[43] China hopes to gradually, though steadily, approach the current breadth of Western uses as well as quality levels and processing capabilities by the 1990s.

The major constraints in establishing an advanced Chinese computer industry fall into four categories: (1) manufacturing capabilities; (2) peripheral equipment; (3) technical personnel; and (4) software. As indicated previously, techniques for mass production of final products as well as computer components are severely lacking in China. Even though advanced components are being developed in the laboratory, many factories lack the necessary production equipment and managerial know-how to produce these items in sufficient quantities and at necessary reliability levels.

Despite the proliferation of computers, there are still obstacles and resistance to the introduction and expanded use of computers. Even where computers have been acquired, underutilization remains a serious and widespread problem. The investment made in the development of application systems is disproportional to that made in the development or import of basic systems. According to sources in Beijing, 32,000 microcomputers were manufactured in 1985, while there were still 40,000 stocked in warehouses with no customers in sight.[44] Officials in the computer industry have suggested that in Beijing municipality, for example, the utilization rate of installed microcomputers is only 26 percent, while the national average is in the range of 15–20 percent.[45] The problem of poor utilization has its roots in personnel shortages, though other key factors include organizational rivalry and intense bureaucratic jealousy, poor maintenance, limited software availability, and poor after-sales service.[46]

Foreign Involvement in the Chinese Electronics Market. Firms from a number of countries are actively pursuing opportunities in the Chinese electronics industry. Japan has been the most active, having become the major supplier of both final products and production lines (final assembly and components, such as television tubes) for a broad range of consumer electronics goods and appliances. In some respects, China has already become the next battleground for the playing out of U.S.–Japanese competition. NEC, JVC, Matsushita, Sanyo, Hitachi, and Sony have all expanded their presence in China. Until early 1985, the Japanese had generally been reluctant to commit to equity investments in China (with some exceptions), especially since their export push was meeting great success. Moreover, concessionary financing provided by the Japanese government facilitated the purchase of additional goods. Beijing's tightened control over foreign exchange in 1986, however, necessitated a basic shift in the Japanese approach; there has been a sharp increase in Japanese investment and joint ventures in the PRC.

Japanese involvement has not been limited to consumer electronics. The establishment of the discrete IC production line by Toshiba at the Jiangnan facility in Wuxi is an example of Japanese success in this area. In 1985 the factory's output reached 278 million yuan (RMB), an almost 50 percent increase over the previous year. Fuji Electric Company has committed itself under the new export control laws to export high purity silicon wafers to China, hoping that the availability of these raw materials from Japan will enhance the possibilities for the sale of Japanese semiconductor production equipment and facilities to the Chinese. Similarly, Matsushita has agreed to provide a linear IC plant for color television sets to Shandong. The new plant will assemble ICs by processing half-finished silicon wafers supplied by Matsushita. Canon signed a deal in April 1986 to export exposure systems for producing VLSI circuits to China and will deliver two mask aligners to the Beijing No. 3 Semiconductor Factory. This equipment will allow the Chinese to manufacture 64K DRAM circuits. The Beijing plant is expected to produce CMOS-type gate arrays. Similar equipment has been sold, in smaller quantities, to R&D and production facilities in Shanghai and Beijing. According to one report, "the loosening of COCOM restrictions turned the eyes of Japanese semiconductor production equipment manufacturers to China," especially as they have been hurt by the computer slump and trade restrictions in the United States.

China had been reluctant to pursue European technology and products because it believed that much European technology was not state of the art and that much of the know-how used by these firms had originated in either the United States or Japan. Recently, though, the West Europeans, aggressively led by the French, have tried to gain market share in a number of areas such as electronics. The French are pursuing IC-related projects in Shanghai and have proposed through SOFRECOM, a company under the French Ministry of Posts and Telecommunications, the establishment of a computer-aided design IC R&D center in Wuxi. The United Kingdom has also not been far behind, as indicated by the recent agreement involving Plasma Technologies to supply Chinese research institutes with nineteen machines to produce semiconductors and ICs.

The position of U.S. firms in the China market has been somewhat uneven. Many U.S. firms have claimed that the American system of export controls has caused the United States to lose out on potentially significant sales (see the chapter by Sullivan in this volume). With the relaxation of these controls in December 1985, few serious obstacles should remain. Japanese sales have begun to increase, but the Chinese claim that proposed agreements with many U.S. firms have not materialized as originally planned. As indicated by then MEI Minister Li Tieying during his visit to the United States in 1986, China remains dissatisfied with the pace of U.S. electronics equipment sales and technology transfer. The sale of secondhand equipment seems to be one area where some progress has been made. In early 1986, for example, Fairchild sold a used silicon-growing and fabrication equipment system to a Hong Kong firm with the intention that it would make its way into China. In addition, the Chinese regularly read the listings of used equipment advertised in various trade publications. U.S. computer firms such as Burroughs, Hewlett-Packard, and Wang have found that joint ventures are the best way to gain market position in the PRC. While the technology-transfer dimensions of these agreements will probably pose problems for both the Chinese and U.S. sides in terms of the pace of transfer, the fact remains that these firms have used their technology to establish a competitive foothold in China.

Prospects and Conclusions

The critical importance of electronics to China's overall industrial objectives has given the Chinese an added impetus to achieve some tangible progress in a relatively short period of time. Electronics, in general, is to make a quantum leap and achieve those levels by the year 1990.[47] And industry officials hope to expand electronics production at a growth rate of over 10 percent per year so that by 1990 it accounts for almost 4.0 percent of the gross value of industrial and agricultural output in China.

The Chinese have indicated that four tasks will dominate their agenda for electronics development: (1) production of electronics components and devices; (2) strengthening the links between research and production; (3) reform and consolidation of the industrial structure; and (4) improving the use of foreign technology.

Much of China's anxiety about the backwardness of its electronics industry stems from its concerns about the potential for a further widening of the existing technology gap between itself and the industrialized world. It also derives from the realization that a lagging electronics industry could inhibit the potential competitiveness of other industries, such as textiles. In response, provinces such as Fujian, Guangdong, Yunnan, and Gansu, which previously have not had a strong electronics base, have established the organizational network to build up local capabilities, though the research and production capabilities in many of these areas remain weak.

Since the beginning of 1986, China, recognizing the inefficiencies and technical backwardness of its electronics industry, has adopted an "import substitution," infant industry–type of approach to development of parts of this strategic sector.[48] In early 1985, for example, the Chinese announced that they would begin to curb imports of some electronics components as a means of protecting domestic industry. Similarly, they have curtailed imports of assembly-type production lines to manufacture items such as washing machines, refrigerators, televisions, etc.[49] By the end of 1984 more than thirty refrigerator and 112 color television lines had been purchased from abroad.[50] The export of electronics products still figures prominently in Chinese objectives for the industry. Specific plans include quadrupling electronics exports to $800 million per year by 1990, while keeping imports at approximately the current $700 million level. Because poor quality, lack of product sophistication, and poor design (in comparison with places such as Taiwan and Hong Kong) have limited China's export potential, the Industrial and Commercial Bank of China has committed 104.0 million yuan (RMB) to assist with the renovation and overall modernization of existing production lines. MEI has agreed to pay the projected 8.0 million yuan interest attached to these loans.

In spite of continued problems, however, progress is being made. By the end of 1986, China signed contracts for the export of $440 million worth of electronics products, over five times the level for 1985. It also exported $113.35 million worth of electronics goods—a 117 percent increase over 1985. These amounts are extremely modest

107

when one considers the performance of South Korea, which in 1985 exported an estimated $5.25 billion worth of electronics products, and Taiwan, which in 1984 exported over $5.05 billion worth of electronics goods.[51] Nonetheless, they point to substantial growth. Exports of television sets in 1986 reached almost 200,000 units, which far exceeded projections of 15,000–20,000. The main markets were the United Kingdom, the United States, and Canada. Moreover, the contribution accounted for by locally sourced components as a percentage of the price of the complete set (excluding the picture tube) is already over 50 percent and is projected to reach 70–80 percent in 1990.[52]

Can China eventually become a major player in the international electronics industry? The verdict remains uncertain in many respects pending the extent to which China effectively absorbs available foreign technologies and pending its ability to organizationally restructure the industry. Emerging financial barriers will significantly raise the cost to China and other nations of building modern production facilities to manufacture ICs and other similar components. An article in the Shanghai-based Liberation Daily highlighted the difficulties that managers have experienced as a result of the changing signals in the electronics industry. In a survey of 300 factory managers, 62 percent wanted to be relieved of their positions because of the frequently ad hoc and incomplete nature of the reforms and restructuring efforts.[53]

Although the transition to a more competitive, technologically sophisticated, and economically efficient electronics industry will be difficult, there is room for some modest degree of optimism. Local content, for example, is steadily increasing, as is the convergence of Chinese and foreign product and quality standards. Electronics has become the beneficiary of central government attention and nurturing, which is important for technological advancement. In this regard, in its use of industrial policy to launch electronics, China is following some of the neomercantilist approaches to creating competitive advantage that have been followed in the newly industrialized nations. In contrast to many other industries in China, the success of electronics modernization will depend largely on the strength of central control and guidance rather than primarily on decentralization.

Electronics also has the advantage of being exposed to the international market. If the experience of Taiwan and South Korea has taught us anything, it is that international exposure is an important vehicle for building up sensitivity to quality, product diversity, and realiability. The more exposure the industry has, combined with central government assistance, the more likely electronics will play a strategic role in China's modernization. The key measure in this regard will not be China's ability to compete with the United States or Japan in foreign markets—though exports will continue to be a high priority objective and China will likely be able to establish a niche for itself in the low-middle segment of the electronics industry that will gradually be vacated by the newly industrialized countries. A more significant indicator of electronics modernization will be the PRC's increased ability to meet its domestic industrial and consumer electronics needs with decreasing dependence on foreign inputs. The main opportunities for foreign electronics firms in China, therefore, will be in helping the Chinese meet this objective.

Appendix A: Development Goals for China's Electronics in the Seventh FYP, 1986–1990

1. *Gross Production Value:* In 1990 share of 3.7 percent of national industrial and agricultural gross production value. Annual growth rates of 16 percent.

2. *Overall Goals:* Focus on *consumer electronics* as the largest market. Application of *industrial electronic products* notably in traditional industries; emphasis on development of software, systems engineering, and consultant services. Emphasis of *components development* on consumer electronics needs; other areas include telecommunications, computers, instruments and military electronics. Priority also on measuring instruments, special technology equipment and special materials. Strengthening of *military electronics;* technology transfer into civilian sector to be continued.

3. *Regional Policy:* Focus on a few technologically advanced regions, especially in *East China.*

4. *Large Project Areas: Integrated circuits* (especially enlargement of domestic technological capabilities in color TVs and related picture tubes); *computers and telecommunications; electronic products for export* (not specified).

5. *Emphasis on five techniques: Large-scale production* (focus: CAD, CAM, CAT), *miniaturized processing* (VLSI, 1-2 micrometers line width); *telecommunications* (digitalization and switching); *industry-oriented electronics* (technical transformation of traditional industries); military *electronics.*

6. *Organization:* Establishment of *branch development centers* for microelectronics, computer software, telecommunications, industry-oriented electronics and military electronics. Set-up of more than *ten export bases.* Structural reforms (divestiture) to be continued.

Appendix B: China's Proposed Three-Stage IC Plan

PHASE ONE (1986–1990): Foundation-Laying Stage—Master 3-inch silicon chip and 3.5 micron processing precision—and begin work toward the 2.0 micron level. Also ensure that items such as 4K MOS RAM, 16K DRAM, 4K CMOS RAM, 8-bit and 16-bit microprocessors, 1,600–2,400 gate CMOS gate array logic circuits, and low power TTL Schottky can be mass produced. Development work should focus on 2 micron technology and CMOS circuits.

PHASE TWO (1991–1995): Continuing Development Stage—Continue to focus on LSI circuit production capability, mastering 4-inch silicon chips and 2 micron technology. Bring about large volume production of 64K MOS RAM and 6,400–12,800 gate CMOS arrays. Continue to concentrate on 16-bit microprocessors with some work on 32-bit processors and 256K MOS RAM. Also begin work on GaAs circuits. R&D work should focus on 5-inch, 1 micron technology.

PHASE THREE (1996–2000): Production of VLSI Stage—Form VLSI production capability. Production capabilities should include ability to manufacture 256K and 512K MOS RAM and 32-bit microprocessors in large quantities. Also some production of 1 Mb memories. R&D work should be focused on new generation ICs, such as high TC value superconductors and bioelectronic circuits. During this phase China's IC industry should strive to attain the U.S. level of 1990.[54]

Notes

1. Tom Forester, ed., *The Microelectronics Revolution* (Cambridge, Mass.: MIT Press, 1980).

2. Hans Kühner: *Die Chinesische Akademie der Wissenschaften und ihre Vorläufer 1928–1985* [The Chinese Academy of Sciences and its Predecessors, 1928–1985] (Hamburg: Mitteilungen des Instituts für Asienkunde, no. 146, 1986).

3. Manfredo Macioti: "Scientists Go Barefoot," *Successo* (January 1971), quoted in Jon Sigurdson, *Technology and Science in the People's Republic of China* (Oxford: Pergamon Press, 1980), p. 38.

4. According to Cheng Chu-yuan's study of China's machine-building industry, "the technology of electronics, which has made great strides since 1958, was first of all to satisfy the demands of national defense." See Cheng Chu-yuan, *The Machine-Building Industry in Communist China* (Chicago: Aldine Publishers, 1971).

5. According to one source in Shanghai, before the post-Mao economic reforms, military factories produced on a "cost plus 5 percent" basis, with the achievement of the tasks always superseding considerations of economic efficiency and cost.

6. Xiu Jinya, "Push Vigorously the Research, Production and Application of Computers," *Jingji Guanli*, no. (1984), pp. 12–15.

7. Jon Sigurdson: "Technology and Science—Some Issues in China's Modernization," U.S. Congress, Joint Economic Committee, *Chinese Economy Post-Mao*, vol. 1 (Washington, D.C.: Government Printing Office, 1978), pp. 476–534, especially pp. 519–24.

8. Harlan Jencks, *From Muskets to Missiles: Politics and Professionalism in the Chinese Army, 1945–1981* (Boulder, Colo.: Westview Press, 1982).

9. For details of this divestiture effort see *China Daily*, August 2, 1985.

10. "Electronics Ministry Decentralizes Authority," *Xinhua*, May 8, 1986, translated in *JPRS-CST-86-025*, July 1, 1986.

11. The principle of dual leadership may also apply to enterprises that are jointly administered by provinces and cities or by cities and counties. It is also possible for a combination of such "local" entities along with a central government ministry to administer an enterprise, e.g. city, province, and the ministry. A good example of the latter is in the "Zijin Information Industry Corporation" in Nanjing.

12. Li Peng, "The Electronics and Information Industries Should Serve the Construction of the Four Modernizations," *Jingji Ribao*, January 14, 1985.

13. Quoted from Jonathan Pollack, *The Chinese Electronics Industry in Transition*, A Rand Note, N-2306 (Santa Monica, Rand Corp., May 1985), p. 21.

14. *Jixie Zhoubao* (Machine-Building Weekly), no. 149 (July 29, 1983), p. 2.

15. "Gu Mu Attends Electronics Conglomerate Opening," *Xinhua*, January 6, 1986, translated in *FBIS*, China: *Daily Report*, January 9, 1986, pp. K9–10.

16. In Western terminology, we would refer to the term "corporatization" as part of the process of vertical integration; but in the PRC, the term explicitly refers to the process of horizontal integration across heretofore insurmountable vertical barriers.

17. Fang Yi, "Report at the National Science Conference (Extracts)," *Renmin Ribao*, March 29, 1978.

18. See Li Peng, "The Electronics and Information Industries;" see also *Xinhua*, January 11, 1985, and *FBIS-China*, January 15, 1985, pp. K25–27.

19. Li Tieying, "Continue the Reform, Speed up the Development, Actively Invigorate the Electronics Industry," *Zhongguo Dianzi Bao*, no. 59 (January 21, 1986).

20. Chen Jiyuan, *"Diqu jingji jiegou duice"* (Measures regarding the regional economic structure), in Sun Shangqing, ed., *Lun jingji jiegou duice* [On measures regarding the economic structure] (Beijing: Chinese Academy of Social Sciences Publishing House, 1984), pp. 318–60.

21. *Zhongguo Kexue Jishu Zhengce Zhinan* (Primer on China's S&T Policy) (Beijing: S&T Publishing House, 1986), p. 137. By 1990, China hopes to produce 400 million ICs per year.

22. Xu Daorong, "Remarkable Electronics S&T Breakthroughs in the 6th Five-Year Plan," *Zhongguo Dianzi Bao*, no. 101 (June 17, 1986), p. 3.

23. Sun Tingcai, "A Discussion about the Selection of Microcomputers," *Dianzi Jishu*, no. 7 (1982), pp. 5–78.

24. Chinese officials, led by Vice-Premier Li Peng, believe that massive

imports of ICs have seriously injured the domestic IC industry. In 1985, for example, estimates were that China would need a total of 170 million ICs, but close to 200 million pieces were imported. At the same time, over 53 million pieces were domestically produced, creating an excess of nearly 85 million. Foreign ICs tend to get used first unless otherwise instructed from above.

25. According to a March 1986 report, China's immediate goal is to develop three-micron technology for mass production while continuing research on one-micron technologies.

26. These capabilities correspond to the U.S. manufacturing level of 1967 and the Japanese manufacturing level of 1969. See *Zhongguo Kexue Jishu Zhengce Zhinan* (Primer on China's S&T Policy), loc. cit.

27. In late 1985 Qinghua University received certification for production of China's first 16K static RAM, which measured 28 square millimeters, was 0.003 mm thick, and contained 108,000 transistors and other devices. In addition, a 64K NMOS DRAM was also developed by MEI Institute #24 and the Jiangnan Radio Factory in Wuxi. The chip, whose size was 3.96 × 7.56 square mm, contained 150,000 elements and attained a minimum line width of 2.5 microns. Finally, in September 1986 the completion of a 16-bit CPU developed by the CAS Shanghai Institute of Metallurgy in cooperation with the MSI Lishan Microelectronics Corporation and the Shanghai Jiaotong University was announced. See *Guoji Dianzi Bao*, June 11, 1986; *Guoji Dianzi Bao*, September 11, 1986.

28. Currently, the Chinese are working with X-ray lithography in order to move ahead into VLSI technology. Some of this work is being carried out at the Institute of Semiconductors under the Chinese Academy of Sciences, a facility that was recently completely refurbished and that imported a number of pieces of new testing and manufacturing equipment from Japan.

29. State Statistical Bureau, *Statistical Yearbook of China 1985* (Beijing: China Statistics Publishing House, 1985), pp. 565 and 573.

30. "China Must Make Own Color TVs," *China Daily*, December 30, 1985, p. 4.

31. "Electronics Industry Booming," *China Daily*, March 6, 1986, p. 4.

32. "Foreign Tape Parts Go to Reverse Speed," *China Daily*, January 8, 1986, p. 3.

33. "Last Year, Chengdu's Electronics Industry Realized the Best Level in History," *Zhongguo Dianzi Bao*, March 21, 1986, p. 1.

34. "Great Wall Computer Group Corporation Established in Beijing," *Zhongguo Dianzi Bao*, December 16, 1986, p. 1.

35. "New Computer Giant Eyes Home Market," *Beijing Review*, January 19, 1987, pp. 5–6.

36. The description of these goals was provided by Li Rui, former general manager of the department of computer industry under the MEI. See "Computers in China," *Summary of World Broadcasts/Far East* (FE/W1201/A/13), November 10, 1982, pp. 13–14.

37. Ibid., p. 14.

38. "Minister Jiang Zemin on China's Developing Electronics Computer Industry," *Zhongguo Xinwen She*, February 21, 1984, translated in *FBIS*, China: Daily Report, February 12, 1984, pp. K8–9.

39. Li Peng, "Electronics and Information Industries."

40. For an earlier commentary on this latter point see Ge Zhangyi, "A Discussion of the Countermeasures of the World's New Technological Revolution," *Guoji Maoyi Wenti* (September–October 1984), pp. 6–10.

41. "Push Vigorously the Domestic Production of Microcomputers During the Seventh Five-Year Plan," *Renmin Ribao*, July 21, 1986, p. 1.

42. "Beijing Area Chosen to Manufacture Mainframe and Medium-Scale Computers," *EDP China Report*, vol. 4, November 30, 1985, p. 18.

43. Lü Dong, "Report at the National Work Conference for Computer Applications (Extracts)," *Zhongguo Keji Bao*, no. 75, June 25, 1986, p. 2.

44. "Computers Facing Glut in Market," *China Daily*, January 11, 1986.

45. Ibid. According to one source, a survey in Beijing revealed that of the 14,000 microcomputers in place most are used fewer than three hours a day. "Beijing Has Future as Computer Capital," *China Daily*, January 18, 1986, p. 2.

46. There are only approximately 10,000 people involved in computer services in China. The creation of the China Computer Services Corporation in 1984 is a positive step toward improving computer use, though the number of people and their skill levels remain inadequate. Chen Liwei, "The Position and the Role of Computer Services in the Computer Industry," *Dianzi Xuebao*, no. 5 (September 1984), pp. 65–67, translated in JPRS-CST-85-009, April 9, 1985, pp. 57–61.

47. According to Li Tieying, the goal for 1990 is to bring 70 percent of the country's major electronics goods up to 1970s and 1980s levels.

48. This policy, which in Chinese is known as "baohu zhuyi" (protectionism), was officially announced by Vice-Premier Li Peng in January 1986.

49. The large number of these lines has proved problematic because many of them rely extensively on imported components. In recent months, because of the revaluation of the yen, some factories have had to curtail production due to a shortage of foreign exchange. The Fujian-Hitachi joint venture, for example, will reduce television production by 100,000 sets in 1986.

50. A list of forty-five items, mainly in the consumer electronics area, requiring import licenses was issued in March 1986 by the MOFERT.

51. "Asia: The Four Dragons Rush to Play Catch-Up Game," *Electronics Weekly*, May 6, 1985, p. 48–56.

52. "Chinese Color TV Industry Enters International Market," *Renmin Ribao* (overseas edition), December 16, 1985, p. 3.

53. "Managing a Factory Is Difficult," *Jiefang Ribao*, August 23, 1986, pp. 1, 3.

54. See Wang Yangyuan, "Discussion About the Technical Goals of China's IC Industry in the 1990s," *China Computerworld*, no. 9, May 8, 1984, p. 3.

Commentary

Chia Siow Yue

If we were to look at the economic implications of China's electronics industry, we would, of course, have to look at the effects of both trade and investment. On the trade side we must consider both imports and exports. China has imported tremendous amounts of consumer electronic goods and technology, although these imports have declined somewhat in the past two years because of foreign exchange difficulties. The result is that there is tremendous overcapacity in the consumer electronics industry in China today, particularly in television and other assembly plants. In this area, I imagine there will be strong pressure for China to export in addition to importing and producing for the domestic market. There have also been dramatic changes in China's ability to import technology now that the United States has removed constraints on exports of high technology.

Regarding exports, I disagree somewhat with Dr. Simon's statement that China should focus on producing electronics for the domestic market and forget about exports. I think there are tremendous economic pressures for China to export. If we compare China's import requirements over the next few decades with China's export prospects, I think it becomes clear that electronics will have to play an increasing role.

Traditionally, China has exported large amounts of textiles and garments, but textiles and garments cannot expand at the rate that will be necessary to meet China's foreign exchange requirements. In the case of textiles and garments, as we know, there is the problem of increasing protectionism in the OECD markets. I believe China will be forced to export an increasing range of consumer electronics, taking the path that South Korea, Taiwan, Hong Kong, and Singapore have taken.

Having said that, the question then becomes, What is the comparative advantage of China in the exports of such products? China may find itself in a much more unfavorable position than that of the four Asian NICs (newly industrialized countries). It has the factory intensity or the low labor cost, low wages, and abundant labor supply, but the Chinese laborer is not as productive as laborers in the NICs. Moreover, when we talk about competition in consumer electronics, price is only one factor, and nonprice factors will become very important. The Chinese socialist economy being structured as it is, and given the type of enterprise and sectoral structure that has been outlined by Dr. Simon, I am not very optimistic about the ability of the Chinese industry to adapt its product designs and so on.

Since, essentially, a socialist economy does not believe in consumer sovereignty, how should it produce and compete in the world market?

With regard to competition, therefore, China's position in the world market would be below that of Japan, of the United States, and of Europe. I would even rank it below that of the NICs. The question is, apart from consumer electronics, in what other segments of the electronics industry may China specialize and have a comparative advantage? Here I am much more pessimistic because competition in the semiconductor industry, for example, occurs only between the two giants, Japan and the United States. Even Europe has fallen far behind. China, therefore, cannot compete in that field, and to some extent I agree with the idea that without a technological lead in the semiconductor industry a country cannot play a major role in the rest of the electronic segments. China would have to play a secondary role, and it is in this regard that I think a lot of the institutional reforms at the price level will be essential if China is to compete in the world market in consumer electronics vis-à-vis that of the NICs or vis-à-vis even that of the emerging Association of Southeast Asian Nations (ASEAN) exporters.

With regard to investment, what implication can we see from the growth of the Chinese electronics industry? There's no doubt that great priority will be placed on the electronics industry for various reasons: The production of domestic electronic products would be a means of improving the standard of living of the Chinese masses. In addition, it is widely recognized that electronics is a growth industry and is therefore worthy of promotion in its own right. But more important in the Chinese context, electronics is seen as the means for the modernization of the whole industrial sector. Therefore, I agree with Mr. Simon that great emphasis will have to be placed on the importation of foreign technology. A lot of emphasis will have to be placed on how China can promote a favorable investment climate that will attract the types of foreign investment and technology it requires.

115

And I agree with Mr. Simon that the problem is not as much of technology acquisition as of technology assimilation and technology diffusion.

Roger W. Sullivan

The adjectives "optimistic" and "pessimistic" do not have much relevance to me in this discussion. Whether China is going to be a major player in international electronics trade or not does not strike me as an issue that can be reduced to those terms.

First, some have assumed that China wants to compete. I am not sure the evidence is there for that. We have talked to the Chinese for some time about their electronics industry. When the State Council Leading Group on Electronics was established, we tried to make contact with it and to talk about ways American industry might be helpful. I do not think Vice-Premier Li Peng was very interested.

By contrast, the State Council Leading Group on Foreign Investment, with which we work very closely, is very anxious to get our views. The State Council Leading Group on Foreign Investment is interested in improving its investment climate. Li Peng is not necessarily interested in what we have to say on electronics because his primary goal seems to be import substitution. He may be conscious of the pressures that will come to bear on China to get into the export business in electronics, but he may also be conscious of some of the points that have been treated in the World Bank analysis of China—specifically, that it is not necessarily going to be China's decision whether it can be a player in the international market in electronics products. The decision will probably be made for it, and a lot of people in China believe the decision has already been made.

There are so many biases against exporting from China, and there is so much advantage in selling on the domestic market that it is going to be very difficult indeed for China to develop the level of quality that would make it competitive with the NICs. We see this even in the bicycle industry in China where trying to get a factory manager interested in exporting bicycles is very difficult. You can make a good living selling on the domestic market in China.

Through exchange rates and protectionism, the Chinese system adds to those biases. The World Bank pointed out the real danger of China's practice of putting protection in place the minute it becomes capable of making any kind of product. This is true in the electronics industry and in small computers, for example. Wham!, the minute China makes something, no matter how bad it is, consumers can no longer buy the product from abroad, putting the manufacturer in the position of producing a lot of products that are good enough. Somebody has to buy them. Because his customers cannot import, the industry has no outside stimulus to force an improvement in quality or design or anything else that would make it more marketable.

This is quite different from what happened in Singapore, Taiwan, Korea, and Japan. None of those places had domestic markets big enough to absorb the production of their industries. They were forced right from the start to cope with the pressures of the international marketplace and either be competitive or get out of the business.

China doesn't have to be competitive or get out of the business. China can be very successful with something between the European and the Soviet models of producing the electronics they need for their military and the electronics they need for their industry. As soon as they can make something that does the job—it may not be as good as an IBM model or a Honeywell—that is what they continue to make. It is unlikely therefore that even if China decided it would be a good idea to turn some of the excess capacity into export earnings that it could pull it off. Someone in China said to me one time, "We can tell people they can't make something. We can tell them they can't export something. But we can't tell them *to* export it. We can't tell them to sell it if they don't make it in a way that makes it competitive on the world market."

I do not think that is a pessimistic conclusion. I think it is a realistic conclusion based on the fact that China is and will for quite a long time be limited in certain areas in its ability to produce goods that are up to international market standards.

Discussion

ARTHUR H. ROSEN: If we agree with all these pessimistic assessments, we must wonder why so many American companies are rushing out to rent space in satellites that the Chinese are able to put up, which I presume require a certain amount of sophisticated electronic gear. The Chinese have certainly demonstrated a capacity, when they wish to, to mobilize human and material resources in, for example, the nuclear and rocket industries.

And also, of course, China is not working in a vacuum. There is a role for American industry, and American industry is taking part in Chinese modernization. The two constituent elements of UNISYS—Burroughs and Sperry, for example—both have computer plants going up or already operating in Kunming and Wuxi, respectively. IBM is also involved in China, and a number of other American companies, including high-tech electronics industries, are moving in.

It seems inevitable to me that the benefits of technology transfer are going to be diffused throughout the country. My impression is that a number of smaller American firms in Silicon Valley, Boston, and elsewhere are also rushing into this business in China and that this will have a rather substantial cumulative effect in the next several years, as will Chinese scientists and technology specialists in the computer industry who are returning to China after studying in the United States and other countries.

The Chinese do seem able to develop quality, even for the domestic market. It has been shown in a number of computer industries and in other competing consumer areas such as televisions, bicycles, sewing machines and so on, that competition does develop in the domestic market. The Chinese consumer is now often able to choose on the basis of quality rather than simply take something because it is on a shelf; he is able to be brand conscious. That will increasingly be the case in even more advanced industries such as electronics.

ALBERT KEIDEL: I want to explore two factors. First, there should be a link between China's ability to produce sophisticated chips and its ability to produce electronic goods or final products.

It seems to me that electronic chips are going to be like the steel and coal of the early industrial revolution. Since these are so capital intensive, couldn't China import them in large numbers, use more labor-intensive methods to put them into electronic consumer goods, and then reexport them?

The second factor is the notion of China's need to focus on import substitution because of the lack of incentives to export. That is not only a factor in the electronics industry but it has also been true for cameras, wristwatches, and a whole host of products for which the Chinese domestic price system discourages exports at the current exchange rate because pre-price reform prices for so-called luxury consumer goods make the international price ratio about fifty to one as opposed to one to one, where it should be.

Already we have seen some evidence of price reform: wristwatch prices dropped 40 to 50 percent in rural areas last year, and sewing machine prices dropped as well. If price reforms continue so that poor quality, lower quality, or mediocre manufactured goods drop in their domestic price, and at the same time there is an exchange rate adjustment or a series of exchange rate adjustments by the 1990s, the prospect of exporting some of these mediocre quality electronic goods would be rather attractive.

DENIS FRED SIMON: Why does China continue to be attractive, for example, to foreign firms—firms that want to go in and manufacture computers or manufacture television sets? What has happened is that because of the import substitution policy the Chinese government has set up a sort of quid pro quo—that is, technology transfer in return for market access. In fact, I would argue that we are in for a big shock and that firms are starting to see that already. Good examples are Hewlett-Packard and IBM, which have reached so-called manufacturing agreements with China. Although the "manufacturing" is mostly assembly at this stage, the expectation of the U.S. firms is that this will give them greater market access and that they will be able to sell their machines in China.

The Chinese expectation is technology transfer, and what we have already seen is a contradiction. The pace of technology transfer is not fast enough from the Chinese perspective, whereas from the foreign firms' perspective moving any faster cannot be justified. The result is products that are good only for internal consumption. That's one of the reasons why U.S. firms are operating in China. Otherwise they would have no way, particularly in microcomputers, for example, to sell their products in large numbers in the Chinese market.

Some firms are looking to the long term and hope to capitalize on the learning curve in China; they hope to be able to produce items in which they could send components elsewhere and put them into some kind of global product network. But right now that is just not possible. Foxboro, for example, has been faced with the problem that their pace is not fast enough for the Chinese. Hewlett-Packard has also been faced with that. Wang, which just started, is faced with the problem of technology transfer not occurring fast enough and a problem of product quality. So they are all in this dilemma. The Chinese have pushed the situation so that there is this quid pro quo.

On the other side are the end users. You have to distinguish between so-called technology developers in China and end users. End users in China want foreign-made computers, foreign-made televisions, foreign-made components. Ninety-nine percent of the components for the Chinese supercomputer were imported. There were almost no domestically made integrated circuits or semiconductors in it. In the 757 computer, which is another supermini built by the Chinese, again they restructured the machine so that the majority of key components are imported.

The Chinese will import chips for high priority national projects such as the building of a supermini or a main frame. But the Chinese have stated unequivocally that they do not want to import large amounts of chips because there will then be no market for their own domestically produced chips. For them, it is sort of a Catch-22: domestically produced chips have low yields, low performance, and low reliability, so the domestic users do not want to use them, and the leaders do not want to import foreign ones. The Chinese probably should not start to build lots of chip plants, but the requirements of electronic self-reliance are central to the thinking of the leaders today. Therefore, they're not going to break out of that mold.

I do think China is serious about becoming a big player in consumer electronics exports. They are pushing very hard on it. They talk a good line, but they are not there yet and are not going to be there for a long, long while.

ROGER W. SULLIVAN: An earlier comment raises an interesting point: I said that the products China makes in the electronics area would serve their domestic needs but would not be up to international standards; that does not necessarily mean, however, that the products are poor quality in some kind of an objective sense, or even that that interferes with their ability to incorporate some of these things into other kinds of products and sell them abroad.

The Soviet Union, for example, makes some pretty horrible aircraft, including their military aircraft; the Fox Bat bomber would be a joke in the U.S. Air Force, but it shoots planes down. It has vacuum tubes and cheap metallurgy, all kinds of other problems, but it does the job. The same could be said about the Ilyushin, but that doesn't mean that Singapore Airlines is going to buy Ilyushins to fly across the ocean. The same can be said about China. It is making a lot of things for its domestic market that do the job. But they are not necessarily going to be salable in the international market.

The disincentives to export, such as price, apply across the board—to sewing machines and bicycles as well as to electronics. But something special seems to apply, to consumer electronics and to some other kinds of products. If the Chinese continue to clamp on protectionist measures—and they will—the minute somebody can make an adequate computer or any other kind of a product, the Chinese manufacturer has no incentive to improve the quality, the design, the appearance, or the user friendliness of his product. He will just continue to make "clunkers" and ship them out to a captive consumer. But that doesn't mean that they cannot make sewing machines with some kind of microprocessors in them.

Many of the things that the Chinese want to import in semiconductor manufacturing equipment from the United States, for example, are things American firms would not even be making if it weren't for the Chinese market. American manufacturers no longer use the components the Chinese want.

Just because China will not be competing with Japan and the United States or even with Western Europe in electronics does not mean the Chinese are not going to be able to put up satellites, does not mean they are not going to be able to make sewing machines with microprocessors in them, and so forth. It just means they are not going to be in the front line of electronics.

MR. SIMON: As a final comment, the Chinese imported lots of equipment with the expectation that the magic of technology would enhance competitiveness. But because they did not have the people or the managerial know-how, there was a tremendous waste of equipment and money. They believed, mistakenly, that technology alone would create competitiveness and did not pay attention to the need for effective management.

We have seen that management makes technology work, in whatever industry, and in China that's been the biggest lesson so far. As a result the Chinese economy is going to develop, but it could develop faster. Right now the growth that is taking place is not filled with a lot of substance. That's where, I think, the problems are going to come in the future.

5

China's Role in the World's Aircraft and Airline Industry in the Year 2000

Adam M. Pilarski

The demand for aircraft is a derived demand that depends on the health of the airline industry, which in turn is a function of traffic. Growing traffic increases the demand for additional aircraft as well as generates funds to pay for them. This chapter therefore first forecasts traffic and then estimates the number of planes needed to carry the traffic in China in the year 2000. A short description of the aircraft industry follows. All of the forecasts and analyses form the basis of a speculation regarding China's role in commercial aviation in the next century.

A central question is whether standard economic theory and econometric practice can be of use in analyzing China's air transportation. Is it relevant to estimate demand in a system whose central authorities make decisions without regard to economic realities? The facts documented in this chapter are that air transportation in China depends on economic factors in a way that most countries in the world do. Empirical econometric analysis supports my position that air transportation in China can be analyzed successfully with standard economic tools.

The opinions expressed are those of the author only and do not necessarily reflect the views of McDonnell Douglas or its management. I would like to thank Mr. Yan Shanfa of SAIC (Shanghai Aviation Industrial Corporation) and Mr. Fu Shula of CARITE (China Aero Research Institute of Technology and Economics) for their help in the analytical part of my project. While my opinions surely differ from theirs, I could not have accomplished much without their input, knowledge, and support. My appreciation also goes to Yao Ying Zuo and Ma Fengshan of SAIC, Ji Xiaohua of CARITE, Chen Feng of CAAC, and Young Chai and Eric Macklin of Douglas Aircraft. Jan Roman, as always, did a marvelous job typing the manuscript.

Traffic

Domestic Traffic. Domestic traffic in all countries of the world depends on two major factors: income and price. Generally, the more money people (or governments or businesses) have the more they fly. Moreover, the higher the relative price of flying the less people will fly, other things being equal.

Airline traffic in the People's Republic of China (PRC) is substantially different from any other in the world for many reasons. Clearly, the PRC is unique in its size, geography, organization of its airline industry, fleet composition, etc.—but so is every country in the world. Every country has unique characteristics differentiating it from others. What makes PRC traffic forecasting more difficult, however, is that most native travelers are on business trips. Hence, the government both pays out and collects most of the money from the industry. This does not mean, however, that economic factors do not matter. Economic constraints still exist. Even if they do not affect individual citizens, they exist for the economy as a whole. As national income rises, more resources can be devoted to air transportation and more people are flown. As costs rise, other things being equal, the government should raise fares and restrict flying. The analysis for the whole economy is similar to the one relevant to the individual.

In the same way that an individual decides whether to buy an airline ticket, shoes for the children, a new television set, or a present for a relative, the government must decide how to allocate the limited resources available to a nation. It can spend money on education, health, defense, or many other public services. Allocating more resources for air transportation means building fewer parks—and vice versa, of course. Although every government is faced with difficult choices, the availability of more funds makes the choices a little easier. But the fact is that economic factors do matter in determining the amount of resources a centrally planned economy devotes to air transportation in a manner similar to that employed in the rest of the world.

We find a very consistent picture when observing the developments of air transportation all over the world. Study after study in country after country shows the same basic relationship: as incomes grow, so does air traffic. Not only does this happen, but air traffic grows much faster than income, at a rate of one-and-a-half to two-and-a-half times as fast in fact. Why does this happen? There are at least two purely economic explanations. The first is related to the concept of "value of time." As people's levels of productivity and

123

education rise, the value of their time increases too. Today, for example, although many tourists can afford the price of a transatlantic cruise, almost nobody takes a ship from the United States to vacation in Europe. They cannot afford the time, and so they fly. The second explanation for the rapid growth in air traffic is that air traffic is a luxury item. When our incomes go up we can afford more than our most basic needs.

Both of these explanations are universal and apply to the PRC in the same way that they apply to the rest of the world. As the number of highly educated and productive people in China increases, the government has to provide means for them to spread their knowledge throughout the country. The valuable time of such people can be used more productively if these individuals spend a short time in transit. And after satisfying the basic needs of the population (food, shelter, and clothing), the government can spend part of the increase in national income on "luxuries" like developing remote areas, supplying fresh fruit and vegetables (via air cargo) to cities, or creating emergency evacuation facilities in case of earthquakes or flooding.

Data and models. Theoretical considerations and the availability of data suggested the possible use of two independent explanatory variables: Chinese macro income and the price of a ticket (yield). The raw data consist of DRPK (domestic revenue passenger-kilometers), in billions of dollars, GIAP (gross industrial and agriculture [index] product), and YRPK (yield per DRPK [index]). GIAP and YRPK are index numbers calculated from constant 1980 yuan.

Traffic in our study was measured by DRPK (which is defined as number of passengers multiplied by the distance they fly). DRPK and GIAP were obtained from the *China Statistical Yearbook*. The yield index, measuring the cost of flying one person one kilometer, was obtained from the Civil Aviation Administration of China (CAAC), the national airline. Both the yield series and the income series are adjusted for inflation.

The relationship between traffic and independent variables is formulated using regression analysis. Numerous such relationships can be established—for example, variables can be run in linear fashion, or a regression can be estimated using logarithmic transformations of all variables or any other mathematical transformations. Moreover, data can be analyzed over different time periods. Using data for the post–Mao Zedong period only (1976 on) reduces the number of observations and hence reduces our confidence in the validity of the results. When analyzing the whole 1949–1985 period, however, we use some data that may be of little relevance to today's China. The same problem, of course, exists when analyzing any other country. How relevant to today's traffic are developments in the United States in the pre–jet airplane era? There is no one best equation. Many possible specifications are analyzed statistically and are scrutinized to determine whether they produce reasonable forecasts.

The equation used for forecasting is a logarithmic transformation of the variables, which reduces the importance of statistical outliers. Even more important, it produces elasticities. In the case of logarithmically transformed data, regression coefficients become elasticities, which indicate the responsiveness of the dependent variable as a result of a change in the independent variable.

The regression produces a coefficient of 1.935 in regard to GIAP and of -0.262 with regard to yield. The GIAP coefficient of 1.935 indicates that as income (measured by GIAP) increases by 6.7 percent a year, traffic will rise by 12.97 percent (1.935×6.7); the YRPK coefficient indicates that as yield decreases by -3.0 percent traffic will rise by 0.79 percent (-0.262×-3.0). This income elasticity of close to two is consistent with that found in many other countries and regions. The price (yield) elasticity has the expected negative sign but is smaller than that of many other countries, indicating that travel in China is less price sensitive—a reasonable conclusion since most travelers are on official government business.

The regression shows that the relationship of traffic and economy is a statistically significant one. Adjusted R^2 is 0.9543, t values are 15.7 for GIAP and -1.6 for YRPK coefficients, F value is 345.8. The Durbin-Watson statistic is very low (0.54), but a Cochran-Orcutt fix-up does not change the coefficients materially.

Traffic forecast. Generating a traffic forecast requires an input regarding the explanatory variables. The following forecasts of independent variables were used: a 6.7 percent annual growth of real GIAP for the 1986–1990 period, followed by 6.0 percent for 1991–1995 and 5.3 percent for 1996–2000. The forecasts for real yields for the same time periods were annual decreases of 3.0 percent, 1.8 percent, and 1.2 percent.

These numbers are official forecasts of PRC officials. The GIAP forecasts, for example, predict a quadrupling of the economy between 1980 and 2000 in accordance with official PRC government forecasts but clearly below forecasts generated by others, notably Albert Keidel of Rock Creek Research, Inc. (see his chapter in this book). The results of the model developed using forecasts of independent variables are displayed in table 5–1.

International Traffic. Chinese international traffic grew at unprecedented rates in recent years. Domestic traffic skyrocketed by an aver-

125

TABLE 5–1
GROWTH OF DOMESTIC AIR TRAFFIC, PEOPLE'S REPUBLIC OF CHINA,
1980–2000

	Domestic Traffic (billion passenger kilometers)	Average Annual Compound Growth Rate (percent)
1980	2.96	
		21.6
1985	7.88	
		13.7
1990	15.00	
		12.1
1995	26.53	
		10.5
2000	43.85	

SOURCE: Douglas Aircraft Co. Forecast, historical data from CAAC. Methodology described in text.

age annual rate of over 25 percent, resulting in a level in 1985 twenty times higher than in 1972. Such an increase is truly exceptional in aviation history. At the same time, however, international traffic grew almost 240 times, or over 50 percent annually. Although I make no international forecasts here, I believe that in the future domestic systems will still generate substantially more revenue passenger-kilometers (RPKs) than the international network will.

China Fleet Forecast

Methodology. A macro analytical method based on the Douglas Aircraft Strategic Analysis Model was specially modified to generate a fleet forecast for China.

Total revenue passenger-kilometers are equal to domestic RPKs plus international RPKs. The passenger capacity requirement measured by available seat-kilometers (ASK) is obtained by forecasting the percentage of seats filled (the load factor) year by year. This passenger capacity is achieved by ASKs generated by the existing fleet, by orders, and by generic new aircraft. Aircraft productivity changes are taken into account in the analysis.

The data used in the China fleet forecast were provided by Chinese representatives and obtained from officially published CAAC statistical data.

Load factor. In recent years, CAAC's load factors were substantially higher than those of other airlines of the world. In 1985 the average load factors on the majority of CAAC routes reached over 70 percent, in some cases over 80 percent. This high load factor reflects the fact that in China the air service cannot accommodate the rapidly increasing demand. Load factors were assumed to decrease through the study period to a 65 percent average, which is more in line with other airlines in the world.

Passenger capacity. From traffic forecasts and load factor assumptions, we can obtain passenger capacity. The results predict increases from 15.84 billion ASKs in 1985 to 35.83 billion in 1990, to 60.48 billion in 1995, and finally to 101.72 billion ASKs by the year 2000. These increases imply an average annual growth of 13.2 percent.

Existing fleet. By the end of 1985 CAAC had 144 aircraft in route service. Seventy-six feeder aircraft accounted for about 11 percent of total RPKs, forty-five domestic trunk aircraft (aircraft used to fly between major cities) produced 56.3 percent of total RPKs, and fifteen international aircraft accounted for the remaining 32.7 percent RPKs.

China's existing fleet consists of eighteen types of aircraft, most of them very old. As a result the average productivity is rather low in comparison with that of other airlines.

Retirements. CAAC plans to improve its fleet structure. The IL-14s and IL-18s, for example, have been in use for over thirty years. Older aircraft are being phased out in favor of newer equipment with more efficient operating economies.

CAAC fleet retirement projections are based on assumptions that aircraft were retired after twenty to thirty years of use. By the year 2000 most of the current CAAC aircraft will be retired, leaving only thirty-five aircraft of today's fleet flying.

Orders. CAAC has announced firm orders for sixty-nine new aircraft, sixty-one of which have been ordered for deliveries before 1991. During the 1986 to 1987 period, the rapid addition of new planes may actually result in higher RPK growth than is forecast.

Generic aircraft. The existing fleet (minus retirements) coupled with firm orders will not satisfy the forecast traffic growth. The difference between the forecast demand and current fleet plus existing commitments must be satisfied with new orders.

Productivity growth. The capacity requirements in terms of ASKs are satisfied by changes in use, seat size, and aircraft units. The productivity of existing equipment was analyzed and projections made assuming realistic productivity changes for both existing and future aircraft.

Block speed was kept the same through the study period. The utilization was increased monotonically for every type of aircraft. The average annual growth rate of aircraft utilization was between 3 and 4 percent. Increases in utilization alone satisfy 27 percent of additional capacity requirements in the 1986–2000 period.

Departures (the number of flights) are assumed to have an average annual growth rate of 11 percent. This unusually high rate of departure growth is acceptable in the case of CAAC, because China's current level of service is still very low compared with that of other countries.

New passenger aircraft requirements. China's new passenger aircraft requirements for all planes, including feeders, will be forty-one units for 1986–1990, 163 for 1991–1995, and 154 for 1996–2000, for a total of 358 planes for all of 1986–2000.

The new passenger aircraft requirements are mainly in the small, short-range categories during the first five years of the forecast. A predominance of smaller planes continues during the 1991–1995 time period, and between 1996 and 2000, larger aircraft gain favor.

Discussion of Forecasts

The forecasts for China developed here suggest changes of large magnitudes. Traffic is expected to grow substantially at rates that will double domestic traffic in less than six years. In fact, the levels achieved in 1985 will be surpassed over five times by the end of the century. Similarly, the CAAC fleet of 144 planes in 1985 is expected to grow to a total of 462 planes. To achieve such a large fleet an expenditure of over $7 billion (in 1986 dollars) will be needed.

Are the forecasts described here reasonable? Do they predict levels that seem feasible by the end of the century? Are the forecasts too optimistic and too high? As a matter of fact, the forecasts use quite conservative official PRC inputs. Therefore, I believe the probability is higher that I underestimate rather than overestimate the future of air transportation in China. Listed below are the reasons for my belief and some general discussion of the implications of the forecast.

• Domestic air traffic would grow to about five-and-a-half times the 1985 level and would surpass the level of domestic traffic in Canada by the end of the century. But despite such healthy growth, traffic in the year 2000 would amount to only 12.5 percent of the level achieved by the Soviet Union in that time period. It would be less than 5 percent of the level of the United States. As a matter of fact, it would equal only slightly more than 10 percent of the level achieved by the United States in 1985. This is in absolute terms. In per capita terms, the air traffic level in China in the year 2000 would equal only a little more than 1 percent of the U.S. level in that year and about 2.5 percent of the 1985 level.

• An informative way to look at air transportation in China in general and at the feasibility of our forecast in particular is to compare it with the world as a whole. By 1985, according to the McDonnell Douglas data sources covering most of the world, China had 21.3 percent of the world's population, 4.6 percent of the world's production (gross domestic product), and only 1 percent of total air traffic. Similar numbers forecast for the year 2000 are 19.5 percent, 7.1 percent, and 2.1 percent. In other words, despite doubling its share of total air traffic, China will have one-fifth of the world's population, one-fourteenth of the world's production, and only one-fiftieth of the world's air traffic.

• The high levels of air traffic growth will cause its share of total traffic in China to increase from 2.6 percent to 4.7 percent in the relevant time period. For comparison purposes, the share of air traffic in the United States out of total traffic is today estimated at about 15 percent. If intracity automobile traffic is excluded, air traffic's share of total traffic approaches 90 percent in the United States.

• Excluding feeders and considering only jets, China's requirements for an appropriate fleet to serve the expected demand will be 186 units, which constitutes only 3.3 percent of anticipated world aircraft demand (China will make up 19.5 percent of the world's population, 7.1 percent of the world's production, and 2.1 percent of the world's air traffic). The capital required to acquire that number of jets will be $5.7 billion, or roughly 2 percent of the total estimated world requirement. These numbers, although substantial, seem quite plausible.

China's Position Today

China has the third largest aviation industry in the world, employing over half a million people. (The U.S. aviation industry employs almost a million workers.) Historically the focus in China was concentrated on military products—the F-6, F-7, and F-8 fighter planes, the B-6, the A-5 planes, and others. Overall China has produced about 5,000 military aircraft.

In the 1970s the development of commercial aircraft was acceler-

129

ated. The twelve-passenger Y-5 general aviation plane has been produced since the 1950s, but several planes have been introduced recently. The turboprop Y-12 (engines made in China) entered service in 1985. China already has sold six units of the seventeen-passenger plane abroad. The Y-7, a fifty-two passenger and 1,900-kilometer-range turboprop that entered service in 1984, together with the smaller Y-12 are used by CAAC in China. The largest commercial aircraft built in China is the Boeing 707 variant called Y-10 with a seating capacity of 147 and a range of 8,500 kilometers. After the test prototype flew in 1980, the Chinese suspended work on it to concentrate on more advanced technology. In addition to the passenger plane, China has produced a cargo Y-8 aircraft since 1982. It is powered by the WJ-6 engine, has a range of 5,600 kilometers, and can carry twenty tons of cargo.

Although precise statistics are not available, it is quite clear the Chinese industry lags behind that of some of the more developed countries. This is especially true in the case of manufacturing technology and in management. The existing gap is a function of the Chinese infrastructure, and attempts are being made to reduce it, although that necessarily takes time.

Official Plans for the Future

After a series of conferences were held to discuss the future of commercial aircraft production, the official state policy was declared to be one of vigorous development of commercial aircraft. It was decided to pursue a balance between imported foreign equipment and technology and that produced domestically. Feeder planes, for example, will be primarily produced in China. The Y-7 and Y-12 will be further developed, and new derivatives will be produced. The Y7-100 derivative, as another example, is being modified in Hong Kong. It has winglets and is equipped with more advanced electronic instruments. CAAC has ordered forty Y7-100s to be delivered by 1990.

Larger trunk aircraft will rely on both cooperative ventures and imports. The McDonnell Douglas Corporation (MDC) MD-82 is being licensed and produced in Shanghai by SAIC (Shanghai Aviation Industrial Cooperation) in cooperation with MDC. At least twenty-five planes will be produced, and an option for an additional fifteen is currently being considered. Planes are also being purchased from the United States (MDC and Boeing), the Soviet Union, Europe (Airbus), and the United Kingdom (BAe). There is talk of a desire by the Chinese to design and produce their own trunk aircraft before the end of the century. For long-range aircraft suitable for international traffic,

China will continue to rely on imports, mainly from Boeing and MDC.

During the 1986–1990 period, a sum of between $300–350 million is provided in the Chinese government budget for development of commercial aircraft programs. The money will be used to improve the Y-7, Y-8, and Y-12 and maybe to develop a new trunk plane. China plans to build a total of 200 commercial aircraft during that period, including the Y-7, Y-8, Y-12, MD-82, and general aviation planes.

Speculations

Before I speculate about the future, a few remarks are in order. Although some of my comments may appear negative, they should be taken in conjunction with my great admiration for China, for its people, its culture, and its history. I appreciate China's tremendous social and economic achievements. Although I stress here some of the problems, I generally see China's future in air transportation in a very positive light.

Most forecasts of China's role in anything are extreme predictions of all or nothing—China becomes either the world's greatest power or a totally insignificant pawn. The reason for diverse predictions is the enormous size of China: the physical size, the natural resources, and the huge mass of people all create vast opportunities, which seem to some observers to be unlimited. The low level of income, skill, and education and the lack of a sufficiently large group of managers skilled in up-to-date methods create a pessimistic view for some observers, which, again, seems to be unlimited.

The positive predictions center on China's huge population. Executives and politicians all over the world commonly express the belief that if every Chinese would buy, for example, just one hamburger, one pack of chewing gum, one car, or one plane their firms would earn vast amounts of money. Everybody wants to "be in China" in order not to miss the huge market opportunities just about to explode there. McDonnell Douglas, for example, realizes that if the Chinese were to fly on average only one-tenth as much as the Americans do right now, they would need at least 1,000 jet planes. Since China has only about ninety jet planes now, the demand for additional planes would be phenomenal. So, to many, China appears to be the future of the world, and McDonnell Douglas, for one, sees its future there as particularly bright.

The immense size of China also fosters an overwhelming pessimism about its future. The necessity to feed over a billion people and the lack of understanding of basic managerial concepts by many managers lead pessimists to naturally conclude that China cannot achieve the status of a world economic leader.[1]

The truth, as always, is someplace between the two views described above. Air traffic will grow in China at very high rates into the next century. Such high rates occurred in many Asian countries in the past (for example, traffic on Singapore Airlines grew by an average annual rate of 41 percent between 1969 and 1979, Korean Air grew by an annual average of over 38 percent, and the Malaysian Airline System grew by an average of over 31 percent a year in the same time period). But China has the potential to continue such high rates of growth well into the twenty-first century, which will generate a sizable demand for new planes. The Chinese leadership will continue to be interested in producing a trunk aircraft locally. The Chinese possess, or will acquire, sufficient technical knowledge to plan, design, and manufacture such a plane.

The nonrecurring costs of developing an all new plane, however, will be well over $2 billion. Added to it are investments in tooling, purchases of components, production in process, and many other costs. From the time a decision is made to start thinking about an all new aircraft until money comes in for the first delivered aircraft, large amounts of money are spent—$5–10 billion is not an overstatement. This number is consistent with the high capital cost foreseen by William J. Spencer of the Xerox Corporation to establish integrated circuit facilities in the electronics industry.

The Chinese aircraft authorities are most interested in designing and producing an all-new state-of-the-art aircraft as well as its engines and in providing full product support. Because aircraft production is a cooperative venture today, the Chinese understand that they have to start as collaborators with an already well established producer. McDonnell Douglas MD-80 planes, for example, have the elevators produced in Australia by Hawker de Havilland, the wings produced in Canada by MDCAN, the fuselage panels, rudders, and ailerons in Italy by Aeritalia, the emergency exit doors in Spain by CASA, the wing trailing edges in Japan by Mitsubishi, the forward attendant seats and the modular lavatories in Japan by Jamco, the inboard slats/tracks in Switzerland by Swiss Federal, the spoilers and the inboard flaps and vanes in Sweden by Saab-Scania, and the landing gear doors in China by SAIC. Major U.S. subcontractors include Pratt & Whitney for engines, as well as Westinghouse Electric, Sundstrand Aviation, Rohr, Calcor, Cleveland Pneumatic, Delco, Sperry, Garrett, and many other large corporations. In fact, final assembly labor accounts for only about 5 percent of the value of the plane. The story is very similar for the other major McDonnell Douglas product, the

DC-10. Parts are produced in various countries, and final assembly accounts for about 5 percent of the value of the plane.

So, in the modern world of complex international interdependence no planes are produced exclusively in one country. The value added of subcontractors' work is significantly higher than the value added of the final assembly producer whose name goes on the body of the plane. And the cooperation of major producers is increasing. McDonnell Douglas talks to the Chinese, Boeing cooperates with the Japanese, and Airbus is trying to get additional partners. Similar trends are evident among engine producers, primarily because of the enormously high development cost of new products, which, if not shared, could bankrupt one company if markets developed slower than forecast.

An additional reason for shared production is related to marketing advantages. It is taken for granted that KLM will buy Fokker products and that Air France will order any Airbus plane produced or even dreamed up. India, Indonesia, Brazil, and numerous other countries are interested in a minor producing partner status, usually in exchange for marketing consideration.

China, in the early part of the next century, will definitely play a role in the international aircraft production market. The question is— what role? Will it be a major role because of the substantial increases in demand, the huge labor force already involved in aircraft production, the determination of the Chinese leadership for technological advances, and the relatively low wage rates? Or will it be a minor role, stressing marketing advantages rather than manufacturing and engineering advantages? As mentioned previously, the truth will lie somewhere between these two possibilities.

China's role in the production of airplanes will be greater than that of Indonesia, Brazil, and other countries with developing aircraft industries. But first we must analyze the factors in China's favor. The size (demand factor) is obvious and is being played up by the Chinese, although they virtually ignore all the supply factors. The availability of half a million employees in the airplane production industry and the existence of relatively low wages merit some considerations.

My personal experience with a few economists and marketing analysts in China has been extremely rewarding. They are hard working, well educated, smart, skilled, and eager to learn more. Their skills and training compare very favorably with those of their counterparts in the United States. The same, I presume, is true for those in other professions, including engineers designing planes.

Progress, however, is not determined by the existence of skilled top professionals. Nor is technological progress a function of Nobel

Prize laureates or the number of inventions patented in the capital city by university professors. Rather, progress is achieved by the ability of peasants to load a truck, of a clerk in a provincial city to handle a hotel reservation, and so on. Although China clearly possesses some "cream of the crop" professionals, what really matters are vast numbers of efficient mid-level managers and professionals.

Out of the half a million people working in the aircraft industry some are, no doubt, first rate. But the overall efficiency is probably very low because low productivity is part of the socioeconomic system and the experience of the workers. Both of these factors take a substantial amount of time to change. The Chinese, I believe, are not aware just how complicated improvements in productivity really are. Let me illustrate the above point with a personal example. While working with the Chinese on traffic forecasting I was repeatedly asked, especially by higher ranking personnel, to give them "the formula." Of course, the statistical formula exists in every textbook and the necessary software to run the regressions is widely available. But the true value of a good forecaster lies not in the use of straightforward formulas. Rather, it is the forecaster's knowledge of the industry, the ability to see causal relationships, intuition, and the ability to select the proper variables, time period, and functional form. All of these skills, of course, are a function of experience. The Chinese, however, seem to believe that secret formulas exist and that with them they will immediately catch up with the West. The Great Leap lesson seems to have been forgotten. And, if one company will not deliver the secret formula, they will try to get the information by transferring their business to a competitor. In summary, the majority of the Chinese labor force does not have enough experience to improve rapidly on the low level of productivity. Management skills are also missing, as evidenced by the insistence on quick-fix solutions to problems that have to take time.

The second element of labor involves wages. Low wages with high productivity would make China a formidable aircraft producer. The Chinese should put greater emphasis on this advantage. Instead of luring foreigners with promises of a great market, the Chinese should stress more positive factors—if, that is, low wages and high productivity are planned to be characteristic of the industry.

Low wages are a problematic issue. For coproduction purposes, are wages defined as the amount of money a worker receives or as that amount plus a surcharge to compensate the state for subsidies for education, health care, and so on? If the former is true, will the second definition be adopted after some time? Another unknown is the general level of wages in China. Clearly, however, the government's interest in raising the standard of living of the population, together with a healthy appetite of the Chinese for consumption, may lead to an early death of the low-wage concept.

The last point I want to discuss is the role of the government. Transportation and the acquisition of modern technology are clearly top government priorities. Although similar priorities affect decisions in Indonesia, India, Brazil, and other countries, China's goals seem to be much more ambitious—to catch up with the world's top producers before the end of the century. I am not convinced that this goal is well thought out: there is a limit beyond which foreign producers will not go even when lured by promises of high future sales. There also is a limit to which the Chinese government would be willing to spend its scarce resources once it fully understands the financial commitment necessary to achieve its goals.

Summary

I believe that China will become a player to be reckoned with in the field of aviation early in the next century. It will coproduce a plane (or several planes) with a major producer. China will be ahead of India, Indonesia, and other countries trying to join the ranks of aircraft producers, but it will still be substantially behind the major producers of the industry. Attempts to go it alone will not produce a product capable of competing in the world. Trying to close a gap of decades in too short a time will produce only frustration, waste of large amounts of money, and a product similar to those produced by the Soviet Union today, ones that cannot be sold without substantial political pressure even in the technologically least-developed countries of the world.

Note

1. Let me stress that McDonnell Douglas does not take such a view. This is manifested by the company's longstanding and continuous cooperation with China in coproduction, joint studies to produce future aircraft, and sales of McDonnell Douglas planes.

Commentary

Albert Keidel

My comments fall into three categories: some fairly technical ones, some more general methodological ones, and a few that involve judgment. Looking for biases, I got a sense that McDonnell Douglas is like oil men who sit and drink their beer and say, "There's no oil in this ground," and then look sideways to see if anybody's listening to them. The question is, How much oil is there in China's aircraft industry? What's the future of that industry? How big is it really going to be? Adam Pilarski's comments using the quadrupling target for total Chinese gross output as a guideline to the future of the Chinese aircraft industry may indicate some biases. They make the Chinese aircraft industry look as if it will not be as big as, in fact, it could be.

I'd like to explore some of those, but first let me go through a few technical points. Mr. Pilarski should use national income instead of gross value of agricultural and industrial output. It's a better measure. There's more information on it now. The use of this regression is a good statistical basis for trying to find out what the Chinese characteristics of their own aircraft industry and its trends are. But if you look, for example, at the period around the Great Leap, some of those numbers in 1959 to 1964 are very unstable. There's a lot of jumping around that involves political events so I would say that the revenue passenger kilometers and the gross value output figures, and so forth, are caused by a third force. Instead of one causing the other, they are both being caused by a third force. This is one of those causality links that needs at least to be checked on, or commented on, in the paper.

One also sees it in the numbers for 1966, which is, of course, the year the Cultural Revolution had its impact on industrial output. I would suggest that (and I noticed on the slides that you actually had some results from 1975 to 1985 that reduce your freedom) perhaps you should just back up and start with 1970. In that sense, you probably can clear away a lot of that Maoist jumping around and have a certain amount of stability. You might put in a dummy for 1976, the year Mao and Zhou Enlai died.

The notion that econometrics could provide a solution that reaches across all countries and people is intriguing. I think, however, we need to be careful. What we have here is a variable in the equation that is not formally allowed for—time or perhaps a trend. In other words, there is a trend of growth over time. The gross output variable is growing with time, and the cost variable is declining with time. I think those are factors to take into account.

The process of working from seat needs, seat-kilometer needs, and load factors back to aircraft raises questions that we really cannot answer without knowing a great deal more about the aircraft industry in China. In some places, those factors change dramatically in ways that would keep down the growth of the aircraft fleet in the overall projections. I would like to have a little more comment on that, but it may not be allowable within the security arrangements of McDonnell Douglas.

I wonder whether the historical process has, in fact, been demand driven, with the kind of causality implied in the regression analysis. Have incomes, costs, and demand determined growth of the number of aircraft, or has the supply been constrained? My worry is that the aircraft growth in the past twenty or thirty years in China has been seriously supply-constrained. Anybody who has traveled in China knows the tremendous excess demand for transport of all kinds in China. Political decisions about the level of investment in the aircraft industry, and about keeping airports open, together with the unwillingness of the government to allow a great deal of travel, may have determined the growth of the aircraft industry more than income and cost did.

If that has been true in the past, to what degree might it also be true in the future? Is the growth of the Chinese aircraft industry and passenger and freight transport by air going to follow trends, or is it manipulable by Chinese policy decisions? If the international section, by which they can earn foreign exchange to pay for more airplanes, is fungible to a degree, we should think more about supply constraints and policy decisions in the future of the Chinese aircraft industry, rather than only income, though income is very important.

Finally, I'm interested in the comparisons with Singapore and Korea and in the whole range of comparisons in the "reasonableness" section of the paper. Are these numbers reasonable? I think what was really being asked was, Are these numbers too high? In other words, the worry was that people would say the numbers couldn't be that high. By comparison with the United States and with the Soviet

Union, however, China appears to have quite a small slice of the airline and aircraft industry pie in the year 2000.

If, however, we want to look in the other direction and ask if these numbers aren't really much too low, then some different comparisons could be in order. I was intrigued that the combined growth of Singapore and South Korean Airlines is equivalent to the growth expected for China between now and the year 2000. In fact, the Singapore and South Korean airlines' projections are for economies that in population are infinitesimally small in relation to China. A great deal of their mileage comes from international traffic. In ten or fifteen years China will probably try to duplicate the volume of traffic that Singapore and South Korea have captured, by offering bargain flights or by making tremendous efforts to improve quality.

We need to shift away from comparisons either to South Korea and Singapore on the one extreme or to the Soviet Union and the United States on the other. We should focus on China's aircraft industry in relation to countries that are large and developing, such as India and Brazil. Perhaps we should use some per-capita bases as well. In relation to the per-capita incomes of these various countries, what will the Chinese air traffic load look like?

Lee Soo Ann

Although Dr. Pilarski does not go very much into international air traffic, I think that domestic and international travel are linked. In a large country the volume of international traffic would affect the demand for domestic traffic—just think of anyone entering or leaving the United States. If international traffic doubles or triples, surely domestic air travel will be affected.

Dr. Pilarski identified income and price as the two main variables in every country, but a third variable is geography. I was astonished to find that Aeroflot is the biggest airline in the world, although it is hardly known outside Russia. Because of the size of the country, the airline serves as a means of communication and control.

In China, will airlines be the mode of control throughout the country? It depends very much on alternative means of transport. To what extent will railways and roads develop, and at what level of sophistication?

Another factor is the amount of freedom people have to move around in the country. In the United States it is not merely income that creates flying demand, but the freedom of people to change location and to change jobs. That is now impossible in China, so trips are made largely for business purposes. If there is a movement toward freedom to relocate for employment or residence, it would add a demand for air traffic not based just on income growth.

Given the supply constraints, I do not see China going very much into aircraft production. Other countries in Asia—Japan, Indonesia, and India—are going into it. I do not know to what extent China would turn to these countries, which have similar experiences in airline growth and some experience in aircraft production, for joint ventures or some other means of joint production.

In conclusion, I do not think China will have much of an aircraft industry, although it will have a very large airline demand. The two things are quite different.

Discussion

DAVID M. LAMPTON: We have several members of the audience who would like to ask questions. Perhaps we should hear all of them first and then let Dr. Pilarski respond.

QUESTION: To any of us who have been to Chinese airports lately, it is clear that immense amounts of investment are required in ground facilities for these airplanes to fly. The equations before us don't seem to include any variable for that. How does the author deal with that need?

DENIS FRED SIMON: First, I think that a change in psychology should be considered, as well as the need to move goods and services across the country. In China today it takes people three days on a train to get from Chongqing to somewhere else, and they do not seem to care how inefficient it is. Isn't a psychological change in the society needed?

Second, do you include Hong Kong in your statistics as a domestic route as of 1997? What will happen then with the traffic? For example, now there are only one or two Cathay flights and a couple of CAAC flights, but demand will grow tremendously, won't it?

Third, what about military carriers? The Chinese now allow civilian planes to land at military airports, which increases the ground capacity to some extent. But if the Chinese military is going to be more efficient and more mobile, then it will have to have a greater capacity for troop transport as well as for the transport of goods. Is there any consideration of those load factors within this?

ADAM M. PILARSKI: I should make the point that we were working with the constraint of having to produce numbers that the Chinese government would accept. This is the first time I have been accused of having numbers that are too low. Usually we are accused of forecasting too high, to sell our planes. So I try to justify why the numbers are as high as they are, not as low. Clearly, if there were a bias, it would be on the high side.

Someone suggested that we compare China to India and Brazil on a per capita basis. That is exactly what the Chinese wanted, and that is exactly what we did. Using national income or other measures, we tried a whole bunch of measures. The numbers in the paper were the numbers that the Chinese felt comfortable with. We also tried CIA estimates of GDP. The results are similar, which made us feel good.

There is a need for a psychological change regarding time. Clearly, the older leaders still feel better going on the train and working while they're doing it. It takes time, but the economy also takes time. So yes, that is a very good point.

Hong Kong was not included in our figures. International growth is more complicated than domestic growth for many reasons, and the variables that we used were quite different. One of the big questions is, How much money will the Chinese government have in foreign reserves? How much would they be willing to spend on flying into National Airport with foreign money? This is a very big question.

On the supply constraints question, we tried a lot of statistical analysis of load factors, but the results were not as significant as I had expected. Many people pointed out that Chinese methods are totally different. Growth is not driven by demand. If we used the demand-driven model, we were told we would never come up with reasonable results. But surprisingly, we did come up with reasonable results. That convinced me that it might not be purely supply driven. People told us it was like taking money from one pocket and putting it in another. The government would decide who would fly and how many planes would fly, and who cared about demand?

Somehow, though, it is related to the economy. I don't know why, but it is the way it is in every other country. The government can decide whether to build more hospitals or to expand air transportation, but there are still the classical economic limitations.

6

The Nature and Implications of United States–China Trade toward the Year 2000

Roger W. Sullivan

Trade between the United States and China has grown faster than most Americans anticipated. Even under very conservative assumptions bilateral trade is likely to triple by the year 2000. With trade in approximate balance and China's exports increasingly consisting of products competing less with American producers than with other foreign suppliers to the U.S. market, United States–China commercial ties are likely to support rather than cause problems for overall Sino-American relations.

This paper argues that China was significantly motivated to establish such normal relations with the United States by a perceived need for capital, technology, and markets. That need will continue and indeed grow into the next century. The levels of trade projected in this paper will be sufficient to ensure continued Chinese interest in an expanding Sino-American relationship. Such trade, however, is not likely to be of sufficient importance to the United States to sustain the high-level attention American policy makers have given China since 1972. What explains that attention is the perceived strategic benefits to the United States and its allies of friendly relations between China and the United States.

The significance of growing Sino-American trade and investment, then, is in reinforcing the symbiosis that has existed between China and the United States since 1979 as China has gained technology, capital, and access to the American market and the United States has enjoyed significant strategic benefits. As in U.S.-Japanese relations, the American perception of the importance of these strategic benefits will continue despite thaws and tactical shifts in U.S.-Soviet or Sino-Soviet relations.

Myth and Reality

The myth is that economic relations between the United States and China today fall far short of the euphoric expectations of 1972, when President Richard Nixon made his historic China visit, or 1979, when diplomatic relations between the United States and China were restored. In fact the expectations were modest, and even the most optimistic projections of earlier years fall far short of today's reality.

A study published by the National Committee on United States–China Relations in 1971 concluded that "potential Sino-American economic relations will be quite small," even under the most optimistic assumptions.[1] The estimates in that study for total United States–China trade in 1980 ranged from a "plausible" $25 million each way to "optimistic" U.S. imports of $200 million and exports of $325 million, for a total of $525 million. Even allowing for inflation, these were gross underestimates. United States–China trade in 1980 approached $5 billion.

In fairness to the authors of the 1971 study, the absence of reliable data on the Chinese economy and on the relations between domestic economic activity and China's foreign trade reduced their projections to what they themselves called "informed speculation." We are in a better position today, but some humility is still in order. The projections in this paper are also crude ones based on informed speculation and will, I believe, like those of earlier years, by the year 2000 prove to have been conservative.

Forecasts can also be wrong because they are based on faulty assumptions, such as that China has little the United States is willing to buy or that protectionism will severely limit China's access to the American market. A 1982 study predicted that

> the growth of China's exports to the United States . . . will be hindered by the limited range of goods the PRC has to offer. Increases in Chinese exports of textiles, which currently account for 30 percent of the PRC's total exports to the U.S., will be restricted . . . by the U.S.-PRC Textile Agreement.[2]

In fact, by 1985 China's textile exports to the United States had doubled.[3] In 1986 China's clothing and apparel sales to the United States increased another 79 percent.[4]

Still forecasters continue to confuse the intent of U.S. restraints on imports of textiles from China with their actual effect, which may well have been to facilitate Chinese penetration of the American market. A study prepared for the U.S.Congress in 1986 noted the dramatic increases in Chinese textile exports to the United States since controls were first imposed in 1982 and concluded that with little difficulty "the PRC will be able to continue its textile expansion program in accessing the U.S. market." The quantitative controls, the author commented, only force China to become more flexible.[5]

The point here is not to disparage forecasting. Forecasts can be useful and informative, even if the numbers predicted turn out to be wrong. The projections of the early 1970s contained a great deal of useful data and speculation about the prospects for United States–China trade. Particularly interesting was the observation in the National Committee study that at its peak in the 1920s China's trade with the United States constituted 15 percent of its trade worldwide, suggesting that this might be a "natural level" if all restraints on trade were removed.[6]

At the time the report was written, United States–China trade was projected to rise to 5 percent of total China trade by 1980.[7] With the removal of the U.S. trade embargo against China, the extension of most-favored-nation status, and the substantial liberalization of U.S. export licensing requirements for China, United States–China trade has risen to 12 to 13 percent. Whether it will stay in that range, drift down to 10 percent, or rise toward the 1920s level of 15 percent will depend on how the two countries manage the various obstacles to full realization of the complementarity in their economic relationship. It seems reasonable to assume that the U.S. share through the year 2000 will be in the 10 to 15 percent range. What that will mean in dollars depends on what China's total trade is likely to be.

Estimates made in the 1970s of China's trade prospects, particularly of its trade with the United States, were wrong largely because the analysts underestimated the growth of the Chinese economy. Trade is, of course, not an independent economic activity but a sector that reflects changes in the domestic economy. The amount of trade is determined in part by economic development and the size of the gross national product. It is also determined by the size of the country. As many economists have observed, foreign trade ratios (exports and imports as percentages of gross domestic product) tend to be no greater in large high-income countries than in large low-income countries. China is similar to many other low-income countries in the composition of its trade, but its foreign trade ratios (about 10 percent) are like those of the United States and India and quite different from those of smaller countries or areas, such as South Korea (37 percent) and Taiwan (55 percent).

United States–China Trade in the Year 2000

Many observers believe that China is likely to experience growth rates to the year 2000 comparable to those of Japan in the 1950s and 1960s and Korea in more recent years. Of the three possible growth rates for China projected by the World Bank, even the "moderate" projection of 5.4 percent is high by international standards—but no higher than the growth rates attained by China during the 1952–1982 period. Indeed, the World Bank does not rule out the prospect that China's economic growth will approach 7 percent.[8]

For purposes of estimating China's trade worldwide, this paper assumes a GNP in the year 2000 of approximately $1,000 billion. This is a crude estimate but well within the range of estimates by economists studying the Chinese economy. The World Bank assumes that China's foreign trade ratios, currently about 9 percent, will increase only modestly, to 10.6 percent for exports and 10.9 percent for imports.[9] For the sake of simplicity and since precision is not possible in such projections, this paper assumes ratios of 10 percent. In other words, by the year 2000 China's world trade should be on the order of $200 billion in 1985 dollars. If, as this paper projects, United States–China trade is somewhere between 10 percent and 15 percent of China's total trade, Sino-American trade should range from about $20 billion to $30 billion in 1985 dollars.

U.S. Share. What will determine the precise U.S. share of China's trade? One important factor will be the extent to which China's needs and U.S. comparative advantage are compatible. Also important will be the extent to which the United States is likely to act more positively than its competitors to encourage trade through export financing or other government programs. On the negative side, the U.S. share of China's total trade will also be a function of the degree to which the United States acts to restrict trade flows, through either protectionist measures on the import side or export licensing requirements on the export side. These factors are difficult to measure; estimates must therefore be made on the basis of past trends with some allowance for likely changes in the U.S. regulatory environment.

The United States is China's third largest trading partner, after Japan and Hong Kong.[10] Since the normalization of U.S.-Chinese relations in 1979, America's share of China's total two-way trade has remained remarkably stable in the 11 to 13 percent range while trade increased rapidly from $2.3 billion in 1979 to $8.3 billion in 1986 and U.S. exports shifted dramatically from agricultural products to man-

TABLE 6–1

TRADE BETWEEN THE UNITED STATES AND THE PEOPLE'S REPUBLIC OF
CHINA, 1979–1986
(millions of U.S. dollars)

	U.S. Exports[a]	U.S. Imports[b]	Total	U.S. Trade Balance	U.S. Two-way Trade[c]
1979	1,716.5	592.3	2,308.8	1,124.2	8
1980	3,749.0	1,058.3	4,807.3	2,690.7	13
1981	3,598.6	1,895.3	5,493.9	1,703.3	13
1982	2,904.5	2,283.7	5,188.2	620.8	13
1983	2,163.2	2,244.1	4,407.3	− 80.9	10
1984	3,004.0	3,381.1	6,385.1	− 377.1	12.5
1985	3,855.7	4,224.2	8,079.9	− 368.5	13
1986	3,106.2	5,240.5	8,346.7	− 2,134.3	11

a. Free alongside ship (f.a.s.). Customs value and f.a.s. approximately equal to free on board (f.o.b.).
b. Customs value.
c. As percentage of China's total trade.
SOURCE: U.S. Department of Commerce, Bureau of the Census, *Highlights of U.S. Export and Import Trade*, FT 990.

ufactured goods (see table 6–1).[11] In 1981 American sales of agricultural products to China (principally wheat, soybeans, and cotton) totaled over $2 billion. That figure dropped by 1985 to under $150 million and in 1986 almost to zero.[12] U.S. exports of manufactured goods, however, which were an anemic $273 million in 1981, soared to $2.2 billion in 1985,[13] belying the untested assumption of early forecasts that the United States could not expect to be a major supplier of manufactured goods to China.

The prospects for continued growth of American sales to China remain promising because the sectors China has designated as having high priority are in many cases those in which American technology and equipment are preeminent or at least competitive. The list is long and impressive, including onshore and offshore oil exploration and exploitation, mining, electrical power generation, rail and airline modernization, telecommunications, and electronics. American investment commitments in China, already over $2.7 billion,[14] are likely to grow substantially as China moves to improve its investment climate. American investment in China should also lead to increased sales of U.S. equipment and services.

On the import side China should continue to be successful in selling a wide range of products to the United States. Sales of textile goods should increase as China diversifies from controlled to uncontrolled categories and improves quality (and therefore price). Sporting goods and equipment, toys and games, furniture, luggage, and other light industrial products already enjoy growing demand in the American market. The strong market for textiles and other light industrial products enabled China to register a 23 percent increase in exports to the United States in 1986[15] despite a sharp drop in revenues from sales of petroleum and petroleum products, which constituted China's second leading export in 1985.[16]

China will move up the product sophistication scale, though perhaps not at the pace experts have predicted. The existence of a large, protected domestic market and the Chinese bias against exporting will unfortunately slow the process of bringing quality and design of more sophisticated products up to international standards.

Protectionism in the United States may be a serious problem for individual companies and for particular products, to say nothing of its deleterious effect on consumers. But damaging as it may be at the micro level, it is difficult to make the case that it has a significant effect on aggregate trade figures. Therefore, while we must be concerned about legislative and administrative measures in the United States to restrict the import of certain products, such efforts have not seriously affected China's ability to generate foreign exchange earnings in the U.S. market.

Protectionist measures of the kind that gain acceptance in the United States are unlikely to be any more effective in the future than in the past. Most are intended, however they might be abused from time to time, as remedies against unfair trade practices, such as dumping, or as a means of giving a domestic industry time to readjust either by improving its competitiveness or by retraining its workers to produce a different product. Chinese concern about protectionism in the United States is understandable, given China's heavy concentration on light industrial exports, particularly textile products. But such concern, based on "what if" rather than on what is or is likely, is not a sound basis for analysis or projection.

China has been able to adjust to the bilateral textile quota system now going into its seventh year to expand its exports significantly. What the Chinese fear is not the current system but the prospect that restraints along the lines of the 1985 Jenkins bill might be imposed. The Jenkins bill, which was truly protectionist in that it proposed to roll back imports from all major suppliers to 1984 levels (a 50 percent cut for China over its 1986 sales), did not become law. The vote in the U.S. House of Representatives to support the president's veto appeared close only to those who do not understand the peculiar folk-ways of the U.S. Congress, members of which often seek to appear to be in favor of a measure only when they are confident that it will not become law.

Of course, a turn to protectionism in the United States cannot be ruled out. But even in that unlikely event, there are sound reasons for believing that United States–China trade would not be a major target of such measures. First, imports from China are not large in relation to the size of the market or to imports from other suppliers. Second, United States–China trade is likely to remain in near balance without the massive deficits that fuel calls for retaliation against other U.S. trading partners. Finally, as China continues to diversify its exports to the United States and labor-intensive industries shift from Korea and Taiwan to China, the products China seeks to sell will increasingly be competing with those of other foreign suppliers rather than with products made in the United States.

What might inhibit U.S. exports to China? Protectionism in China is certainly a danger as China tries to balance the costs and benefits of further opening up its relatively closed domestic economy. Self-reliance as a principle has strong appeal in China. Chinese leaders are learning, however, from China's experience and from the advice of disinterested organizations such as the World Bank, that without the stimulus of international competition domestic producers would be less likely to bring their products up to international standards or to produce them efficiently enough to be competitive on the world market.

The Japanese could afford to close their domestic market because they were producing largely for the world market and therefore had to be competitive. Chinese manufacturers, by contrast, are producing largely for a domestic market. If they were not subjected to outside competition, they might well be satisfied to produce whatever would meet the minimum quality, design, and price demands of that market. The long-term effect of such an enclosed economy would be both to reduce export opportunities for the United States and other countries and to erode China's ability to earn hard currency and thereby to undermine the economic modernization movement. It seems reasonable to assume, therefore, that China will not become protectionist enough to invalidate either these projections of China's world trade or the U.S. share of that trade.

U.S. Export Controls. Another determinant of U.S. exports to China will be the management of the U.S. government's export administration system. The executive branch of the government, through a

148

licensing system, controls the export of "high technology," whether in the form of products or of technical data, to all countries in the interests of national security. Very tight controls are applied on technical data and on virtually all products destined for the Soviet Union and other members of the Warsaw Pact. Until 1980, because of a combination of history and bureaucratic inertia, the same rules that applied to exports to the Soviet Union controlled sales to China. It was not until December 1983 that China was designated by the U.S. government, for export control purposes, a "friendly, nonallied" state.

That decision was a momentous one politically as well as economically. It meant that the United States was finally ready, more than ten years after signing the Shanghai communiqué, to acknowledge explicitly that China was a friendly country and that a strong, secure China was in the interest of the United States. The liberalization of the export control system that followed this policy decision removed the absolute ban on the transfer of technical data to China, making American participation in offshore oil exploration and exploitation in China possible. The new regulations also made possible the rapid expansion in 1984 of American sales to China of computers, semiconductor manufacturing equipment, and other controlled products.

Bringing the export control system for China in line with national policy did not keep pace with changes in the China market and the evolution of technology. What seemed like advanced technology in 1983 is, in many areas, obsolescent in 1987. Some products licensable for sale to China in 1983 are no longer even manufactured, and upgraded models cannot be sold under the technical guidelines approved in 1983. These guidelines were supposed to have been updated periodically, but such updates have not been forthcoming. As China continues to modernize, products and technologies that were neither appropriate nor needed by China when the earlier review of the American export control guidelines was completed were added to China's growing list of priority needs. The reform of the U.S. system has not kept up.

Telecommunications are a case in point. China plans to import over $4 billion of telecommunications equipment and services over the next four years alone and even larger amounts during the 1990s.[17] Under current U.S. export control procedures, much of the sophisticated equipment China seeks, such as optical fiber and advanced digital switching gear, is not licensable for sale by American firms. Unless that situation changes, American companies will be shut out of a major opportunity in China.

In contrast, the export control systems of other nations give their exporters a competitive advantage over American firms. This is true even for the member countries of the Coordinating Committee (COCOM), the Paris-based organization made up of the members of the North Atlantic Treaty Organization and Japan, all of which supposedly follow the same rules on sales to the Soviet Union, the Warsaw Pact countries, and China.

American companies are at a disadvantage not because America's allies cheat but because the U.S. government enforces stricter controls than the COCOM agreements require. For example, in December 1985 COCOM removed the requirement of COCOM approval for sale to China of twenty-seven categories of products previously restricted. These product categories could henceforth be sold at "national discretion," without referral to COCOM. What this means for the other members of COCOM is that their companies can export without a license, since in most countries a firm is free to export unless there are overriding national interest reasons to prohibit a sale.

The United States, however, continues to require licenses for products in those twenty-seven categories, in effect placing the burden on the exporter to show that the export will not damage the national security. The delays involved in processing such licenses, averaging over five months and in many cases extending to over a year, put American firms at a serious disadvantage.[18]

In other cases differences of interpretation of the COCOM rules result in disapproval by the U.S. government of sales of products other member countries routinely allow under national discretion. The extent of this difference of interpretation is suggested by U.S. Department of Commerce data showing that in 1985 the United States referred 3,612 China cases to COCOM for approval. The number submitted by all other COCOM members was slightly over 990.[19] Given that exports of the European Economic Community (EEC) to China equal those of the United States and that sales from Japan are three times those of the United States, it seems a fair inference that U.S. officials interpret the COCOM rules far more strictly than officials of other countries, to the detriment of the competitive position of American companies. The implications for American participation in future Chinese development are obvious. If China cannot get what it needs from the United States, it will go elsewhere, because in the low- to medium-range technology China seeks, the United States is simply one potential supplier among many.

U.S. Participation in China's Modernization. American ability to participate in China's economic development will also depend on the extent to which the United States will be a source of financing for China or will have access to capital from other foreign sources. Americans will most likely continue to be significant investors and to be competitive for projects with an economic return on investment. For these it is reasonable to expect China to draw on private commercial financing. China will look to international concessionary financing, however, for projects of infrastructure and institutional development, such as the Yangzi River hydropower, flood control, and navigation projects, airport modernization, and port and railroad development. They do not earn a commercial return and are therefore not expected to be considered appropriate by the Chinese for private commercial financing. A large proportion of the funds for such projects will come from the World Bank, and American companies have been competitive in bids for Chinese projects financed by the World Bank.

Nevertheless, because the United States does not have a bilateral aid program for China, American participation in China's infrastructure development projects will presumably depend on the size of the World Bank program, since the only other source will be bilateral aid from other countries. Not surprisingly, American suppliers are generally unable to gain access to funds provided under another country's bilateral aid program, whether that aid is formally tied or not.

Japan is the major supplier of bilateral aid to China. In two agreements (in 1979 and 1984) Japan has committed over $3 billion in soft loans through 1991.[20] France, Germany, Belgium, Italy, the United Kingdom, Canada, and Australia also have aid programs for China, though on a much smaller scale than Japan's. The direct and indirect commercial benefits of an aid program, however, while difficult to quantify, are likely to be many times the amount of the aid. A small sum for engineering services, for example, usually means that the recipient country will be more likely to look to the donor country for the equipment necessary for the project. Since countries often try to standardize equipment for ease of maintenance and availability of spare parts, one large purchase on a project can mean many more purchases in future years.

These limitations affecting the likely American share of China's trade must be kept in perspective. Americans have import competitive advantages in China that will continue to operate through the end of this century and beyond. Nevertheless, how the United States deals with the issues of export licensing and export financing will determine whether American companies can realize the full potential of the American competitive position.

Even under a pessimistic projection, in which the American share of China's trade in the year 2000 drops to 10 percent, United States–China trade would rise from the current $8.3 billion to $20 billion in 1985 dollars. If the United States merely holds its current share, United States–China trade would be about $22 billion. Under an optimistic projection, in which the U.S. share rises to the 1920s "natural" level of 15 percent, United States–China trade at the end of this century would approach $30 billion. That is a substantial amount, particularly for those sectors of American industry (for example, transportation, telecommunications, and electronics) that could be expected to benefit disproportionately.

To put matters in perspective, although China will probably become one of America's top ten trading partners by the year 2000, surpassing Australia, Italy, and India, United States–China trade will not compare to trade with such major U.S. partners as Canada, Japan, Mexico, and the EEC. What, then, is the significance of United States–China trade, and what are its implications? To answer such questions, we must consider what each nation was looking for when it sought improved relations with the other.

Motives for Seeking Improved Relations

The United States. There is little mystery about the benefits the United States hoped to gain from improved relations with China. In a briefing held at the Department of State on January 15, 1979, Zbigniew Brzezinski said, "Normalization [of United States–China relations] consolidates a favorable balance of power in the Far East and enhances the security of our friends." The Fifty-ninth American Assembly, cosponsored by the Council on Foreign Relations, concluded in March 1981 that the

> normalization of United States relations with the People's Republic of China in the 1970s constituted a major and positive development in U.S. foreign policy. Normalization removed major burdens from our international relations and national security planning, enhanced United States security flexibility, [and] imparted greater stability to the Asian region.

This has been the consistent view in the United States of the value of the China relationship since 1969. The United States sought strategic gains. Few Americans expected economic and commercial relations to go very far; to the extent that anyone in government thought about them at all, it was as a means to an end.

American political leaders have often tended to view economics and commerce only as means to political ends. Space does not permit examination of the historical and philosophical reasons why Americans think in these terms. Nevertheless, the United States frequently uses trade and economics for political purposes (for example, the grain embargo or export controls) and as instruments of foreign policy but rarely uses foreign policy instruments to advance commercial interests. Because this is the U.S. bias, Americans assume that others share it.

China. Concern over the Soviet threat drove U.S. policy in the process leading toward the establishment of diplomatic relations with China in 1979. Americans assumed that the same concern motivated China. Certainly China was concerned about the threat from the Soviet Union and saw improved relations with the United States as a useful way of deterring that potential source of aggression. But China's motives in the late 1960s were more complex than Americans realized at the time.

Economic and commercial considerations played a far larger role in the Chinese decision to seek improved relations with the United States than is generally understood. Well before Nixon's 1972 trip to China, the Chinese leaders directing China's foreign policy in the 1970s, including Zhou Enlai, Deng Xiaoping, and probably even Mao himself, realized that China had to devote a greater effort to economic development and modernization—an effort that required the expansion of trade and economic relations with the non-Communist world and that could be successful only through improved relations with the United States, because of America's real and assumed influence over Japanese and European policy.

In the early 1960s, well before most Americans were conscious of any change in China, a dramatic shift was taking place in China's economic relations with foreign countries. The geographic and political direction of China's trade was changing from East to West, from the Communist world to the non-Communist world. Even at that early stage Zhou Enlai and others in the dominant Chinese leadership faction saw the need for greater emphasis on economic development and modernization and understood the importance of foreign trade in promoting that modernization. Trade began to surge, and by 1965 Japan had replaced the Soviet Union as China's principal trading partner.

During the Third Five-Year Plan, from 1966 to 1970, a period generally thought of almost exclusively in terms of Red Guard fanaticism, xenophobia, and the Maoist fundamentalism of the Cultural Revolution, China was returning to the trading patterns that existed before 1937, with the exception, of course, of trade with the United

States, which was still nonexistent because of the U.S. trade embargo against China. Sino-Soviet trade fell to its lowest point in 1970 and has not exceeded 2.5 percent of China's trade since that time.[21]

China's economic requirements could not be satisfied simply by this shift in the direction of trade. Trade with Japan had developed reasonably well under private auspices, but there were restrictions stemming from the absence of diplomatic relations. Since Japan made no secret that it was coordinating its China policy with the United States, it must have been obvious to the Chinese leadership that there was little chance of establishing diplomatic relations with Japan in the absence of improved relations between China and the United States.

Of course, China wanted diplomatic relations with Japan for many reasons, but economic reasons were surely high on the list. By 1971 China had gone about as far as possible in developing commercial ties with Japan without official relations. If trade was to expand any further, trade financing was needed. And without a change in political relations the Japanese government would not extend the necessary export-import bank financing. The specific obstacle that China sought to remove was the Yoshida letter of 1964. That letter, written by the prime minister of Japan to the government on Taiwan, promised that Japan's trade with China would remain private and that there would be no government involvement and no government credit.

Then came President Nixon's trip to China in February 1972. Japan-China relations, which had been frozen in private channels, began to move forward again. The Yoshida letter was canceled in June 1972, and in September Japan and China established formal diplomatic relations. As a consequence Japan-China trade expanded rapidly, as did trade with Europe. The United States ended its embargo on trade with China and even abandoned the China differential, which applied greater restrictions on exports to China than on exports to the Soviet Union. China achieved these goals without compromising its position on Taiwan. For several years China seemed satisfied with a policy of opening the doors to trade, capital, and technology transfer from Japan and Europe through improved relations with the United States.

The Establishment of Diplomatic Relations

Why then did China decide to move toward full diplomatic relations with the United States when it was clear that to do so might require compromise on the sensitive Taiwan issue? Some analysts argued at the time that it was a tactical move to gain a measure of protection against the Soviet Union to China's rear during its incursion into Vietnam. It seems clear now, however, that China had long-term, not tactical, objectives in mind. It is unlikely that Deng Xiaoping would have attempted to justify moving to full diplomatic relations, with all the political risks at home, solely on the basis of a presumed need to resist or gain protection against the Soviet Union. What China particularly needed at that time was technology transfer from the West.

In March 1978 Vice Premier Fang Yi told a national science conference in Peking that China "needs science" and a "vast army of scientists and technicians who are first rate by world standards." Reporting on the draft "Outline National Plan for the Development of Science and Technology, 1978–1985," Fang emphasized that the coming eight years would be critical to China's modernization. China must therefore strengthen scientific and technical cooperation with all other countries so that it could advance in such key areas as energy production and conservation, computers, lasers, and high-energy physics. In June 1978, formal U.S.-Chinese negotiations on the establishment of diplomatic relations began. In July, in meetings with the president's science adviser, Frank Press, on technology transfer, training, and exchanges, the Chinese signaled that those normalization negotiations would be successful.

It was no coincidence that Fang's call for an opening to the outside world in technology and rapid progress toward diplomatic relations with the United States occurred simultaneously. China's goal of dramatically increasing the flow of technology from the developed world could not be accomplished without diplomatic relations with the United States. Indeed, the Chinese probably exaggerated the extent to which diplomatic relations with the United States might be helpful to them in this area. They were correct, of course, that the United States exercised very tight control over technology transfer, not only directly to China from the United States but indirectly through the COCOM mechanism from Japan and our allies in Europe. It was in China's interests, then, as China defined them, to go beyond the 1970s effort to reduce tension with the United States as a way of gaining access to Japanese and European trade and credits and to seek full diplomatic relations with the United States.

The Chinese almost certainly assumed that the establishment of diplomatic relations with the United States would lead not simply to a relaxation of U.S. restrictions on trade and technology transfer but to a lifting of those restrictions. Normalization together with the extension of most-favored-nation treatment would mean, if not automatically at least rather quickly, that China would no longer be classified as a real or potential enemy under the export licensing systems of the

United States and its allies. That this did not happen explains China's angry reaction during the 1980–1983 period to the slow pace of change in American and allied technology transfer policy toward China. It was not until 1983 that the United States declared China a friendly, nonaligned nation for export control purposes, and it was not until 1985 that COCOM agreed in a formal way to distinguish between China and the Soviet bloc.

This is not to minimize the importance of geopolitical factors in the normalization process. China, of course, shared the U.S. interest in resisting Soviet power. The United States shared China's interest in the economic benefits of normal relations. But the economic benefits were primary in China's eyes. For the Americans the strategic and geopolitical gains were predominant. It is in this complementarity of interests that the significance and implications of the growing United States–China economic relationship can be found.

At the risk of some oversimplification and exaggeration, U.S.-Chinese relations can be reduced to the following propositions. The United States has gained a major strategic benefit from the Sino-Soviet split and from the virtual elimination of the risk of conflict between the United States and China. Differences remain, but both sides have worked successfully to manage those differences so that they have not interfered in any serious way with the expansion of their mutually beneficial relationship. The United States under four presidents has followed a policy toward China not unlike American policy toward Japan in the 1950s: deny it to the Soviet Union (the most important objective) and work for increased security cooperation insofar as this does not create political problems that could jeopardize the primary objective. China, meanwhile, has been following a policy toward the United States startlingly like that of postwar Japan: committing itself to remain at least neutral if not in support of the United States in any U.S.-Soviet conflict in exchange for deterrence against Soviet aggression, economic support, and the time necessary to develop the Chinese economy.

There are, of course, important differences between China's and Japan's relations with the United States, but the parallels are striking. We know that China has been intrigued by Japan's economic model, although there is controversy over the extent to which the economic and trade policies of an island nation could be relevant to a country like China with a large landmass and low trade ratios. It appears, however, that in foreign policy rather than in trade policy China has chosen to follow a Japanese model, albeit with Chinese characteristics.

China, like Japan, wants to preserve its independence from the

United States while also preserving the economic benefits of the relationship. It dissents from U.S. policies around the world, though generally on areas far from China and on which China's views exert little influence, thereby minimizing any adverse effect on United States–China relations. In the realm of Sino-Soviet relations, China both asserts its independence and illustrates the limits it imposes on that independence to preserve the more important benefits of the United States–China relationship.

In the 1979–1980 period, when Deng Xiaoping was talking publicly about security cooperation with the United States, China may well have been exaggerating its anti-Soviet rhetoric to convince the United States that China's break with the Soviet Union was real, deep, and irreparable. Chinese officials were clearly intent on reassuring U.S. officials and the American public that China was not pursuing a short-term tactical advantage but was seeking a strategic (that is, a long-term) relationship with the United States. Overcoming lingering American suspicions that the two Communist giants might somehow patch up their differences was critical to China's effort to gain a rapid and substantial relaxation of American restrictions on the sale of so-called high technology to China.

China was convincing, and the restrictions on technology exports began to fall. The pace of change may have been slow, but the explanation for that can be found more in bureaucratic inertia than in any lingering concern over the possibility of a Sino-Soviet reconciliation inimical to U.S. interests. China is well aware of the limits to how far it can go in improving relations with the Soviet Union without jeopardizing its access to American technology and capital.

The United States has also demonstrated that it realizes the limits to its own freedom of action imposed by the imperatives of the United States–China relationship. During the 1980 campaign Ronald Reagan campaigned on a platform critical of the United States–China normalization agreement and in support of the restoration of official relations with Taiwan. Any so-called upgrading of the United States–Taiwan relationship would, of course, have been an abrogation of the United States–China agreement on the establishment of diplomatic relations, and the Chinese wasted no time in pointing that out. What is interesting for purposes of this analysis, however, is that the Chinese continually linked the Taiwan and technology transfer issues as problems that threatened the relationship. In that way they raised the U.S. failure to relax export control on technology sales to China to a level of seriousness comparable to a violation of our agreement to recognize "one China" and the People's Republic of China as the sole legal government of China.

Since 1981, when President Reagan met with Chinese Premier Zhao Ziyang at Cancun, steps taken by the administration indicate a realization that efforts had to be made to restore the United States–China relationship and preserve its important strategic benefits. In January 1982 President Reagan authorized negotiations with China, which culminated in the August 17, 1982, joint communiqué on arms sales to Taiwan. In the spring, while those negotiations were under way, he wrote letters to the Chinese leadership reaffirming the normalization understandings and giving assurances that the United States would "not permit the unofficial relations between the American people and the people on Taiwan" to violate the American commitment to a one-China policy.[22]

In the same year Reagan ordered a review of U.S. controls on exports to China. In June 1983 Secretary of Commerce Malcolm Baldrige, during an official visit to Beijing, announced that China was being moved from the potential enemy to the friendly, nonallied category for export control purposes. A few months later the details of a substantial liberalization of export controls for China were announced. Both these steps were taken, despite their controversial nature in the Reagan constituency, because the president and his foreign policy advisers came to the same conclusion as his three predecessors: that friendly relations with China contribute significantly to American security interests in Asia.

The Future of U.S.-Chinese Relations

Since 1983 growing American confidence in the stability of China's foreign policy orientation and the way in which it defines its national interests has made the United States much more tolerant of China's recent efforts to increase trade and negotiate a reduction in tension with the Soviet Union. This more relaxed American view has given China greater flexibility and confidence that it can proceed with a more evenhanded approach to the Soviet Union without risk of damaging its relationship with the United States.

Up to a point, it is probably useful for China to keep alive in American minds the thought that its foreign policy direction might change. While a return to alliance with the Soviet Union is unlikely and certainly not something the Chinese government sees as in China's interest, there is leverage for China in the thought that such a change in foreign policy could be "forced" on China by an American failure to provide the expected benefits of closer relations with the United States (for example, access to markets, technology transfer, and capital).

China realizes, however, limits to how far it can go in pressing that point without jeopardizing Beijing's more important relations with the United States. Were China to act in such a way as to raise serious concern in the United States about either China's long-term foreign policy orientation or the risk that technology supplied to China might leak to the Soviet Union, the progressive relaxation of U.S. and allied restrictions on technology exports to China would stop and probably reverse. At the same time, China can feel reasonably sure that the United States will continue to pursue policies in the areas of greatest current concern to China—export control and protectionism—that will "induce Chinese leaders to develop a degree of confidence in the long-term benefits of closer relations with the United States and will avoid the danger of driving the Chinese into dependence on the Soviet Union."[23]

The mutual benefits are these: China gets a peaceful environment in which to develop, thanks in part to American deterrence of the Soviet Union. It also gets technology, access to the American market, and capital from international institutions and American investors. The United States gets significant strategic benefits. With the likely expansion of United States–China trade projected in this paper, this symbiotic relationship will strengthen and become increasingly important in the coalition strategy of containing the outreach of Soviet military power in Asia.

As the China–United States economic relationship grows, it will become increasingly linked with the objectives and chances for success of China's economic modernization program. The United States and other nations will then have greater confidence that China would change its foreign policy alignment only in the unlikely event that its leaders decided to abandon the effort to modernize altogether or concluded that they could achieve modernization in the international atmosphere that existed in the 1960s without significant technology transfer from the West and in the face of American hostility. In the absence of a change in Chinese policy, the United States can be expected to take any steps necessary to preserve and develop its strategic relationship with China as long as the Soviet threat persists.

Tensions will of course exist between the United States and China. Both sides will try to gain the maximum advantage. China will press for economic benefits, and the United States will be accommodating enough to satisfy the minimum requirements of the partnership. China will work to preserve its independence, particularly in its dealings with the Soviet Union, but will be careful not to press that independence to the point of jeopardizing the flow of technology from the West. The United States will press China for more cooperation in defense and will encourage it to strengthen its military forces. Like Japan, China will do the minimum and concentrate, at least in

159

the medium term, on economic development, leaving deterrence of the Soviet Union to the United States.

Notes

1. Alexander Eckstein, ed., *China Trade Prospects and U.S. Policy* (New York: Praeger Publishers for the National Committee on United States–China Relations, 1971), p. 268.

2. Damian T. Gullo, *China's Hard Currency Export Potential and Import Capacity through 1985* (Washington, D.C.: U.S. Congress, Joint Economic Committee, 1982), p. 106.

3. National Council for United States–China Trade, *United States–China Trade Statistics* (Washington, D.C., 1986), p. 15.

4. U.S. Department of Commerce, *U.S. General Imports: World Area and Country of Origin by Schedule A Commodity Groupings*, December and annual, p. 698; December, p. 700.

5. Joseph Pelzman, *PRC Textile Trade and Investment: Impact of the U.S.-PRC Bilateral Textile Agreements* (Washington, D.C.: U.S. Congress, Joint Economic Committee, 1986), p. 407.

6. Eckstein, *China Trade Prospects*, p. 248.

7. Ibid., p. xxvi.

8. World Bank, *China: Long-Term Development Issues and Options* (Baltimore: Johns Hopkins University Press, 1985), p. 36.

9. Ibid., p. 102.

10. Ibid., p. 8.

11. National Council for United States–China Trade, *United States–China Trade Statistics*, p. 8.

12. Ibid., p. 12.

13. Ibid.

14. National Council for United States–China Trade, Beijing Office, *United States–China Trade Statistics* (Beijing, 1987), p. 100.

15. Department of Commerce, *U.S. General Imports*, p. 700.

16. National Council for United States–China Trade, *United States–China Trade Statistics*, pp. 14–15.

17. U.S State Department, *China's Telecommunications* (Cleared document, June 18, 1985), p. 1.

18. U.S. Congress, Office of Technology Assessment, unpublished report, 1987 (cited with permission).

19. Department of Commerce briefing, Bell South, Atlanta, Georgia, February 21, 1986.

20. David B. Richter, *Concessionary Financing to China* (Washington, D.C.: National Council for United States–China Trade, 1986), p. 2.

21. State Statistical Bureau, *Statistical Yearbook of China, 1981* (Hong Kong: Public Economic Information Agency, 1982), pp. 357, 363.

22. Letter from President Ronald Reagan to Vice Chairman Deng Xiaoping, April 5, 1982.

23. Atlantic Council, Committee on China Policy, *China Policy for the Next Decade* (Boston: Oelgeschlager, Gunn & Hain Publishers, 1984), pp. 32–33.

Commentary

Albert Keidel

I like the linking of GDP to trade volume. This can help us answer the questions that have been raised about how we can possibly think that China will depend on trade to the degree that South Korea and Taiwan have. A good deal of literature examines the development path of small countries as opposed to that of large countries. An 8–15 percent trade ratio for a country like China, or Brazil, or some other large developing country is very different from the 50 percent export-to-GDP ratios we sometimes see for small or medium-sized countries. So I am in broad agreement with the approach to the trade projection in this paper. I have some technical questions, however.

Roger Sullivan says that China's GDP in the year 2000 will be equivalent to Japan's in 1978. I used to say that until the yen-dollar exchange rates changed. Now we cannot say that; we need to take it back to the late or middle 1960s for the actual size of the GDP, if we are going to keep Japan's rate at about 150 yen, much less 120 or 110 yen to the dollar. In per capita terms, the analysis is very different, and our Rock Creek Research shows that China's development level is equivalent to Japan's in the early 1930s. That is a very different benchmark from the overall economy.

I agree that protectionism will not be a major problem for China. We have to be careful with some of the sweeping language in the paper, however, because protectionism could affect China's exports, perhaps not negatively but positively. I wonder what China's exports of garments and textiles would be if there were no protectionist pressures from the United States and other OECD countries not to admit them. They could be quite a bit larger than they are, although issues of quality may make a difference.

With regard to the author's emphasis on China's need for competitive foreign imports, I would like the author to say something about whether domestic competition in China—Shanghai trying to steal Peking's market, Canton coming up north, and all competing for the domestic market—might be something of a substitute for further opening up to foreign competition.

161

I would also like him to make a little more of the notion that the U.S. advantages in high technology exports and its restrictions beyond what is required by COCOM are what has been limiting trade between the United States and China. It seems to me he has put his finger on something very important.

This point has a number of dimensions. China is going to be as bilateral as it can in its trade, and we are also bilateral. If we tend to have a large surplus with China in high-technology areas, this will reduce some of the pressure to apply the textile and other restrictions on China that we are seeing now.

In the security area the paper is a little strong. For instance, to say that the United States is unique among nations "in viewing economics and commerce only as a means to political ends" is too strong. A lot of people around the world might think that we have a strong interest in making money and in having flows of products, and so forth, coming to the United States.

My strong feeling is that the second half of the paper overemphasizes viewing China and the evolution of Chinese-American commercial relations as part of the U.S.-Soviet equation. The Soviet card that China could play against us is also probably overemphasized a bit. It does not make much sense to me to think that the Chinese would play a Soviet card and we would rush back into their arms. The Soviet technology does not make sense for China, either.

What is critical now is that we have an economy that was centrally planned but is somehow finding its way toward institutions that are much more complex, much more decentralized; an economy that depends more on market institutions. That transition has tremendous value for the United States, aside from the Soviet-U.S. nexus. The lesson that China is giving to the world, without saying it, is that the Western system—the system of markets, of decentralized investment, of freer flows of information—is what works. That sends a signal to the rest of the third world as they choose development strategies and try to persuade one another of what courses to take. All the Chinese have to do is keep doing what they are doing. For us that is of tremendous strategic importance and something that I would also like to see mentioned in the paper.

John Wong

Mr. Sullivan has made an excellent analysis of the nature of U.S. trade with China. I particularly like the way he puts it in the perspective of China's foreign policy framework, the U.S. foreign policy framework, and their strategic positions.

I would like to look at Chinese foreign trade from our own perspective. As a socialist, inward-looking economy, China has always faced tremendous obstacles in expanding trade with other countries.

One can identify three fundamental constraints on China's foreign trade growth. The first is what may be called the basic constraint. This is related to China's huge physical size and resource base. As a continental economy, China tends to be more self-sufficient and less dependent on external relations for its growth.

This can be seen in the very low ratio of trade to GNP, as Dr. Keidel has pointed out. But this does not mean that foreign trade is not important for China. A vast country is also likely to develop dualistic features. And it is likely to experience internal transport bottlenecks.

Some parts of big countries are bound to be more externally integrated than others. So a big country still has great leeway to develop trade. For example, in Shanghai, with a population of over 10 million people, or even Guangdong Province with 60 million, there will be tremendous opportunities for trade.

The second constraint is what I call the structural constraint, which links growth of trade to growth of the economy. Mr. Sullivan has particularly emphasized the importance of China's four modernization programs as a basis for the future expansion of U.S.-Chinese trade. In other words, if China continues its modernization, there will be an opportunity for more trade.

The last constraint I would call policy constraint. This is the most unstable variable in the equation determining China's trade with any other country. Mr. Sullivan has pointed out how the relaxation of U.S. restrictions on technology exports has facilitated the development of U.S.-Chinese trade.

This is the policy on the U.S. side, but all eyes are certainly on the potential policy shifts on the Chinese side because of the recent downfall of Hu Yaobang, the party general secretary. China does not have to abandon its economic modernization programs altogether. Just a change of speed or a small modification of its development orientation toward a more self-reliant posture would be sufficient to have a profound effect on China's trade with any other country.

This points to the nature of China's foreign trade development in the future. Mr. Sullivan has projected the amount of Sino-American trade by the end of this century at $20–30 billion. This is a threefold increase—a big jump but not from the standpoint of many export-oriented economies in Asia and the Pacific. For example, Taiwan's trade with the United States last year amounted to about $24 billion, and by the end of this century South Korea's trade with the United States will be some $80 billion, four times the projected figure for Sino-American trade.

This brings us to a "missing link" in the paper. I think the implications of future Sino-American trade should be considered along with how the Chinese economy can be integrated with the other dynamic Asian-Pacific economies. It may be better to look at U.S.-Chinese trade not just in the context of the two countries but also in the context of how China interacts with these neighboring countries, particularly the NICs. If China should import more advanced technology from Japan, it will obviously import less from the United States and vice versa.

Finally, we find that the two-way trade between the United States and China has for many years been in favor of China. But the Chinese government has long complained that for the fifteen years since 1972 trade has been consistently in favor of the United States except in 1972 and 1977. Chinese exports via Hong Kong are presumably not included in the figures.

Again we see a difference in approach. If China includes its exports via Hong Kong, the figures will be biased against China because U.S. exports via Hong Kong are usually not included and are difficult to account for.

This applies even more to the Japanese. If exports via Hong Kong are taken into account, the deficit in Chinese trade with Japan will be bigger still. A problem thus arises from the different perceptions.

David M. Lampton

I would like to make four points, most of which are not redundant to the preceding remarks. I will start at the end of the paper.

First, it seems to me that Mr. Sullivan is saying—and I agree— that the United States ought to enhance its stable relationship with the PRC and the stability of Asia and go some considerable distance in dismantling or at least liberalizing its export control system. My question is, How far does he think we could go?

Even more interesting is a point that has not yet been raised. Mr. Sullivan talks about the development assistance program that Japan has with China. Under U.S. law such a program is at least conceivable, although we do not now have the budgetary resources for it. What kind of U.S. development assistance program would be desirable in his view?

Second, Mr. Sullivan starts by observing that Eckstein's 1970s projection missed by about a factor of ten the actual United States–

China trade in 1980. What is interesting to me is why Eckstein was off by so much. I went back to past issues of the *China Business Review,* and it seems to me that the economists missed the thing that political scientists are trying to understand; that is, where are the discontinuities going to occur?

If we look at the years in which trade jumped or there were large perturbations—both in Mr. Sullivan's last table and in the longer time series data on China trade—1979, 1982, and 1983 are the years of big discontinuities. Although I do not attribute everything to political factors, I do not think we can understand those discontinuities without reference to political factors in China. We have to begin to look at those factors if we are going to explain behavior in the short periods that are of concern to business people.

Third, I was interested to note the discontinuity between Mr. Sullivan's paper and Mr. Keidel's paper. When Mr. Sullivan talks about Chinese export potential, he is talking about textiles, toys, luggage, and sports gear. When Mr. Keidel talked about Chinese export potential, he was talking about textiles, to be sure, but also about automobiles and electronics. Implicit in those two export potentials is some difference in expectations about how rapidly the sophistication of Chinese industry is going to progress.

My final point concerns the strategic rationale. I agree with Mr. Sullivan's view that the strategic rationale was very important for the United States. My question is, If China is improving its relations with the Soviet Union—as I think is demonstrably the case—and the United States improves its relations with the Soviet Union, what is the new basis of consensus for U.S.-Chinese relations going to be in the future?

Here I think the economic rationale must be the key. Although the strategic rationale was important in the past and could remain central in the future, there is a higher than fifty-fifty chance that the strategic rationale will diminish as the cohesive force on the American side.

Discussion

WILLIAM T. Tow: The COCOM regulations have been significantly liberalized over the past year or so, falling in line with a *modus vivendi* reached by the Departments of Defense, Commerce, and State in the United States in about December 1985. I am not sure how much more liberal we can get in the export of high technology. When I was in Shanghai in October, I had talks with the Shanghai Institute of International Affairs. The general Chinese line—"Give us more, give us more"—was being replaced by a surprising satisfaction on the part of the Chinese political analysts and strategists that I talked to, saying, "You finally got the message, we're getting more, at least in terms of the liberalization of your laws." The extent to which the volume will fall into line with the laws is another question, of course, but I would be interested in some feedback on that.

DENIS F. SIMON: Going back to 1983, when the first major relaxation took place, I would like to get beyond the policy level to the level of the firm, of American industry, and put forth a hypothesis that Mr. Sullivan might comment on.

I agree that until the relaxation in May 1983 the export controls were a major obstacle in the way of expanded United States–China trade and sales by firms. I would argue that after 1983, however, they became a decreasingly important factor and that the inability of American firms to compete in the Chinese market was due more to their own managerial inefficiency and their lesser ability to understand and strategically penetrate the Chinese market than Japanese and, more recently, European firms. The failure of the United States is not the failure of policy in 1987 but a failure of managerial know-how to do business overseas.

If we look at the kinds of technologies that the Chinese really need today, we see a whole spectrum of things that the United States could begin to offer the Chinese that would improve the standard of living of the Chinese people and build an economic infrastructure. Again, the U.S. failure has to do with managerial decisions and know-how on the part of U.S. business rather than U.S. policy.

QUESTION: I have a question about the extent to which China's policy makers are still guided by a sense of history. I am reminded of Fairbank's latest book, in which he says that China is still being run by an emperor and just the names have changed, not the system of power.

China has a very bad history of overseas trade. It was forced into unequal trade treaties, forced to buy this and buy that—opium and so on. To what extent would its future trade policies be influenced by all these considerations? Will China emphasize bilateral rather than total multilateral trade, and will it try to gain advantages to compensate for what it feels were injustices in the past?

ROGER W. SULLIVAN: I was interested in Mr. Keidel's comments on textiles. Yes, a certain amount of the rapid expansion (a 79 percent increase) in textile sales in the United States can be related to licensing. But the expansion is largely due to two things that happen when these kinds of constraints are put on somebody's sales to the United States. It is not unique to China. I do not know why we keep pushing textile restraints. They did not work with Japan or Taiwan, and they are not working with China. Two things happen.

First, as soon as the restraints are put on, the price goes up, because the restraints create a shortage. The next thing that happens, if the suppliers are smart, is that they shift into areas that are not controlled, because only certain categories are controlled. Within controlled sectors they go up market and make better quality goods.

The study done for the Joint Economic Committee is very interesting. It points out that, far from having been a drag on Chinese sales to the United States, the restraints enabled China to penetrate the market to the extent that it has.

Mr. Keidel asked, If it were not for protectionism, what would have happened? If it had not been for protectionism, the study suggests, the sales might have been less. We facilitated Chinese penetration of the market. We helped to induce in them a flexibility and adaptability to market conditions that they would not otherwise have learned.

On the U.S.-Soviet equation, I was not talking about the danger of China's returning to dependence on the Soviet Union. That is not something to worry about, because China knows perfectly well that there are limits beyond which it cannot go without sacrificing its reasons for getting into this relationship in the first place—technology transfer and capital from the United States.

That is all part of the symbiotic relationship. That is why I am not concerned about Chinese efforts to reduce tension with the Soviet

Union, nor is the U.S. government, because that point is now understood.

I agree with Professor Wong. Part of my point when I said that the range of trade is likely to be $20–30 billion is that it is not a lot. I am fully aware of that.

If commerce and economics were the foundation of the United States–China relationship, we would not see the president of the United States spending as much time on it as he does. We would not see the secretary of state or the secretary of defense going to China as often as they do. If we tried to say that the nature of the relationship is really economic and commercial, China would not be a very important country in the foreign relations of the United States. But in fact it is and will remain so because of the security dimension of the relationship.

The Chinese are very well aware that the Soviet Union is the long-term threat to them and to the region and that they are in what I have called a period of relative invulnerability, in which they can afford to focus on rebuilding their People's Liberation Army (PLA) and making decisions on what they need in the way of weaponry, confident that the United States can handle the Soviets while that goes on. But they do not see any fundamental change in the relationship between China and the Soviet Union, nor do they see any fundamental change in Soviet policy in the region, nor do I.

How far would I go on export licensing? Let me include that with Bill Tow's comments and Denis Simon's questions about COCOM. First, there is a tendency to assume that just because the U.S. government announces that it is liberalizing something, something in fact gets liberalized. A lot of false starts have been made in export licensing liberalization, as many people here who have looked at it know and as Denis Simon knows very well. It didn't work in 1980 when we first tried it or in 1981; but 1983 saw a major change.

The 1985 liberalization is a little confusing because it created what the Chinese would call unintended consequences. COCOM took a list of twenty-seven categories of products, on what is called the Commodity Control List, and designated them "green zone." That means that each member country of COCOM is free to sell those products to China at its discretion.

National discretion means to the Germans, for example, that a company can just sell the product; but to the United States it means that the product does not need clearance from COCOM but does need clearance from the Commerce Department and the Defense Department. The United States suddenly found itself at a competitive disadvantage because other countries—the Germans, the Japanese, and the French, for example—say to the Chinese, "Here is a piece of equipment. It may not be as good as what you could get from the United States; but if you order it from the United States it will take eight months, and I can deliver it next week."

This also explains why we do not get so much criticism from the Chinese anymore. There is no longer a question about their being able to get access to high-technology material. They can get it elsewhere. In the paper I was talking about the ability of the United States to get its share of Chinese trade.

Before 1983 the export licensing problem was a political problem between the United States and China, because what the United States was perceived as doing was keeping China from getting access to these goods. Since 1983 it has become a commercial problem. The United States has liberalized the system so that other countries, and theoretically the United States, can sell more than they could sell before, but the United States has kept procedures that have inhibited the ability of American companies to compete.

Some changes should still be made. For example, the U.S. Defense Department decided that China should not get an intercity communications system—a secure communications system and a command and control system. You might ask why we don't want them to have those things, and the Chinese do indeed ask that question. Those are not in the green zone; they are in what is called the red zone, which means that under no circumstances can we sell those things to the Chinese.

Then the British signed contracts to sell this equipment to the Chinese. Margaret Thatcher goes to Ronald Reagan and says, "This is a big ticket item for us. Why don't you approve it?" Reagan tells the Pentagon to approve it, and the Pentagon tells American companies, "This is a political decision, not a precedent for any future sales you have with China."

This comes back to a basic point: if the U.S. relationship with China were purely a commercial one, the U.S. government would lose interest in it. President Reagan does not liberalize export controls to China because he wants American companies to sell equipment to China. He does it for strategic reasons. The United States does not worry about protectionism and how it will affect China because it is worried about the American consumer having to pay higher prices for products from China. It worries about protectionism for strategic reasons.

How far would I go? I would at a minimum put the United States on the same basis as its COCOM partners. Essentially, I would take all the items that we are now supposedly allowed to sell China and allow companies to sell them without having to go through a licensing procedure at all and then look at some strategic assumptions made by the United States and ask the Pentagon why, for example, it does not want the Chinese to have an intercity communications system. Where is the security interest in that?

I am not very optimistic that the United States is going to engage in any kind of development assistance program with China. The budget constraints for the near term certainly make that impossible. American congressmen should think twice before they say we should reduce our contributions to the World Bank, because about the only concessional financing American companies have access to is World Bank financing.

We have some chance of getting a little money for training, and some legislation is pending that would provide money actually earmarked for China. We are getting encouraging noises from the Export-Import Bank indicating that it is prepared to consider doing something that would enable us to match predatory financing by other countries in China. I would not hold out much hope for a major assistance program to China, but at least some help in export financing must be offered.

A multinational company could not care less about the balance of payments of the United States. That is a congressional concern, a taxpayer's concern. The disadvantages that the United States government puts companies under in the United States do not keep IBM from making money. What they do is to determine whether IBM's Japanese employees or IBM's Canadian employees or IBM's American employees are going to benefit, because IBM just goes where the financing is, where the export controls are looser.

7
China's Modernization and the Big Powers: Strategic Implications

William T. Tow

Military modernization in the People's Republic of China (PRC) has been largely driven by factors of cost and technology since that country's first test of a nuclear weapon almost a quarter-century ago. The Chinese have viewed the development of an indigenous strategic force as the most cost-effective means to achieve a credible—if minimal—deterrent against both the Soviet Union and the United States. Indeed, at least one official U.S. intelligence estimate and several independent estimates have projected that up to half of China's entire military research and development funding was directed toward its nuclear weapons program between 1965 and 1979.[1]

Chinese strategist Zhang Jianzhi recently noted that "China's nuclear strategy can be summed up as a strategy of 'limited self-defensive counterattack', which is not aimed at launching and winning any nuclear war outright but opposing and checking its occurrence."[2] Yet while there is little doubt that the PRC has been modernizing its industrial, scientific, and military infrastructure with every intent of closing the strategic gap between itself and the superpowers, a strong case can be made that China's strategic capabilities in relation to those of both Moscow and Washington have actually declined in recent years. U.S. Defense Secretary Caspar Weinberger recently noted in testimony before the U.S. Congress, for example, that China has been able to sustain a relatively small finite deterrent by using camouflage, concealment, and mobility to compensate for its still rudimentary land-based nuclear missile technology. Although the deployment of more Chinese nuclear ballistic missile submarines will allow for greater survivability in China's deterrence forces, the introduction of advanced ballistic missile defense technologies by both the Soviet Union and the United States could seriously diminish the PRC's relative strategic strength over the rest of this decade and

171

beyond.[3] If Beijing attempts to compensate by developing a wider range of nuclear weapons capabilities or by deploying greater quantities of its present systems, the traditional cost-effectiveness appeal of the nuclear deterrence option would be reduced commensurately.[4]

The extent to which China has moved beyond the finite, limited nuclear deterrence capabilities in place and operative against the superpowers since the late 1960s needs to be evaluated in light of its recent measures to reorganize its military force structure, command system, methods for high-technology assimilation, and actual weapons production. The purpose of this paper is to assess what the Chinese strategic deterrent means for the international power balance, now dominated by the Soviet Union and the United States. Initially, a brief evaluation will be offered on how the current pace and scope of the PRC's strategic force programs are developing. This can be undertaken, in part, by comparing China's nuclear weapons program with those of two other intermediate nuclear powers—Britain and France. A second important aspect of China's strategic power is to what extent the United States and its Western allies have a viable interest in facilitating the PRC's aspirations or blocking the PRC from obtaining greater strategic capability through technology transfers at both the global and the regional levels. This issue seems particularly relevant given recent indications that China may be willing to forge at least a qualified rapprochement with the Soviet Union as a key component of Beijing's so-called independent foreign policy. Finally, a brief examination of two other critical but related issues will be presented: first, China's positions on, and impact upon, superpower arms control negotiations; and, second, China's responses to the prospect that Japan will play a greater military role throughout East Asia (Japan's economic power base already makes Tokyo a de facto great power in East Asia and the world despite its lack of extensive military capabilities).

China's Strategic Force Development and Deployment

China, Britain, and France—the world's three intermediate nuclear powers—are embarking on nuclear force modernization programs in an effort to compensate for the superpowers' steady increases in their own offensive nuclear arsenals (and, more recently, as a hedge against Soviet technological breakthroughs in strategic defenses). Zhang Jianzhi cogently assessed the rationales for middle nuclear powers to sustain their own force buildups, even at a time when the United States and the Soviet Union still retain about 95 percent of the world's nuclear stockpile:

In developing nuclear weapons, there is a relatively stable "saturation point" for all countries, which is marked by "sufficient quantity" and "reliable quality." Before their nuclear weapons reach [this] "saturation point," medium size nuclear powers have a deterrent factor too, but they are very liable to have their nuclear force disarmed by the enemy's first attack because the actual combat capability of their nuclear weapons is not yet strong enough. In terms of strategy, this period of time can therefore be regarded as a period of "latent danger." Before the period of "latent danger" is over, their nuclear deterrent is still not reliable and the investment in building their nuclear force should not be readjusted or reduced.[5]

Whether intended or not, China's deterrence strategy appears to rest upon the same elements of ambiguity and bargaining that have predicated the British independent nuclear deterrent as well as the French *force de frappe* throughout much of postwar history. In a strategic nuclear triangle involving two stronger nuclear powers, the independent Chinese force would have to be considered—and, therefore, would be a source of significant influence—because even a technologically primitive nuclear force such as China's could wreak enough damage on the prevailing superpower in a nuclear showdown to render it more vulnerable than the weaker superpower. In such a scenario, either superpower would have less incentive to attack or preempt China's finite deterrent on its own.[6] Stated differently, while China now has only about a 3 percent share of the global nuclear stockpile, the percentage of its share and that of the other middle nuclear powers will increase markedly by the end of the century. The need for China's nuclear force to be taken into greater account by Washington and Moscow will, however, be largely predicated upon what form of technological breakthroughs one or both of the superpowers achieve in their own nuclear force capabilities by that time.

Although China's nuclear capabilities need not be exaggerated at present, projected qualitative improvements in the PRC's nuclear force will add markedly to the significance of whatever quantitative level that force will attain in the near future. It appears useful, therefore, to compare what qualitative advances the Chinese are actually making in their strategic force structure in relation to those emerging in the British and French nuclear arsenals. If the most common measurements used by strategic analysts for comparing lethality and diversity of various strategic forces are applied, China now rivals Great Britain and France as a nuclear power. The PRC's intermediate-

173

range ballistic missile (IRBM) and medium-range ballistic missile (MRBM) inventories, by way of illustration, far exceed those of France (China, according to the International Institute for Strategic Studies, has some fifty liquid-fueled, single-staged, road-transportable missiles with a 600-mile range and an additional fifty to eighty IRBMs with a range of 1,500 miles compared to only eighteen S-3 IRBMs with a 2,000 mile+ range for France) while Britain has virtually no land-based IRBM or MRBM deployments.[7] Both the French and the British, however, remain far ahead of China in submarine ballistic missile (SSBN) deployments (the French have six SSBNs and the British four, while the Chinese have only one or, at the most, two). The quality of British and French nuclear-strike aircraft are also superior as both the Tornado and the Mirage IV far exceed the old Chinese TU-16 in efficiency and penetration capability.

Both London and Paris each have 500–700 nuclear warheads and are currently planning to increase their inventories to over a thousand over the next decade (although the British Labor party would move the United Kingdom toward unilateral nuclear disarmament if it were to assume power in that country and the current party platform were observed).[8] There is some debate over the actual number of such warheads in China; recent estimates by the Defense Intelligence Agency and the Institute for Policy Studies estimate that 250–350 warheads are stockpiled, while Bradley Hahn, a consultant on Chinese defense problems who often writes for Asian defense publications, has cited a figure totaling as high as 1,250.[9] Most estimates, however, credit the Chinese with between 225 and 300 warheads. The confusion about the exact total may well be the result of uncertainty over what has been characterized as "an unspecified number" of atomic demolitions (ADMs), which have been deployed in northern China to deter future Soviet ground attacks against Chinese military positions close to the Sino-Soviet border.[10]

Britain, France, and China have all deployed or are on the verge of deploying multiple reentry vehicle (MRV) missile delivery systems. Certainly Britain's pending deployment of Trident II SSBNs (by the mid- to late 1990s) to replace its aging Polaris fleet would reinforce the clear British lead over the French and Chinese in the categories of nuclear warhead development and missile guidance technology—which can be strengthened only by pending British involvement in the U.S. Strategic Defense Initiative's (SDI) research and development program—as well as in aspects of command, control, communication, and intelligence (C^3I). Presumably, much of this British advantage comes from its access to such U.S. technologies and its work with the Americans in NATO nuclear planning.

France and China, by contrast, have developed nuclear forces largely independent of superpower assistance. Notwithstanding the absence of a highly developed nuclear collaborative relationship with a superpower such as that which the British have developed with their American counterparts, the French and Chinese are still moving toward nuclear modernization at a steady pace. France is deploying multiple independently targetable reentry vehicles (MIRVs) for its five *le Redoubtable* class submarines and is already in the process of *MIRV*-ing its first Inflexible class SSBN, thus keeping pace with Britain's MIRVed D-5 missile (which, in turn, will be deployed on its Trident IIs). Ultimately, the French *Oceanic Strategique* will experience an increase in its warhead delivery capability from 80 to 496, while the planned replacement for the current French IRBM force could add another 100.[11] China, by comparison, conducted its first successful test of a submarine-launched ballistic missile (SLBM) in October 1982, probably from the missile-launching tube of a Golf class diesel—electric-powered submarine (constructed locally in 1964).[12] The 1982 test launch was reported to have a range of up to 1,800 miles, which would give the Chinese North Sea Fleet the capability to hit a number of Soviet targets in Asia from firing points in the Bohai Gulf.[13] The actual and projected size and capabilities of China's SSBN force, however, remain somewhat enigmatic. Official U.S. government estimates indicate that Beijing has deployed one *Xia* SSBN with twelve ballistic missile tubes and armed with a solid-fueled rocket that has a range of over 650 miles. Using both official and private research institute data, however, other analysts have assigned China a more formidable SSBN capability. Asian security analyst Alastair Johnston notes that "the eventual size of the [Chinese] SLBM force is . . . open to question. There are unsubstantiated reports that the PRC plans initially to procure six SSBNs with twelve tubes each at a total cost of ten billion yuan ($6.7 billion). Other reports suggest seven submarines with sixteen tubes each."[14]

Johnston also concludes that the SSBN force may be regarded by Beijing as an even better investment than an upgraded land-based ICBM program for China to achieve minimum deterrence because of greater cost effectiveness and survivability. Robert Sutter, on the other hand, has speculated that the solid-fueled rocket technology inherent to SLBM development could be applied to land-based missiles, which "would likely improve the mobility and reaction times of China's land-based forces."[15] U.S. government analysts have surmised that if China becomes convinced that a minimum deterrent is adequate for preserving China's security against the present Soviet or a future American nuclear threat, the SSBN program could be downgraded as

175

well because its expense would be regarded by a post-Deng Chinese leadership as too prohibitive within the context of China's overall economic reform programs.[16]

The perceptions of the middle nuclear powers concerning how to sustain or strengthen the capabilities of theater-relevant ballistic missiles vary somewhat. British theater nuclear forces are strongly linked with NATO and its mission planning, and the geography of the British Isles renders stationary ICBM/IRBM/MRBM force deployment largely irrational in comparison to the development of mobile sea and air launching platforms. Moreover, British deterrence theories have never encouraged the view of nuclear weapons as extensions of conventional armaments, whereas China, like the Soviet Union, has until very recently held that no dividing line really exists between conventional and nuclear war.[17] Accordingly, Beijing moved toward land-based missile deployment from the outset of its nuclear weapons program. There seems to be little better reason for France to modernize its own highly vulnerable S-3 IRBM force on the Albion Plateau in southeastern France with a mobile S-X *(Danone)* follow-on missile system other than to demonstrate French technological proficiency or (a more generous interpretation) to complicate Soviet targeting during a preemptive strike. Certainly French SSBNs appear to be much more survivable instruments of finite deterrence. By contrast, China has greater land space and lacks a geographic buffer zone such as what West Germany offers to both Britain and France. IRBM/MRBM development makes sound sense for China, because such missiles allow it to strike key military-industrial targets in the central and eastern Soviet Union as well as to exercise possible influence over other potential adversaries in east or south Asia.

The Chinese, of course, are counting on the superpowers to take Beijing's own strategic interests more and more into account as a result of its nuclear force buildup. This is evidenced by Beijing's increasingly activist diplomacy regarding superpower arms control talks. The PRC might well conclude that it must accommodate Moscow before the Russians are able to use their residual nuclear capabilities in the Asian theater to expand their own power and influence at the expense of both China and the West. All this directly relates to Washington's own interests in sustaining a security relationship with the PRC. Whereas the Reagan administration *did* perceive China's major role as supporting U.S. and NATO deterrence efforts in Europe and Southeast Asia throughout 1981–1982, it has more recently advocated Western assistance in strengthening Chinese (nonnuclear) military capabilities on the assumption that by doing so China will continue to serve as a "passive strategic counterweight" to the Soviet military presence in the Asian-Pacific region.[18] The new-found Chinese determination to streamline its military-industrial complex and to assimilate selected Western technology should be weighed in the context of discerning the degree to which long-term Chinese and Western strategic interests may coincide.

Chinese Strategic Modernization and Western Interests

The reality of "people's war under modern conditions" was especially underscored in December 1984 when approximately forty elderly officers were retired from the People's Liberation Army (PLA) General Staff headquarters and replaced by personnel with less intense memories of Mao Zedong's Long March and subsequent revolutionary military programs. This was followed up by a Central Military Affairs Commission meeting in late May–early June 1985 where specific implementing actions were taken, among which were a *ganbu nianqinghua* (cadre "youthification") campaign, as well as subordination of the PLA more completely to Chinese Communist party authority through reducing military representation on the Politburo and by merging Chinese defense industries with civilian production centers.[19] That China is giving high priority to its strategic force development is evidenced by the June 1984 formation of a separate Strategic Missile Force Command to supersede the long-standing nuclear missions of the PLA's Second Artillery.[20] While China's overall military budget remains static, at best, the PRC's leadership showcased a wide array of nuclear delivery systems under the new command's auspices in the course of a military parade held in Beijing during October 1984.[21]

Under the Four Modernizations (agriculture, industry, science and technology, and defense), therefore, the momentum of China's nuclear force programs and the military reorganization accompanying it are critical factors to understanding overall Chinese strategy. Even the military nuclear industry, until now largely beyond the reach of cost-cutting measures, is facing shortages in construction material and increased pressure to be converted into a profitable and fiscally conservative operation. While China's Seventh Five-Year Plan calls for the installation of nuclear power plants capable of generating a total capacity of 10,000 megawatts by the year 2000, program expenditures may actually allow for only half that. To what extent the material shortages and decreased production outlays will affect uranium mining operations critical to nuclear weapons production (China now mines an estimated 1,000 tons of uranium per year for military purposes) remains uncertain.[22]

Underlying these developments seems to be a more relaxed view in Beijing over the prospects that China will become involved in a nuclear conflict with either superpower, at least in the near future. While the U.S. nuclear threat was very real to China's leadership throughout the 1950s and 1960s and the Soviet threat just as predominant from the late 1960s through the early 1980s, Beijing has more recently concluded that the superpower arms race is a seesaw affair.[23] By the middle of President Reagan's first term, the Soviets were regarded as preoccupied with internal economic and political problems, while the Americans were preoccupied with a new arms buildup. Only five years later, a younger and more dynamic Soviet leadership (under the direction of Mikhail Gorbachev) was still attempting to strike a balance between internal political reform and global geopolitics while the United States was reeling from misadventures in Iran, Lebanon, and Nicaragua. With more time now believed to be available for modernizing its industry and technology, China's leaders concluded that they should approach nuclear and conventional weapons development with the care and organization needed to close obvious technological gaps. In late November 1986, a highly placed Chinese aeronautics official described the revised policy in an interview with *Liaowang* (overseas edition):

> Through repeated studies, the CCP central leadership, the State Council, and the Central Military Commission, after consulting the departments concerned, have decided to change the structure of the military industry from the previous one, which merely served defense construction, to a new pattern that serves the development of the national economy as a whole. . . . The State Council . . . will treat the military industrial enterprises in the same way as they treat other civilian industrial enterprises.[24]

The policy implications for the West are clear: in helping to develop China's technological and economic base, it also helps lay the foundation for increased Chinese strategic capabilities, which must be taken into account. The West needs to examine afresh the comforting hypothesis entertained in some circles that "a modernizing China is inherently a good China." Because Chinese policy behavior is so situationally defined, as Lucian Pye argues in his recent article on Chinese "pragmatism," one can have little confidence that today's policies are a good predictor of tomorrow's behavior.[25] It would therefore be wise to remember that China's economic and strategic policies have always been subject to the little-understood vagaries of constant maneuverings among domestic Chinese political coalitions. Regardless of what faction prevails in the latest round of Chinese political shadowboxing, it would be mistaken for either superpower to assume that China's views of deterrence will inevitably come to reflect its own.

Chinese strategists have already served notice to the outside world that such is the case. Professor Zhang from the Chinese Academy of Social Sciences recently wrote that "the degree to which technological advances can overcome natural and social environments, and thus change the style and conduct of warfare in East Asia, may be debatable."[26] Yet, in recent years, Washington has tended to interpret China's military defensive needs as an almost inviolate strategic principle, falling within the framework of a deterrence model along Western lines that could be applied particularly to the Sino-Soviet border. As a result, *the United States*—not China—has emphasized Beijing's need for introducing more sophisticated, Western-produced antitank and artillery systems there. U.S. defense firms have thus cultivated images of China buying large quantities of Western air defense systems and coastal patrol craft, images that proved to be far too optimistic. The Chinese, it turned out, could not (and would not) rely on finished weapons systems. Instead, they have sought to overcome key technological bottlenecks in both their strategic and their conventional forces through highly selective purchases and technology acquisitions. Under such circumstances, it is reasonable to ask why the United States did not from the outset take more literally the thinking reflected in a recent Chinese science and technology journal: "In the view of developed countries, providing advanced technology to foreign countries is equivalent to digging one's grave, and they will strive to stay ten years ahead of us technologically."[27]

It seems more reasonable, therefore, for the West to assume that China regards the potential development of sophisticated strategic defense systems by either or both superpowers to be a major threat to its own national security and strategic credibility. If so, China's incentives to acquire advanced technology from the West will increase even more as Washington and Moscow forge ahead with their respective strategic defense programs. A truly formidable breakthrough by either the United States or the Soviet Union in ballistic missile defense technology would greatly diminish the utility of even the most advanced segments of China's present deterrent. China's leaders, one presumes, must now already be seeking to upgrade the PRC's C^3I, targeting, and survivability capabilities, if for no other reason than to upgrade their deterrence potential. In the absence of such improvements, the present capabilities of China's military and nuclear power, now so impressive in relation to its third world economic base, will wither over time because of its relative lack of technological sophistication. The West, therefore, still remains the source of what high technology would be most coveted by future Chinese strategic planners. This includes "kill mechanism" subcomponents related to ballistic missile defenses, including various advanced computer systems, lasers, particle beams, homing projectiles, and related missile guidance and targeting technologies.

Such considerations outline, in stark relief, the following policy questions. What kinds of Chinese nuclear capabilities are in our Western interest as well as in the interest of stability along the Pacific rim? What *practical* means does the United States have to shape emerging Chinese strategic capabilities? In the absence of such U.S. policy leverage, could China revert to a technology relationship with the Soviet Union for selected military technology, given a continued improvement in overall Sino-Soviet ties? What does all this imply for the future of U.S. technology transfer policies toward Beijing? Is a further relaxation of such policy, as it applies to both commercial (see the chapter by Sullivan in this volume) and the military-strategic dimensions of the Sino-American relationship, justifiable in relation to overall U.S. national security interests? While space limitations preclude an in-depth analysis of these questions here, the broader implications that they raise can at least be briefly specified.

Washington and its allies have every interest in China's achieving deterrence capabilities sufficient to preclude the type of Soviet preemptive strikes that the Soviet Union reportedly contemplated in the late 1960s against Chinese nuclear installations or related strategic facilities.[28] Nor would the partial dismemberment of China through Soviet military occupation of Xinjiang or Manchuria and the subsequent establishment of "enclaves" there be in Western interests, given the inordinate strategic imbalance of power that would then materialize throughout northeast Asia.[29] In addition to China's integral role in fulfilling the requirements for strategic denial of Soviet power projection in the Asian Pacific, at least two other strategic functions of a Chinese nuclear deterrent seem readily apparent: (1) as an increasingly strategic counterweight to the Soviet Union when and if U.S. basing presence in the Philippines and elsewhere throughout the Pacific is reduced or lost and U.S. maritime nuclear projection is affected as a result; and (2) as a type of strategic enforcer to be applied against whatever future Vietnamese intentions may be entertained for aggression against the member states of the Association for Southeast Asian Nations (ASEAN).

If Beijing's nuclear deterrent can be viewed as critical in these ways, analysis of China's ability to maneuver effectively between the superpowers within a so-called strategic triangle so as to exact the maximum benefits possible from Washington—especially in the area of technology transfers—becomes more understandable.[30] In reality, however, China has only a limited ability to exact such leverage from the United States because Beijing is limited in how far it can dangle "the Soviet option" without jeopardizing its access to Western technology. The United States, by contrast, can gauge or calibrate the flow of high technology to the PRC more in accordance with its reading of how willing the Chinese are to apply such technology in checking Soviet military power (this is a separate consideration from the earlier stated problem of Beijing's resistance to Western deterrence rationales for structuring its own anti-Soviet containment strategy). Chinese polemics about "independent diplomacy," moreover, must be tempered by the reality that China still depends, in the final analysis, upon U.S. projection of nuclear deterrence in Asia to guarantee the type of peaceful environment China needs to raise its own economic infrastructure to higher stages of development.[31]

The U.S. expectation that it can continue to link technology transfers to Chinese political cooperation may have to be revised, however, in the aftermath of Deng Xiaoping's future departure from China's political scene. Of most concern in this regard is the qualified but ongoing improvement in Sino-Soviet relations. Sino-Soviet trade relations, for example, have been revived to the point where over $2.6 billion worth of economic transactions occurred between the Soviet Union and the PRC in 1986 alone (Moscow now stands as China's fifth largest trading partner).[32] Throughout 1985–1986, Sino-Soviet relations in the so-called low-technology transfer sector were also enhanced with a Commission on Economics, Trade, Science, and Technology coordinating joint projects in electronics and other basic industries.[33] Although it seems improbable that any future Chinese leadership would move toward a rapprochement with the Soviets reminiscent of the 1950s, it might be well for Washington to remember that most Chinese military equipment, in fact, still originates from Soviet blueprints. The Chinese bias toward military simplicity and gradual military self-sufficiency also appears to be more compatible with Soviet weapons systems than with the relatively complex avionics or antisubmarine warfare technology, for example, that China is now soliciting from the West.

In general, strategic considerations will still play a large part in most decisions Washington makes about Chinese requests for further trade liberalization and technology transfer under the auspices of either the U.S. Department of Commerce Commodities Control List or the U.S. Department of State Munitions Control List. Until the United States gains a better understanding of just what the Chinese perceive to be the critical aspects of nuclear and conventional deterrence, however, these fluctuating category assignments for China either in reviews by the U.S. agencies of concern or by the Coordinating Committee for Export Controls (COCOM) will still tend to obfuscate the overall guidelines of any Sino-American relationship governing high-technology transfers.

China and Arms Control

Speculation about how the PRC could become a greater factor in superpower negotiations pertaining to either European or global arms control has also increased, especially as the United States and the Soviet Union move toward an apparent *modus vivendi* on intermediate nuclear forces. The Chinese, in any case, would still seem to have an abiding desire for the United States to reject Soviet arguments that British, French, and Chinese forces be taken into account as part of the Soviet Union's "equal security" concept, which has been advanced at both the Strategic Arms Reduction Talks and the Intermediate Nuclear Force negotiations. Equal security—as the Soviets have represented the idea—implies that the Soviets must retain at least some marginal advantages within the global strategic balance to offset nuclear capabilities of "hostile nuclear powers" located along its peripheries (this reasoning was spelled out by a Soviet journalist writing in 1980 that "it is hard to see how the USSR and USA . . . can restrict or scale down their strategic armaments while China continues to produce and deploy more missiles").[34]

Nor has Beijing been reticent in advancing its own views on arms control within the United Nations and other international settings. The PRC's overall position, however, has varied little from its first comprehensive proposal advanced at the UN Special Session on Disarmament in 1978. At that time, the Chinese demanded that the superpowers cease all nuclear testing, stop their qualitative improvement and manufacturing of all nuclear weapons, and reduce their nuclear arsenals by 50 percent to demonstrate their sincerity for disarmament politics. Until such reductions in the superpowers' inventories take place, however, China reserves the right to continue its own strategic force buildup.[35] At first glance, such Chinese expectations about superpower arms control behavior seem unrealistic. Yet, one need only recall the landmark proposals for deep cuts in strategic forces nearly achieved at the Iceland summit in October 1986 to realize that Beijing's demands or expectations may not be totally unfounded.

The recent discussions about the abolition of medium- and short-range missiles in Europe are further indication that such moves are not only possible, but perhaps likely.

Even until such time that significant reductions in the superpowers' nuclear arsenals are realized, China stands to gain continued propaganda dividends through portraying both Moscow and Washington as insincere in their arms negotiations. In January 1987, by way of illustration, the *People's Daily* contended that "deadlocks keep emerging in the bilateral talks on disarmament between the USSR and the U.S." It blamed this trend on both Moscow's and Washington's "vision . . . of beefing up [their] military strength," with the United States stubbornly adhering to its determination to develop and deploy sophisticated missile defenses and with the Soviet Union sacrificing the economic well-being of its people through continuing its own global military buildup.[36]

Underlying such polemics, however, is the very real Chinese concern about the implications of the Strategic Defense Initiative or other advances in military technology for China's own military capabilities. China's leadership has reportedly already authorized an in-depth analysis of the implications of space warfare on China's own security.[37] In the meantime, it is pressing for control of space weapons in the UN with proposals for the superpowers to exercise restraint in their space defenses in the same way as China would have them cut back on their existing offensive nuclear weapons capabilities.[38]

The PRC is also developing an Asian-Pacific arms control agenda to supplement its pressures against the superpowers. "Nuclear-free-zone" politics has become the primary means through which the Chinese have implemented this policy. China has endorsed and ratified the South Pacific Nuclear Free Zone Treaty (SPNFZT) and has criticized various American congressmen and military officials who oppose the treaty on the grounds that it compromises U.S. extended deterrence in the western Pacific.[39] Nuclear-free-zone politics naturally reflects China's affinity for representing itself as the "vanguard" of third world security interests confronting superpower hegemony. Interestingly, the Soviet Union is the only other nuclear power that has endorsed the SPNFZT (inasmuch as the treaty language leaves in the hands of the individual signatory the decision to accept naval port calls or aircraft landings without verifying the nuclear status of the ship or aircraft in question). Under present treaty stipulations, nuclear-capable units of the Soviet Pacific Fleet could still transit the treaty area. The United States has rejected affiliation with SPNFZT on the grounds that it must retain the prerogative to determine the composition of its naval and air force weapons without question.

It is, of course, uncertain to what extent Beijing will remain committed to nuclear-free-zone approaches to disarmament, especially when and if its own naval capabilities become more diversified and nuclear dependent in the future. If precedent serves as evidence, however, China has demonstrated remarkable flexibility over the past few years in adjusting its declaratory diplomacy to pragmatic ends. Examples include the International Atomic Energy Agency's new-found authority to inspect China's nuclear installations as well as China's recent and explicit pledge to refrain from atmospheric testing of nuclear weapons. Furthermore, the Chinese have been gradually moving away from an absolute insistence on preserving their sovereign rights in questions relating to arms control and disarmament. This movement reflects Beijing's changing assessments of the global power balance and its own capabilities. China's growing recognition that geopolitics is best reinforced by policy pragmatism is an encouraging development from both the American and the Soviet arms control perspectives.

China, Japan, and the Global Power Balance

China's response to the intensification of Japanese military efforts provides what may be the most important test of its determination to preserve an anti-Soviet defense coalition, while simultaneously enticing NATO Europe and Japan into greater alignment with Beijing's own geopolitics of independence outside the orbit of superpower competition. Overall, Sino-Japanese relations remain fairly stable. Recent political developments in Japan, however, have rekindled historical fears on the part of the Chinese, including a well-publicized visit in August 1985 by Japan's Prime Minister Nakasone to the Yasukuni Shrine where Japanese war criminals are buried, as well as outspoken and revisionist interpretations of Japan's war guilt carelessly expressed by Japan's since-fired education minister (see the Sutter contribution to this volume). Such developments contributed little to mollifying concerns expressed by former General Secretary Hu Yaobang and other Chinese officials that a revived Japanese militarism could yet become a threat in northeast Asia if it is allowed to develop unhindered over time.[40]

Moreover, Nakasone's disclosure at the end of 1986 that Japan's defense budget would exceed 1 percent of that country's 1986 GNP—thus removing a long-standing ceiling of self-restraint on arms spending observed by Tokyo—further intensified Chinese feelings that Japanese defense ambitions could represent a threat to regional stability if left unchecked by the Americans. The worst-case scenario from a

Chinese perspective would be that Japan might be encouraged to adopt a security posture more commensurate with its formidable economic capabilities and more consistent with its prewar identity and behavior. The Chinese Foreign Ministry recently summarized Beijing's concern in this regard: "We express our concern over this development. For reasons known to all, Asian countries all along have been sensitive to the Japanese Government building up its military strength. . . . We hope that the Japanese Government will draw on the historical lesson in earnest on this issue."[41] More recently, at the fifth session of the Sixth National People's Congress, Chinese Foreign Minister Wu Xueqian was criticized by some delegates for having been too supine in his dealings with Tokyo.[42]

Despite such reservations, China still regards friendly relations with Japan as integral to its overall foreign policy. Access to the Japanese market and capital remains indispensable to the realization of Beijing's Four Modernizations objectives. This remains the case, notwithstanding China's $4.5 billion trade deficit with Tokyo in 1985 and a $5.5 billion deficit in 1986.[43] It is also true despite the bitter taste in Japanese mouths, which is the legacy of Chinese "retractions" on financial obligations to Japan over the past few years. In 1981, for example, China's national budget constraints combined with its suspension of major capital construction projects reduced Beijing's demand for Japanese capital goods below those originally envisioned by the February 1978 long-term trade agreement (1978–1985) between the PRC and Japan. Chinese oil production targeted for export to Japan also fell well short of its projected goal (in 1979 China exported only 7.4 million tons of oil to Tokyo, far short of the 15 million ton annual figure originally called for by the trade agreement).[44] The extent to which these difficulties can be overcome must, in part, depend upon how flexible China is willing to be in ultimately accepting a Japan that promises to become more strategically and diplomatically self-sufficient. On Japan's part, its leadership must take great care to demonstrate that incremental increases in Japan's defense budget have more to do with the general momentum of overall Japanese economic growth than with any specific regional design. In return, China must understand Japan's imperative for protecting its economic lifeline against growing Soviet power in the Pacific. Rising American financial problems can work only to increase expectations that Japan ought to shoulder more of its own defense responsibilities.

Even now China has been given reason for concern over Nakasone's interest in hosting Soviet leader Gorbachev, who could yet be the first Soviet postwar leader to visit Japan. This remains true even though Beijing has sought Japanese understanding for its own overtures toward limited rapprochement with Moscow. It seems that at least some breakthroughs in Soviet-Japanese relations are inevitable, indeed long overdue. Certainly, the latest Soviet overtures toward the Japanese are less crude and potentially more appealing to Tokyo than those at any other time in recent history.

Conclusion

China's nuclear force has clearly affected the Asian-Pacific military balance over the past two decades. It has not, however, been as decisive a strategic force globally. In addition, both the United States and the Soviet Union are now deploying or are on the verge of developing weapons technologies that promise to widen the gap between the superpowers' nuclear deterrence capabilities and those maintained by Beijing. As a result, China is principally *reactive* in its strategic policies directed toward both Washington and Moscow because it is now operating in a technological environment where, at best, it and other middle nuclear powers can only hope their finite deterrence will not become eroded to the point of irrelevance.

Equally apparent is that the PRC will not be content in allowing this situation to continue over the long term. It is pursuing a twin strategy of cultivating economic and technological relations with *all* of the world's industrial powers (including the Soviet Union, although at a lower priority than such relations it entertains with the United States, Western Europe, and Japan) to accrue its own high-technology base while simultaneously pressuring for superpower nuclear disarmament in ways that could only enhance China's relative military standing in the process. This policy course constitutes a low-risk Chinese approach to global power status and reflects a much more pragmatic Chinese world view than when China first entered the nuclear club as an unrepentant ideologue. China can no longer afford to be at such odds with the United States or the Soviet Union that one or both superpowers contemplate future adjustments designed specifically to compromise Beijing.

Notes

1. Central Intelligence Agency, *Chinese Defense Spending 1965–1979;* U.S. Congress, Joint Economic Committee, *China and the Four Modernizations* (Washington, D.C.: GPO), 1982), pp. 597–610; and Robert G. Sutter, "Chinese Nuclear Weapons and American Interests: Conflicting Policy Choices," in U.S. Congress, Joint Economic Committee, *China's Economy Looks toward the Year 2000* (Washington, D.C.: GPO, May 21, 1986), p. 172. By contrast, the Defense Intelligence Agency estimates that only 5 percent of China's total

defense expenditures were allocated for the development of the country's strategic offensive forces between 1967 and 1983. See Ed Parris, "Chinese Defense Expenditures 1967–1983," in *China's Economy Looks toward the Year 2000*, pp. 155–56.

2. Zhang Jianzhi, "Views on Medium-Sized Nuclear Powers' Nuclear Strategy," *Jiefangjun Bao* in Chinese, March 20, 1987; in Foreign Broadcast Information Service *(FBIS), China: Daily Report*, April 1, 1987, p. K29.

3. See Weinberger's observation on this point in Secretary of Defense, *Annual Report to Congress Fiscal Year 1987* (Washington, D.C.: GPO, February 5, 1986), p. 65.

4. This may not necessarily be a disappointment to all of China's military services. Gerald Segal notes that just "because nuclear weapons have opportunity costs for other services, the [guardian of] Chinese defense may not appreciate the central elite's efforts to cut costs by deploying nuclear forces." Segal, *Defending China* (New York: Oxford University Press, 1985), p. 76.

5. Zhang Jianzhi, p. K31.

6. This scenario is developed more thoroughly by Alastair Johnston, "Chinese Nuclear Force Modernization: Implications for Arms Control," *Journal of Northeast Asia Studies*, vol. 2, no. 2 (June 1983), p. 17.

7. Sutter, pp. 173–76; William M. Arkin, *Nuclear Battlefields* (Cambridge, Mass.: Ballinger Publishing Company, 1985), pp. 42, 44, 56; and the International Institute for Strategic Studies (IISS), *The Military Balance 1986–1987* (London: IISS, 1986), pp. 57, 64, 142–43.

8. See Sutter, p. 173; Arkin, pp. 38–39, 44; and testimony of Rear Admiral Robert Schmitt, deputy director of the DIA in hearings before the Subcommittee on Economic Resources, Competitiveness and Security Economics of the Joint Economic Committee, U.S. Congress, *Allocation of Resources in the Soviet Union and China—1985*, March 19, 1986, p. 123. Bradley Hahn's higher projections are found in his "Beijing's Growing Global Missile Reach," *Pacific Defense Reporter*, vol. 13, no. 8 (February 1987), pp. 12–13.

9. Arkin, p. 39.

10. For background on the 1982 military exercise simulating tactical nuclear battlefield conditions for Ningxia Province, see Paul H. B. Godwin, "People's War Revised: Military Doctrine, Strategy and Operations," in Charles D. Lovejoy, Jr., and Bruce W. Watson, eds., *China's Military Reforms* (Boulder, Colo.: Westview Press, 1986), p. 7. Also see Sutter, p. 177; and Lawrence Freedman, "The Role of Third Country Nuclear Forces," in Jeffrey D. Boutwell, Paul Doty, and Gregory F. Treverton, *The Nuclear Confrontation in Europe* (London: Croom Helm, 1985), pp. 134–38, for additional comments on Chinese ADMs.

11. Arkin, p. 51.

12. Sutter, p. 177; and Frank Jiardano, "The Chinese Navy," *Naval Forces*, vol. 8, no. 2 (1987), p. 194. Jiardano is an analyst with the U.S. Defense Intelligence Agency.

13. Ibid.

14. Johnston, p. 18; and A. W. Grazebrook, "China's Type 'Xia' SSBN Now Operational," *Pacific Defense Reporter*, vol. 13, no. 9 (March 1987), p. 18.

15. Ibid. and Sutter, p. 177.

16. Jiardano, "Chinese Navy."

17. For the British view, see Freedman, pp. 115–18. For the Chinese thinking, see Gerald Segal, "Nuclear Forces," in Segal and William T. Tow, eds., *Chinese Defense Policy* (Chicago: University of Illinois Press, 1984), pp. 101–102.

18. See Banning N. Garrett and Bonnie S. Glaser, "From Nixon to Reagan: China's Changing Role in American Strategy," in Kenneth A. Oye, Robert J. Lieber, and Donald Rothchild, eds., *Eagle Resurgent? The Reagan Era in American Foreign Policy* (Boston: Little, Brown and Company, 1987), p. 270.

19. On the senior PLA officers' removal, see *Liberation Army Daily* and *Xinhua* reports on December 28, 1984, and reprinted as "Yu Qiuli Comments," *FBIS, China: Daily Report,* December 31, 1984, p. K2. For recent commentary on the merging of civilian and defense industries in China, refer to Tai Ming Cheung, "China's Big Switch," *Pacific Defense Reporter,* vol. 13, no. 5 (November 1986), pp. 27–28.

20. John Frankenstein, "Chinese Weapons Development: Process, Progress, Program?" in Lovejoy and Watson, p. 71. Also see *Xinhua,* July 30, 1984; in *FBIS,* "PLA Organization, Training Entering New Stages," *China: Daily Report,* August 1, 1984, p. K7, where "the artillery" is explicitly differentiated from the "strategic missile forces."

21. Research Institute for Peace and Security, *Asian Security 1985* (Tokyo: RIPS, 1985), pp. 81–82.

22. See Mathew J. Mathews, "Nuclear Power Shapes Up," *China Business Review,* vol. 12, no. 4 (July/August 1985), pp. 23–25; and Hahn, "China's Nuclear History," p. 28.

23. In his speech before the Thirty-Ninth Session of the United Nations General Assembly on September 26, 1984, Chinese Foreign Minister Wu Xueqian declared that China "hopes to see the two superpowers . . . end their nuclear arms race and global rivalry and improve their bilateral relations in the interest of world peace and international security." See "China's Stand on World Situation Outlined," *Beijing Review,* vol. 27, no. 41 (October 8, 1984), p. 25.

24. Zhang Chunting, "Important Reform of the Structure of China's Defense Industry," *Liaowang* (Overseas Edition), no. 17 (November 24, 1986), pp. 3–4; in Joint Publications Research Service (JPRS), *China Report (Political, Sociological and Military Affairs),* No. 87-001, January 13, 1987, pp. 92–93.

25. Lucian Pye, "On Chinese Pragmatism in the 1980s," *The China Quarterly,* vol. 106 (June 1986), especially pp. 221–24.

26. Zhang Jingyi, "Korea to Kampuchea: The Changing Nature of Warfare in East Asia 1950–1986: part II," in IISS, *East Asia, the West and International Security: Prospects for Peace Part I,* Adelphi Papers 216 (London: IISS, 1987), p. 82.

27. Li Baoheng, "A Shortcut to Accelerating Our Technical Progress," *Zhongguo Keji Luntan (Forum of Science and Technology in China),* no. 1 (September 1985), pp. 42–44; JPRS, *China Report (Science and Technology),* 86–008, March 1, 1986, p. 14.

28. H. R. Haldeman, President Nixon's chief adviser, relates that in De-

cember 1969, U.S. intelligence reports were indicating that the Soviets were seriously contemplating a "surgical strike" against Chinese nuclear installations. H. R. Haldeman, *The Ends of Power* (New York: New York Times Book Company Inc., 1978), pp. 88–94. Thomas W. Wolfe has further noted that Romanians blocked a Soviet move to require that each Warsaw Pact member send "symbolic military detachments" to the Sino-Soviet border following the pact's March 1969 conference at Budapest. See Thomas W. Wolfe, *Soviet Power and Europe, 1945–1970* (Baltimore: Johns Hopkins University Press, 1970), pp. 496–97.

29. For an in-depth study of this scenario, consult William C. Green and David S. Yost, "Soviet Military Options Regarding China," in Douglas T. Stuart and William T. Tow, eds., *China, the Soviet Union, and the West* (Boulder, Colo.: Westview Press, 1982), pp. 135–44.

30. Lowell Dittmer, "The Strategic Triangle: An Elementary Game-Theoretical Analysis," *World Politics*, vol. 33, no. 4 (July 1981), pp. 485–515. Also see Gerald Segal, "China and the Great Power Triangle," *China Quarterly*, no. 83 (September 1980), pp. 490–509.

31. See, for example, the remarks of Chinese Vice Foreign Minister Qian Qichen in *Xinhua*, January 3, 1986; in *FBIS, China: Daily Report*, January 3, 1986, p. C1: "China is rock-firm on its independent foreign policy of peace and no big power should expect China to change its course."

32. Figures excerpted from the *Los Angeles Times*, May 5, 1987.

33. For background, consult *Xinhua*, March 18, 1986; in *FBIS, China: Daily Report*, March 19, 1986, p. C1; and *Xinhua*, October 28, 1986; in *FBIS*, October 30, 1986.

34. V. Vasiliyev, "Peking Schemes," *New Times*, no. 23 (1980), pp 22–23, as cited in Dan L. Strode, "Arms Control and Sino-Soviet Relations," *Orbis*, vol. 28, no. 1 (Spring 1984), p. 164.

35. "Chinese Delegation's Working Paper on Disarmament," *Beijing Review*, vol. 21, no. 24 (June 16, 1978), pp. 22–24; and "Who Should Disarm First?" ibid., pp. 25–26. Also see Samuel S. Kim, "Chinese World Policy in Transition," *World Policy Journal*, vol. 1, no. 3 (Spring 1984), pp. 611–12.

36. Fan Min, "Let Us See If the Deadlock Can Be Broken—The Situation Facing the Seventh Round of U.S.-Soviet Arms Control Talks," *Renmin Ribao* (People's Daily), January 17, 1987, p. 6; in *FBIS, China: Daily Report*, January 22, 1987, p. A4.

37. See John Garver, "China's Response to the Strategic Defense Initiative," *Asian Survey*, vol. 26, no. 11 (November 1986), especially pp. 1231–34.

38. Stockholm International Peace Research Institute, *SIPRI Yearbook 1986* (New York: Oxford University Press, 1986), p. 464, describes the Chinese initiative for banning weapons in outer space in some detail.

39. "China Signs South Pacific Nuclear Protocols," *China Daily*, February 11, 1987, p. 1; and "China Backs the 'South Pacific Nuclear Free Zone Treaty'" *Zhongguo Xinwen She*, October 16, 1985; in *FBIS, China: Daily Report*, October 17, 1985, p. E1.

40. See Research Institute for Peace and Security (RIPS), *Asian Security 1986*, p. 166; RIPS, *Asian Security 1985* (Tokyo, 1986), p. 71: and *Xinhua* report

reprinted as "Spokesman Notes 'Concern' For Japan Defense Budget," in *FBIS, China: Daily Report,* January 2, 1987, p. D1.

41. "Spokesman Notes 'Concern'. . . ."

42. Vice Foreign Minister Qi Huaiyan in a briefing to the foreign press on April 3, 1987, noted in response to a question posed by the China Special Dispatch Agency that various NPC deputies criticized the Chinese government for not taking a stronger stand on the Nakasone visit to the Yasukuni Shrine with the implied connotations such a visit would have on China's image of Japanese "militarism." See Beijing Television Service transcript translated and reprinted as "Vice Ministers Discuss Foreign Policy Issues," in *FBIS, China: Daily Report,* April 6, 1987, p. K6.

43. Data from *Ta Kung Pao* as reprinted in "China Economic Statistics," *China Trade Report,* vol. 24, no. 3 (March 1986), p. 15. The 1986 figure is from the PRC's Ministry of Foreign Trade and Economic Relations as cited in Louise de Rosario, "Slashing the Deficit," *China Trade Report,* vol. 25, no. 2 (February 1987), p. 1.

44. James T. H. Tsao, *China's Development Strategies and Foreign Trade* (Lexington, Mass.: D.C. Heath and Company, 1987), pp. 100–101.

Commentary

Mohammed Ayoob

I think we are overemphasizing China as an independent variable. We always get into this frame of mind when we attend a conference focused around one country. When we talk about China's modernizations and their strategic and economic impacts, for example, we see that country as a sort of centerpiece, with all issues revolving around it. In these discussions, therefore, China appears to be the independent variable, which may or may not be the case. In a discussion of the global and regional strategic situation, however, it appears that China is not an independent variable. In fact, it is primarily reactive in its strategic postures and policies, and I make that assumption primarily by looking at the characteristics of the Chinese economy and polity.

This idea came out quite clearly in earlier discussions, which addressed the various economic and political contradictions within China, above all the fact that China is basically a third world country economically and technologically, with all the features that go with being a third world country. The translation of its potential into actual power, as far as China is concerned, is as difficult as in the case of any large third world country. In China, these problems are further compounded by a relatively regimented command economy, which makes for inflexibility rather than innovation, despite all the discussions about how China is moving toward adopting greater innovative techniques in economic and other types of management. Moreover, political uncertainties remain, related largely to the way the system has developed over the past forty years and to the apparent immortality of the Chinese leadership. So, given these limitations on Chinese economic, technological, and, therefore, military capabilities, China's strategic posture through the century, and probably beyond, is likely to be reactive. That is, it will be reactive to the policy and postures of more powerful players that affect and, in fact, determine China's strategic environment.

Therefore, to keep the discussion from becoming an exclusive

China-centric exercise, I would like to look at the regional and global strategic environments in which China has to operate. It is now a common assumption among students of international relations that as long as China continues to view the Soviet Union as its foremost adversary, it will need American support to neutralize Soviet strategic superiority.

Not enough emphasis is laid on the clause "as long as China continues to view the Soviet Union as its foremost adversary." Given the nature of great power behavior and the assumptions that underlie great power behavior, it would be facile to assume that the Chinese would continue to work on that assumption indefinitely. Many other variables will actually affect and, in fact, determine where China goes toward the end of the century and even beyond. Of course, one of the variables that will affect Chinese behavior is the quality of Soviet-American relations.

I argue that those relations will be, by and large, stable, given both the history of Soviet-American relations since the Second World War and, more important, the systemic determinance of superpower behavior. If a country is at the apex of the international pecking order, then obviously the principle of balance of power determines a large part of its behavior. The Soviet Union and the United States, despite the fact that they may occasionally exhibit some cooperative behavior on certain issues, will, for the most part, continue to remain in an adversarial relationship.

Even as we take the Soviet-American relationship, therefore, as a constant influence on Chinese behavior, we must also look at a combination of two other variables, namely, American-Japanese and Sino-Japanese relations. Washington would obviously prefer China to be aligned with Washington than with Moscow. For a number of reasons, however, if we look at the configuration of power in the Asia-Pacific region, Japan is bound to rank much higher in American strategic calculations than China through the rest of this century and probably well into the next.

American reasons for according Japan strategic priority over China are not very difficult to decipher and are primarily related to the essentially third world character of the Chinese polity and economy. Japan's status as an economic and acknowledged superpower is an important consideration in this regard. The greater predictability of Japanese policies—domestic and foreign, economic and political— also has a major influence on American perceptions.

Above all, Japan's impressive technological achievements, which with political will can be quickly and efficiently translated into equally impressive power projection capabilities, constitute the most important factor likely to determine American policy if Washington is ever forced to choose between Beijing and Tokyo. This, in short, is the trump card that Japan holds in its relationship with the United States. As Prime Minister Nakasone put it, Japan is not merely the unsinkable U.S. aircraft carrier in the Pacific: it is, in current American strategic perceptions, the *indispensable* and *irreplaceable* aircraft carrier in the Pacific strategic theater.

In the context of these strategic realities, therefore, the dilemma for Beijing is reconciling what China, in the light of past experiences, would consider to be the optimum level of Japanese power, with the tremendous potential that Japan's technological and economic bases provide Tokyo to mobilize power for its own ends. Despite the public pronouncements that leaders of various countries indulge in, power has its own logic, which usually supersedes all other logic in the behavior of states.

China would like to see just enough Japanese power mobilized to supplement American power in the Pacific, giving China that amount of security from a presumed Soviet threat. At the same time, however, the Chinese leadership must surely be aware that it has little control over the buildup of Japanese military capabilities. Beijing's apprehensions presumably derive from the fact that if this process accelerates, it might become irreversible. The American predilection for burden sharing at a time when American budget deficits and Japanese trade surpluses continue to mount simultaneously might have an impact on long-term American policy toward the region, which the Chinese might interpret as deleterious to their own long-term interests.

Of course, any attempt to make such projections about the strategic scene in the Asia-Pacific region and the likely effects of that scene on Chinese policies must take Japan to be the centerpiece of such an analysis. Japan must be considered because, while Soviet-American relations in the Pacific and around the globe can be expected to be relatively stable—and, therefore, their impact on Chinese policies can be relatively easily defined and measured—the impact of Japan on the strategic scene in the Pacific, and therefore on China's policies, is likely to be volatile.

To conclude, Japan's foreign policy and strategic posture particularly in the next twenty years will have a major impact on Chinese policies. Therefore, Japanese policies will have a dual effect, influencing in a major way, if not determining, both Sino-American as well as Sino-Soviet relations.

John Fuh-sheng Hsieh

I have a few comments on Dr. Tow's paper. The first one is about model specification, that is, how to relate different variables. As I read the paper, I find that the relationships among some variables are not very clear.

If I may be permitted to respecify his model, I think he is probably trying to say that internal politics in the PRC affects, on the one hand, the strategic thinking of its leadership, and on the other, the modernization program. These, in turn, affect its relationship with the two superpowers.

After specifying the model, we have to be more careful about the logic of the relationships. For instance, Dr. Tow suggests that PRC leaders "seem too enmeshed in their own internal power struggles to project their foreign policy interests more cohesively and convincingly." This refers to the relationship between the two variables, internal politics as well as the strategic thinking of the PRC leadership, and the logic of the relationship is unclear in this statement. It is possible that the PRC elites have been so preoccupied with the internal power struggle that they just do not have time to think about the strategic matters or that the various power contenders in the power struggle may have different ideas on how to devise a cohesive strategy. Which one is more likely should be stated unequivocally.

Another comment is on Dr. Tow's claim that China will play by Western rules governing arms transactions and broader geopolitics only until such time as its economy is strong enough for it to revert to a more self-reliant posture. I think that this is actually true; that is, only when China is weak will it play by Western rules.

Roger W. Sullivan

I do not see the PRC's efforts to modernize itself industrially, scientifically, and militarily as aimed at closing the strategic gap between itself and the two superpowers. That is a fundamental difference I have with Mr. Tow right at the start. Nor do I think the Chinese believe any more that they can isolate themselves or insulate themselves from the fallout of superpower competition by emphasizing U.S. strategic preoccupation with Europe. The Chinese are very conscious of the Soviet threat in Asia, and the United States is becoming increasingly concerned about the Soviet threat in Asia.

Dr. Lampton asked me about the PRC's efforts to improve relations with the Soviets and U.S. efforts to improve its relations with the Soviets and wondered if all these considerations were not irrelevant: is this not a late 1970s phenomenon? Quite the contrary. The U.S.-Soviet relationship is not stable in Asia, although it may be stable elsewhere. The Soviet Union is moving very aggressively to expand its forces in Asia, and the process of what the Chinese call isolating and surrounding China has moved very fast.

It is interesting that when Gorbachev made his statement in July 1986 in Vladivostok, the only thing the press picked up was that Deng Xiaoping said he would be willing to meet Gorbachev any time, anywhere. What Deng Xiaoping really said was that Gorbachev made no reference to the Soviet Union's getting out of Vietnam or getting the Vietnamese out of Cambodia and that those things are important to the Chinese. Deng went on to say that if the Soviets were prepared to do those things, he would be prepared to meet Gorbachev any time, anywhere. Now, he's just sticking his finger right in Gorbachev's eye.

The Chinese are calling the Soviet bluff, in effect, getting what reduction in tension they can. If they think they can force the Soviet Union to reduce forces in Afghanistan, so much the better, but they do not really expect to get very far with this, except to hold the Soviets off while they build up their strength. It's no coincidence that in the past several years the U.S.-Chinese security and defense relationship has accelerated very rapidly. In the past few years we have trained Chinese forces in the United States, negotiated joint ventures on weapons production, and cooperated on Afghanistan and Vietnam. One evidence of U.S.-Chinese ties that got very little notice in the press was the visit of a Seventh Fleet ship to China. A Seventh Fleet ship can visit China on terms we could not get the New Zealanders to agree to. That is really dramatic evidence of Chinese interest in continuing this relationship.

As for Mr. Tow's remarks on the reform of the People's Liberation Army (PLA), this reform does not bear so much on the strategic dimension of China's defense. In other words, people's war and nuclear weaponry exist side by side but compartmentalized in China. People's war under modern conditions is part of trying to develop a whole new doctrine for working with a smaller, modern force made up of younger people.

I was going to pick up that *nianqinghua* (youthization) idea too because when we talked to the Chinese about weapons sales, they said that of first importance is to reduce the size of the PLA, significantly, and have generational change. Both those steps are well under way. In fact, the average age of division commanders in China now is thirty-eight, an amazing change in the past few years.

On the issue of doctrine, the U.S. government has said that its policy in this area is to make China more secure against the Soviet threat by giving it some capability to deter the Soviet Union against a preemptive strike against China. This policy will not put China on a coequal basis with the superpowers at all. In fact, the objective, which the Chinese recognize, is to slow the decline in Chinese military capability and conventional military capability vis-à-vis the Soviet Union.

Dr. Tow referred to giving the military factories civilian functions. From a number of visits to military factories in November 1986, I have concluded that the Chinese plan to treat military industrial enterprises the same way they treat civilian industrial enterprises. In other words, they are simply applying the individual responsibility system to the military factories. I did hear some complaints from factory managers that when they used to get orders from the PLA, it did not matter whether the army wanted one hundred tanks or five tanks; it paid all the bills. Now the PLA may order only twenty tanks from the factory; the army will sign a contract, but there may not be enough money there to cover utilities or wages. So some of the managers do not like the change, although some of them like it very much.

I went to an aircraft factory, for example, where the manager was enthusiastic because he gets a lot of scrap aluminum, which he can sell to the hotels for storm windows and doors.

I think Dr. Tow was overgeneralizing to say that there was bureaucratic resistance across the board. The payoff for the military was that unlike any other enterprise in China, the factories with joint military-civilian products are allowed to keep all the foreign exchange and they can use that foreign exchange to import weaponry and technology. Even as early as November of 1986, NORINCO, which is the sales arm of the Ministry of Ordnance, was already selling more than 50 percent civilian products. They were in the export business in a big way.

Thus the Chinese have followed a very interesting two-tiered approach: buying a lot of pre-1975 technology from the United States, using it to upgrade their military products, which they are exporting, and also using that technology to make civilian products. Then they take the foreign exchange generated from that activity and use it to buy artillery from the United States, to upgrade their aircraft, and eventually to purchase anti-aircraft missiles and the like. They have a very clear approach to orchestrating military modernization and the stages they will go through to achieve it—and how they will get the money with the kind of budget constraints under which they operate.

The statement that China's national security interest seems to be self-contained and beyond the reach of any would-be superpower attempt to mesh such interest with its own was demonstrably untrue from 1978 to today, where we have meshed rather well. I disagree with Dr. Tow's comment that providing advanced technology to foreign countries is equivalent to digging one's own grave and that the United States and other foreigners will strive to stay ten years ahead of the Chinese technologically. Of course, more advanced countries will try to stay ten years ahead of the Chinese technologically. The Chinese know that—the military technology we are selling them is actually twelve years old.

In conclusion, the Chinese realize that it would be foolish to try to return to a policy of isolation and the out-dated view that the U.S.-Soviet strategic rivalry is purely a European phenomenon. They know very well that it is now principally an Asian phenomenon.

Discussion

ROBERT G. SUTTER: I do not perceive Japan as a disturbance to the Asian order, at least in a military sense over the next fifteen years, because the forces inside Japan will limit the scope of Japanese defense buildup.

It is true that some Americans, particularly representatives in Congress, will pressure the Japanese to share more of the burden of defense, but the Japanese have proven to be very adroit at limiting that pressure. I don't see any reason for that to change in the near term.

DAVID M. LAMPTON: First, the discussion of China's nuclear forces leads me to question whether China's nuclear strategy hasn't really been one of minimal deterrence. In other words, isn't the purpose of nuclear forces just to prevent nuclear attack against China? And why would China change that? I see no reason or logic why China would want to enter the nuclear competition beyond limited deterrence objectives.

Second, Dr. Tow mentioned that China did not have a clear foreign policy strategy. What strikes me about China's external behavior, however, is the very clear strategy that it, indeed, does have. That strategy does two things: it maximizes China's ability to derive resources from the external environment, whether it is technology, or capital, or sending students abroad and the like, and it reduces regional threat. China's external strategy seems to be quite precise and well executed.

Third, I agree with Professor Ayoob that Chinese foreign policy is primarily reactive and not initiatory.

Fourth, we do know that the United States is developing a security relationship with the People's Liberation Army. Certainly part of that is attributable to the strategic problem we face with the Soviet Union. But another consideration is the need of the government to bring the PLA into a coalition supportive of the open policy. In other words, there has to be something in this relationship for the military so that it does not play a disruptive role in the overall program.

Some of the rationale for involving the military in this relationship has to do not so much with the strategic equation as with the political necessity of maintaining the coalition to support the open policy.

ROGER W. SULLIVAN: I think that is a fringe benefit. It is also a way that the U.S. Defense Department sells it to the U.S. State Department, but it is not the kind of thing that will motivate the Joint Chiefs of Staff. The Joint Chiefs do not operate merely to educate people. They have a very definite view of how improving relations with China affects the support structure and very definite ideas about what kind of cooperation we can engage in and what the payoff will be.

COMMENT: The conventional wisdom about the reformers and the military is that they do not have a very good relationship and that Hu Yaobang's weakness was that he could not get the support. As for Mr. Sullivan's comment that the divisional commanders are now relatively young because of this rejuvenation exercise, my understanding also is that there should be much more empathy between the young military officers and the reformers because of their youth. Therefore, the proper way to look at this situation is that Hu Yaobang's weakness vis-à-vis the military is really with the top brass, that is, the two Yangs, Yang Shangkun and Yang Dezhi in the Central Military Affairs Commission (MAC), because they are older. The difficulty is that they consider themselves more senior than Hu Yaobang, and the fact that he had been appointed to general secretary did not change matters for them. It would have been quite unacceptable for him to become chairman of the MAC.

Mr. Sullivan, will you comment on the Russian presence in Asia? This is something very topical and very controversial in ASEAN countries. In ASEAN we have a problem deciding whether Russia or China, particularly since we are examining the impact of China's modernization on the security in this area, poses the bigger threat to ASEAN countries. Please separate the short-term threat from the long-term threat.

MR. SULLIVAN: Clearly in the short term, maybe medium term, there is no question but that it is the Soviet Union. I know the ASEAN countries have been concerned for some time about Vietnam, for example, and if we judge by what the Soviets are doing in Vietnam, it certainly does not seem to suggest that they plan to get out any time in the near term or, indeed, ever. They are investing a great deal of money in the Cam Ranh Bay facility, which is now a major naval base, much larger than anything the United States ever had in Vietnam. It is a major projection base for air power; moreover, according to an article I saw recently, it is a purely Soviet base to which Vietnamese are not even allowed admittance.

The Soviet Union has the power now to project both air and sea power throughout the Southeast Asian area and into the Indian Ocean from that base. It will continue to remain there and to balance its position with Vietnam, to support Vietnam in almost any way that Vietnam asks, because relinquishing that base would carry a huge global strategic cost for the Soviet Union. The idea in China, or even in ASEAN, that somehow the Soviet Union could be persuaded to lessen tension in the area by moderating Vietnamese behavior is visionary. Clearly, the Soviet Union is the major threat.

It is more difficult to assess China; it is obviously a major weight in the area. We have to make many assumptions about what will happen to Chinese economic development and what will happen in the Soviet Union over the long term. If China became a major power, however, given its size, it would be a major force to contend with. That possibility is so far in the future that I cannot quite come to grips with it. At what point could China compete as a superpower? Certainly not by the year 2000, which is what we are talking about here. By the year 2050? I don't know.

DENIS FRED SIMON: What seems to stand out in Dr. Tow's paper and Mr. Sullivan's comments is a totally different interpretation of the Chinese willingness to cooperate and whether Chinese military modernization is innocuous.

What Dr. Tow seems to suggest is that the Chinese really do not trust the United States. They may trust us more than the Soviets, but they are not willing to get too close.

It seems Mr. Sullivan is suggesting a much closer relationship there, a better meshing on some security interests, and, indeed, the possibility that the relationship could proceed farther.

QUESTION: As for the nuclear strategy of China, the basic strategy seems to be deterrence, minimal deterrence against the Soviet Union—a "counter-value option," that is, targeting cities. With a counter-value type of nuclear strategy, given China's resources, it is extremely unlikely for it to move into the upper end of the technology spectrum to the "counter-force strategy," that is, attacking military targets.

The number of warheads Dr. Tow cited, over a thousand, is a very uneven triad. Therefore, since the majority of the warheads are on more vulnerable land-based missiles and manned-bombers, they could be neutralized by a very advanced nation like the Soviet Union. I see no reason, then, for China to change its strategy by modernizing its nuclear force in qualitative terms, or even in quantitative terms.

MOHAMMED AYOOB: I agree that at the moment Japanese domestic compulsions will provide important brakes on any aspirations to move Japan toward acquiring more power. But are these compulsions immutable? If the strategic situation changes and if Japanese domestic public opinion, with rising Japanese power, undergoes change, wouldn't those compulsions be transformed into different ones?

After all, in 1932 not many people would have predicted that a decade later the United States would have been involved in a major European military adventure. Now that the 1 percent defense budget barrier has been scaled, the other psychological barriers in Japan might not be especially difficult to scale either, particularly in the context of American pressure on Japan to build up its military capabilities. This pressure seems to extend from an American concern that Japanese power will not act merely as a supplement to American power, but within the burden-sharing context, will come to substitute for certain types of American power in the Pacific. If that happens to be the case, that will have a major influence on Chinese perceptions, both of Japanese capabilities and of Japanese intentions, because quite often capabilities determine intentions rather than vice versa.

Chinese perceptions of Japanese intentions and capabilities, particularly compared with the capabilities and intentions of the Soviet Union, will be determined by two major factors: one is the greater economic and technological dynamism shown by Japan vis-à-vis the Soviet Union, and the other is Japan's potential as a revisionist power. Despite all the Chinese rhetoric against the Soviet Union and all the verbal tirade about the unequal treaties China was forced into signing by the tsars, the Chinese leadership recognizes that the capabilities of the Soviet Union are quite extended and that the Soviet Union is basically a status quo power. Japan, however, given its historical experiences with China and its defeat in the Second World War, can be classified as potentially revisionist.

WILLIAM T. TOW: The question is whether China isn't really a counter-value or city-busting nation as opposed to a war-fighting nation. First, any country that's moving towards MIRV development raises questions.

Second, the latest documents coming out of the new National Defense University (NDU) in Beijing also raise questions about that assumption.

Regarding Dr. Lampton's question about why China would want to change its strategy of minimal deterrence, the answer is essentially that deterrence changes over time. Its purpose is to increase costs and

201

risks to geopolitical opponents. And if there is an exponential increase in the capabilities of one's opponent, then one has to think about one's own force structure and simply buy greater influence in the most cost-effective way. Nuclear weapons are the most cost-effective way, which is related to Mr. Sullivan's point about the military's desire to move ahead with conventional modernization.

The Chinese are intelligent enough to realize that precision guided munitions and other "smart" weaponry are much more expensive in the long run than moving toward a nuclear option. And again, the NDU documents indicate that we have to think seriously about tactical nuclear weapons as perhaps the most cost-effective way to plan for future battlefield situations.

In his second question, Dr. Lampton indicated a clear twofold strategy: maximize technological acquisition and reduce regional threat. These are means, not ends. These are increments, not broad strategy. That is to say, strategy has to do with a broad view of national purpose and a sense of national identity within that purpose. In that sense, frankly, the traditional, historical military writings of Sun Tzu come about as close to any strategy the Chinese have concocted over the past few milleniums by way of national identity and strategy. That, by the way, was a point reiterated with a delegation that came through the University of Southern California two weeks ago. They wanted to talk about Sun Tzu as a strategist.

In answer to Mr. Simon's question about the divergence of Mr. Sullivan's and my interpretations, I will address very quickly some of Mr. Sullivan's comments. The PLA is not just in the civilian marketplace. It is well to remember that the PLA, or the Chinese military, is now the fifth largest arms salesman in the world. All one has to do is take a look at this morning's *Straits Times* to talk about the Silkworm antiship missile, which Caspar Weinberger has threatened to destroy in the Persian Gulf.

Mr. Sullivan doesn't see PRC modernization as a means to close a strategic gap with the superpowers. Chinese ideology, I believe, inherently holds that there has to be a closing of the gap with the superpowers over time, if one believes in correlation of forces, the Marxist dialectic, and the like.

8

Implications of China's Modernization for East and Southeast Asian Security: The Year 2000

Robert G. Sutter

The Dilemma for East Asia

The lessons of geography and history show that China's modernization is likely to have stronger implications for the region of East Asia, including Southeast Asia, than for any other region of the world. Past strong Chinese governments have used China's geographic proximity to great advantage in exerting influence in this region. At times they have employed peaceful diplomatic, economic, and cultural exchange; at other times they have used force and intimidation to pursue their interests in the area.

Thus, the government and peoples of East Asia face a dilemma posed by China's recent drive toward economic development and modernization. On one hand, the recent Chinese preoccupation with conventional nation building has been widely seen as reinforcing Chinese policies of accommodation with most of their Asian neighbors. (A notable exception has been Soviet-backed Vietnam.) China's need for a "peaceful environment" in which to pursue economic modernization and accompanying political reform seems to mandate a more cooperative policy toward its non-Communist neighbors, some of whom represent important sources of economic assistance and trade.

On the other hand, as the Chinese modernization effort continues to advance, so does the national power of the People's Republic of China (PRC). Some observers in the region worry that Chinese development may reach a point over the next fifteen years at which China will use this enhanced national power more forcefully to assert its influence in East Asia. Such action could seriously disrupt the security and development of smaller Asian states. A more assertive Chinese policy could involve instruments of power used by Chinese governments in the past, including direct intervention by ground forces, support for pro-Chinese Communist insurgencies, and support for Overseas Chinese minorities, in countries of Southeast Asia in particular. In addition, successful Chinese economic development and related military modernization could strengthen other levers of influence including trade restrictions against certain countries and increased air and naval capability.[1]

In short, the key task for this paper is to assess whether China's recent generally moderate and cooperative policy toward the governments of East Asia is likely to continue into the twenty-first century or whether China will be more inclined to use its increased national power in ways that would disrupt the security of the region.

To offer a balanced assessment of this question, the paper first examines the main determinants of recent Chinese foreign policy toward East Asia and then reviews prospects for change in the policy coming from developments inside China and from events elsewhere in the region. It concludes that forces favoring continuity in recent Chinese policy appear stronger than forces favoring substantial change. It notes, however, that because a large number of variables determine Chinese foreign policy, it remains a distinct possibility that significant changes in one or more of these variables could prompt unanticipated adjustments in Chinese foreign and security policy in East Asia.

Determinants of Recent Chinese Policy in East Asia

The objectives of Chinese foreign policy in East Asia, and of Chinese foreign policy generally, are determined by a small group of top-level leaders who reflect the broad interests of the Chinese state as well as their own parochial concerns.[2] In the past, Mao Zedong, Zhou Enlai, and other senior leaders exerted overriding control over foreign policy. In recent years, the number of officials involved in advising on Chinese foreign policy has increased, but key decisions remain the preserve of a small group of leaders, especially Deng Xiaoping.

The primary concerns of these leaders have been to guarantee Chinese national security, maintain internal order, and pursue economic development. Especially since the death of Mao in 1976, the top priority has been to promote successful economic modernization. Because this development represents the linchpin determining their success or failure, officials have geared China's foreign policy to help the modernization effort.

To accomplish economic modernization, however, as well as to maintain national security and internal order, Chinese leaders recognize the fundamental prerequisite of establishing a relatively stable strategic environment, especially around the nation's periphery in Asia. The alternative would be a highly disruptive situation requiring much greater Chinese expenditures on national defense and posing greater danger to domestic order and tranquility. China does not control this environment. It has influenced it, but the environment remains controlled more by others, especially the superpowers and their allies and associates. As a result, China's leaders have been repeatedly required to assess their surroundings for changes that could affect Chinese security and development, and they have been repeatedly compelled to adjust foreign policy to take account of such changes.

At the same time, Chinese leaders have nationalistic and ideological objectives regarding irredentist claims (such as Hong Kong, Taiwan, offshore oil rights, and the like) and a desire to stand independently in foreign affairs as a leading force among "progressive" nations of the third world. These goals have struck a responsive political chord inside China. Occasional leadership discussion and debate over these and other questions regarding foreign affairs have sometimes affected the course of Chinese foreign policy. In the Maoist period, for example, leaders sometimes allowed these nationalistic and ideological objectives, and other questions of political debate, to jeopardize seriously the basic security and development interests of the nation. A notable example was the negative effect the highly nationalistic and ideological "Red Guard diplomacy" of the late 1960s had on Chinese relations with key Communist and non-Communist governments in East and Southeast Asia. The disruptive activities of Chinese diplomats, Red Guards, and others at this time led to crises in PRC relations with North Vietnam, North Korea, Burma, Cambodia, and Indonesia.

China's move toward greater pragmatism in foreign and domestic policy since the late 1960s did not develop smoothly; it was often accompanied by very serious leadership debates over which foreign policy goals should receive priority. Since the early 1970s, however, the debates have become progressively less serious, and the foreign policy differences raised in them have become more moderate and less challenging to the recent dominant objectives of national development and security. In this context, nationalistic and ideological objectives have generally been given secondary priority when they conflict with the recent dominant objectives of national development and security.[3]

China's top foreign policy priority has thus remained the pragmatic quest for a stable environment needed for effective modernization and development. Chinese leaders since 1969 have seen the main danger of negative change in the surrounding environment posed by the Soviet Union. At first, China perceived Soviet power as an immediate threat to its national security. Over time, it has come to see the Soviet Union as less an immediate threat, although it remains a long-term threat, determined to use its growing military power and other sources of influence to encircle and pressure China into accepting a balance of influence in an Asia dominated by the Soviet Union and contrary to PRC interests.

China's strategy against the Soviet threat has been both bilateral and global. Bilaterally, China has used a combination of military preparations, political discussions, economic and cultural exchanges, and other interaction to minimize Soviet pressure while China gains whatever material or technological advantage it can from its neighbor to the north. China also uses such interchange to encourage the Soviets to moderate their military-backed expansion around China's periphery in Asia. Globally, China's strategy has focused on developing, either implicitly or explicitly, an international united front designed to halt Soviet expansion and prevent the consolidation of Soviet dominance abroad. During the 1970s, China focused explicitly on developing such a front. In recent years, the perceived immediate threat from the Soviet Union has lessened, and Chinese leaders are satisfied with an implicit anti-Soviet arrangement focused on areas of Asia of greatest concern to China.

As the most important international counterweight to Soviet power, the United States has loomed large in Chinese calculations. Under terms of the Nixon Doctrine announced in 1969, the United States seemed determined to withdraw from its past policy of containing China in Asia and thereby ended a perceived U.S. threat to China's national security. In response, the PRC was prepared to start the process of Sino-American normalization. The process has been complemented in recent years by China's enhanced interest in pragmatic economic modernization, which has emphasized the importance of technical and financial help from abroad and access to foreign markets.

Thus China views the United States as economically important, not only for its own sake, but also as an influence on Japan, Western Europe, non-Communist countries in East Asia, and international financial institutions providing the economic aid, markets, and technical assistance needed to promote Chinese economic modernization. In recent years, China has also broadened its economic interchange with the Soviet bloc, and Sino-Soviet trade has grown more rapidly (from a much lower base) than Sino-U.S. trade. No leader in China has suggested, however, that contacts with the Soviet bloc could rival the importance of economic interchange with the non-Communist nations led by the United States.

Closer Chinese ties with the United States have continued to be complicated by Chinese nationalistic and ideological concerns over Taiwan and third world questions, as well as by fundamental differences between the social-political and economic systems of the United States and the PRC. Most notably, U.S. support for Taiwan is seen as a continued affront to China's national sovereignty. Chinese leaders, though, have differentiated between substantive threats to their security, posed by continued enhancement of Soviet military power and military-backed influence around China's periphery in Asia, and threats to their sense of national sovereignty, posed by U.S. support for Taiwan.

In short, China has worked hard, and continues to work hard, to ensure that its strategic environment, threatened mainly by Soviet expansion, remains stable, so that it can focus on economic modernization. The Soviet Union is perceived to have an expansionist strategy that uses military power relentlessly but cautiously to achieve political influence and dominance throughout its periphery. China has long held that the focus of Soviet attention is in Europe but that NATO's strength requires Moscow to work in other areas, notably the Middle East, southwest Asia, Africa, and East Asia, in order to outflank the Western defenses. China is believed to be relatively low on Moscow's list of military priorities, although Chinese leaders clearly appreciate the dire consequences for the PRC should the Soviet Union be able to consolidate its position elsewhere and then focus its strength to intimidate China.

The ascendancy of the new Gorbachev leadership in the Soviet Union has prompted some Chinese commentators to note the possibility of a major change in Soviet policy in Asia. Of course, a substantial shift in the Soviet pressure on China would have a corresponding impact on calculations that have governed Chinese policy in Asia since the late 1960s. Thus far, however, the Soviets have only begun to address the so-called three obstacles that Beijing says lie at the heart of its security concerns vis-à-vis the Soviet Union: Soviet support for Vietnam's occupation of Cambodia, Soviet military occupation of Afghanistan, and the buildup of Soviet forces along the

207

Sino-Soviet and Sino-Mongolian borders. In particular, Moscow carried out a token withdrawal from Afghanistan, engineered a unilateral cease-fire there, and promised to withdraw one of its several divisions in Mongolia.

As a result, China's strategy of deterrence and defense continues to depend on international opposition to Soviet expansion and raises the possibility of the Soviet Union confronting a multifront conflict in the event it attempted to attack or intimidate China in particular. Chinese leaders see their nation's cooperation with the United States as especially important in strengthening deterrence of the Soviet Union and in aggravating Soviet strategic vulnerabilities. Beijing also encourages anti-Soviet efforts by so-called second world, developed countries—most of whom are formal allies of the United States—and by developing countries of the third world. The intensity of such Chinese efforts has varied, with more intense efforts accompanying Chinese perception of more immediate danger from the Soviets. At the same time, Beijing uses a mixture of political talks, bilateral exchanges, and other forms of dialogue to help manage the danger posed by the much more powerful Soviet Union.

Within this overall strategy to establish a stable environment in Asia, Chinese leaders have employed a varying combination of tactics to secure their interests. These depend on international variables, such as the perceived strength and intentions of the superpowers, and Chinese domestic variables, such as leadership cohesion or disarray. When Chinese leaders have judged that their strategic surroundings are at least temporarily stable, for example, they have seen less immediate need for close ties with the United States, and they have felt more free to adopt strident policies on Taiwan and other nationalistic issues that appeal to domestic constituencies but offend the United States. (This type of logic was in part responsible for China's tougher approach to the United States over Taiwan and other issues in 1981–1983.)[4] When the Chinese leaders have judged that such tactics could seriously alienate the United States and thereby endanger the stability of China's environment, however, they have put them aside in the interest of preserving peaceful surroundings. (Such reasoning is seen by some as having undergirded much of China's moderation in approach to the United States in 1983–1984.)[5]

The implications of recent Chinese foreign policy for the governments and peoples of East Asia have been clear. On one hand, Beijing has continued to do its part to check the expansion of Soviet power around its periphery in Asia. This has involved Chinese military pressure along Vietnam's northern border, support for Cambodian insurgents resisting Vietnam's occupation, and backing for Afghan resistance to the Soviet military occupation of that country. It has also involved continued strong Chinese support for Thailand and Pakistan—countries that provide the key channels for aid to the resistance forces in Cambodia and Afghanistan—and the maintenance of a credible Chinese military deterrent against Soviet military power in the north.

On the other hand, Beijing greatly values political and economic ties with Japan and the ASEAN countries, as well as the United States, and is inclined to keep continued tensions with them under careful control. It has also, notably, moderated its stance on South Korea, while developing important unofficial economic contacts with Seoul. Beijing has attempted to use the successful completion of negotiations with Great Britain regarding the future of Hong Kong to encourage Taiwan to respond positively to repeated PRC peaceful overtures, using the mainland's "one nation–two systems" framework employed in the Hong Kong negotiations.

In attempting to strike an appropriate balance between its sometimes forceful but usually moderate policy in the region, Beijing has used the image of independence in foreign affairs. This posture has several advantages for the PRC under current circumstances:

- It allows Beijing to explore for possible Soviet concessions and to exploit Sino-Soviet economic-technical interchange advantageous to Chinese development, without jeopardizing Chinese security and economic conditions with non-Communist states led by the United States.
- It allows China to develop closer ties with the United States, Japan, and other non-Communist states, including military ties in some cases, without prompting a strong Soviet response.
- It preserves a balance of forces in East Asia generally favorable to Chinese development and modernization, without major additional Chinese expenditures on their military forces.

Whether the governments and peoples of East Asia can expect a continuation of this kind of Chinese policy into the twenty-first century will depend on two major factors:

- the course of the Chinese reform program
- the actions of other key states affecting East Asian security

Prospects for China's Reform Program

Many observers view China's recent preoccupation with internal economic and political reform as having a positive, stabilizing influence on East Asian security. They are concerned, though, that China may change course during the next decade. (A good example of two competing perspectives on this question of possible change in the direction of China's reform program is seen in the articles by David M. Lampton and Albert Keidel in this volume.)[6] A change in domestic policy could lead to a turn toward a more assertive and potentially destabilizing posture in the region. Such a stance could involve, for example, the use of force to claim jurisdiction over Taiwan and to reinforce Chinese territorial disputes with states in the region, strong support for the interests of Overseas Chinese in East Asia, or the use of insurgencies or mobilization of Chinese military power in an effort to intimidate nearby smaller states.

Developments inside China that could cause such a change in foreign policy include:

- a major economic failure or change in political leadership that would prompt Beijing leaders to put aside their current conventional and generally moderate approach to nation building in favor of a more assertive policy toward the countries of East Asia
- the achievement of such a high level of economic success that Chinese leaders would feel confident that China was now strong enough to pursue its interests in the region with less regard for the reaction or concerns of other countries there

From one perspective, it would appear to be good for East Asian stability if China continued to make progress toward economic modernization but failed to achieve rapid success. Under these circumstances, Beijing leaders would likely continue to see their interests as best served by pursuing a moderate, conventional nation-building program. They would likely remain preoccupied with the difficulties of internal modernization and would not achieve the success that would allow for a more forceful policy in East Asia for some time to come. In fact, an examination of variables governing China's reform efforts shows that Beijing appears to face just such future prospects.

The reforms initiated in China since the death of Mao Zedong ten years ago represent pragmatic, trial-and-error efforts designed to undo policy blunders of the past to achieve greater national growth and material well-being for the Chinese people. Recognizing that their political standing rests fundamentally on their ability to achieve tangible economic results, Chinese reformers led by Deng Xiaoping have sharply modified the economic model developed in China since the 1950s. That model was based on principles of egalitarianism, national self-reliance, and strong central control. The modifications of the reformers have created a greater role for economic profit and individual enterprise and for decentralized decision-making; a reduced role for centrally administered prices, production, and investment; and a greater reliance on market forces and contacts with more developed countries to achieve economic progress. In the process, the reformers have carried out administrative initiatives involving gradual but sweeping changes in leadership. These have helped Beijing to effect economic policy changes more competently and with greater political support.

Beijing is likely to remain preoccupied well into the next decade with dismantling and modifying stultifying economic and administrative procedures of the past thirty years. Chinese leaders plan to follow the decollectivization of rural land and increased use of incentives in agriculture of the past seven years with a multiyear effort to introduce incentives and greater efficiency into the more important and complicated urban economy. The key to change in the urban sector rests in China's ability to modify substantially its centrally controlled system of mandatory plans that has an arbitrary and, by market standards, grossly irrational price system. At the same time, Beijing has followed major retirements and shifts in the ranks of the government and army with a full-scale reexamination of all the 44 million members of the Chinese Communist party. Thus, both the economic and political reforms are generally seen as correcting past excesses and exploring new options, rather than fundamentally altering China's Socialist orientation or challenging the monopoly of power exerted by the Communist party. In particular, the main means of production, the major share of the gross national product, and the sources of political power remain under state control.

Beijing leaders are unlikely to achieve fully their current reform objectives until well into the 1990s, if then, because of significant economic constraints, the complications from efforts to implement proposed reforms, and possible leadership instability. Major short-term economic constraints include an inadequate transportation system, insufficient supplies of electric power, and not enough trained personnel. Longer-term impediments include growing population pressure (the population growth rate increased in 1986), the difficulty of obtaining enough capital to develop available energy resources and general industry, and the likely slowdown of agricultural growth after the rapid advances in recent years.

Meanwhile, planned changes in prices have been delayed in part because of their serious consequences for Chinese internal stability, since such changes could trigger inflation and cause hoarding. Closing inefficient factories will force workers to change jobs and perhaps remain unemployed for a time. Decentralized economic decision making means that local managers can use their increased power for personal benefit as well as for the common good. The result of these kinds of impediments has been a slowdown in the economic reforms.

Accompanying political reforms also made substantial progress, but serious problems remain, especially regarding leadership succession. On the one hand, the reforms have given Deng Xiaoping and like-minded reform leaders a firmer hold over both the policy-making and policy-implementing organs of power in China than they have had in the past and they have also increased the odds that the reform efforts will continue following Deng's death.

Nevertheless, repeated political difficulties over the results of the economic and political reforms continue to demonstrate the potential volatility of politics in China. Political demonstrations in several cities in China during late 1986 and early 1987 by students favoring greater democracy appeared to represent a long-term challenge to the Communist party's use of political power. Some in the Party leadership viewed the demonstrations as highly undesirable consequences of recent political and economic reforms that should be firmly repressed, whereas others protected the reform efforts from such charges and moderated Beijing's response to the student demonstrators. In any event, the subsequent resignation of Party General Secretary Hu Yaobang called into question the leadership succession arrangements of recent years and increased the likelihood of leadership uncertainty when Deng Xiaoping, now eighty-two, dies.

Other Key Actors in East Asia

Whether China will be inclined to follow policies that exert a stabilizing or destabilizing influence on East Asia will also depend heavily on the actions of the United States, the Soviet Union, and several important countries in East Asia.[7]

If one assumes that China will remain preoccupied with internal modernization, then one can posit a largely reactive Chinese foreign policy. That is, since China appears basically satisfied with the current situation in Asia and is desirous of moving ahead with internal programs, it will likely not change course in the region unless so compelled by such outside forces as a substantial shift in U.S. or Soviet military deployments or smaller but still important steps like changes in policy by Thailand, Taiwan, or other entities.

The United States. U.S. policy appears, on the whole, to be likely to continue to encourage Chinese preoccupation with domestic modernization and reform. U.S. security policy in East Asia enjoys broad, generally bipartisan support in the United States. It involves incremental efforts to increase cooperation between the United States and its allies (Japan, South Korea, the Philippines, Thailand, and Australia), to establish closer cooperation among these states, and to encourage closer military ties with other East Asian countries, including China.

U.S. economic and political policies in East Asia are somewhat more controversial in the United States, suggesting that the U.S. posture in these areas may be more volatile. Some U.S. officials favor stronger American retaliation against trade restrictions in East Asia to force nations there to reduce their trade surpluses with the United States. Others favor an active U.S. support of opposition politicians challenging authoritarian governments in the region. In contrast, other U.S. officials resist what they view as protectionist trade measures and assert that the United States generally should allow Asian governments to handle their own political affairs.

Listed below are some U.S. measures that could prompt a significant change in China's current policy toward East Asian security. The chances of the United States adopting these measures seem remote.

• Failure of the United States to maintain an active military presence in the region. This could happen in conjunction with a U.S. withdrawal from bases in the Philippines or in other circumstances. It would force Beijing to reassess its security position vis-à-vis the growing Soviet military presence in Asia.
• Strong U.S. measures designed to reduce sharply access to U.S. markets or technology by countries like China. Such restrictions could prompt Beijing to reassess the importance it now places on smooth economic interaction with the United States and other developed non-Communist countries.
• Strong U.S. efforts to encourage separatist-minded opposition politicians in Taiwan to move toward independence or strong U.S. efforts to promote political democracy and free enterprise on the China mainland. Either approach could represent such a serious challenge to the Chinese Communist leadership's sense of national unity and development as to bring about a major reassessment of the pros and cons of smooth U.S.-Chinese relations.

The Soviet Union. Soviet policy may be more likely than U.S. policy to effect a change in Chinese policy toward East Asia. Current Soviet policy toward China, and toward Asia in general, is potentially volatile largely because it reflects a serious contradiction. On one hand, Moscow's leaders do not want to give up the gains the Soviet Union has made as a result of its military-backed expansion in Asia over the past twenty years. Thus the Soviets continue to occupy Afghanistan; to modernize their land, sea, and air forces along China's northern frontier and in the Western Pacific; to support Vietnam's occupation of Cambodia; and to deploy forces out of Vietnam's Cam Ranh Bay. In addition, Soviet leaders continue to be willing to use military power to exploit targets of opportunity that emerge from time to time. Thus Moscow has used military aid to obtain overflight rights in North Korea and to improve its influence, relative to China, in Pyongyang.

On the other hand, Soviet leaders are increasingly aware that these military actions are of great concern to China, Japan, and other Asian countries; that they increase anti-Soviet feeling to such a point that these states are very reluctant to respond positively to Soviet overtures for improved relations unless Moscow takes some actions to reduce its military threat; and that they encourage the Asian states to work more closely with the United States to offset the perceived danger posed by the Soviet Union.

To break out of their relatively isolated position in Asia, Soviet leaders have launched a series of political, economic, and military moves to reassure and improve relations with East Asian countries, but without giving up recent Soviet military gains. Soviet leader Gorbachev has appeared particularly adroit in using such moves to improve Moscow's diplomatic position. He has focused these efforts on China. Although Beijing has responded positively to Soviet offers of increased trade, technical assistance, and cultural exchanges, it balances this by continuing to confront Soviet and Soviet-backed forces around China's periphery and by developing closer political, economic, and military ties with the United States, its allies, and friends.

For the longer term, Moscow clearly has the option to promote a major change in Chinese policy toward East Asia by reducing the threat to China. It appears, however, that Moscow would, in the process, have to meet at least some of the Chinese demands regarding the three obstacles. Yet significant Soviet movement on the three obstacles could jeopardize important Soviet interests in Indochina, Afghanistan, and elsewhere. Thus the key question for Soviet leaders will remain: would the likely benefit of improved relations with China justify the likely risks associated with movement on one or more of the three obstacles?

Japan. Among the key actors in East Asia, Japan seems most likely to follow stable policies that would encourage a continuation of current moderate trends in Chinese policy. Thus the Japanese appear likely to continue to rely on the United States for security support and to use their economic might and slowly growing military power to support allied interests in the region. Accordingly, so long as Sino-U.S. relations remain cordial, Japan is expected to support Chinese modernization efforts actively through extensive trade, aid, and technology transfers. Alternative Japanese policies that would force a major reassessment by Beijing could involve rapid growth in Japanese military power, strong Japanese government ties with Taiwan, or significant Japanese accommodation of the Soviet Union. At present, Tokyo appears to have little to gain from adopting such policies.

It is important to add, however, that as Japan becomes more confident in its leading economic role in world affairs, it can be expected to be more confident and assertive in international political affairs. The result could be a Japanese policy less deferential to periodic Chinese demands over sensitive bilateral issues. This, in turn, could lead to Japanese actions that offend Chinese sensitivities and evoke sharp PRC reactions. Such disputes, similar to those seen in recent years over revised Japanese history text books, should not have a fundamental impact on Chinese foreign policy, although from time to time they could prove difficult to manage discreetly.

Other Asian Countries. Perhaps the greatest source of potential change in Chinese policy toward East Asia rests with the medium-sized and smaller Communist and non-Communist countries in the region.

In Southeast Asia, for example, Vietnam and Thailand are two nations whose policies regarding the current Indochina impasse could be expected to change over the next decade and a half; and change here could have a substantial effect on Chinese policy. Although there is little concrete evidence of any significant compromise in Hanoi's position on Cambodia, the new generation coming to power in Hanoi may eventually be more flexible than the retiring old guard regarding a possible settlement over Cambodia. The declining fortunes of the Vietnamese economy and Vietnam's heavy dependence on the Soviet Union may push the Vietnamese to seek a negotiated way out of the impasse.

The Vietnamese could meet an accommodating response from Thailand. It is conceivable that Thailand will tire of its role as a frontline state and hope to come to terms with Hanoi over Cambodia in such a way as to strengthen Thai independence of China, without seriously jeopardizing Thai security vis-à-vis Vietnam.

Meanwhile, the volatile situation in the Philippines raises the possibility that the Manila government will request U.S. withdrawal

215

from Subic and Clark military bases. Such a U.S. pullback would greatly hamper the U.S. military posture in the area and almost certainly would bring about a major Chinese reassessment of its position between competing U.S.- and Soviet-backed forces in East Asia.

In northeast Asia, meanwhile, political succession seems likely to compound an already unpredictable situation on the Korean peninsula. In North Korea, Beijing will watch with at least some uneasiness as Kim Il Song attempts to improve relations with Moscow and gain Soviet endorsement of his son, Kim Chong Il, as his successor. Beijing has also registered concern over Pyongyang's demonstrated willingness to use force to assert its interests against South Korea. As Kim Il Song ends his rule of four decades and attempts to pass power to his relatively inexperienced son, the chances for North Korean actions threatening to Chinese interests could increase.

Related to this is continued political uncertainty in South Korea. Any instability in South Korea might encourage North Korea to engage in provocative action vis-à-vis the South. Such action, of course, could lead to a great power confrontation on the peninsula. If China were to honor its security commitments to North Korea for fear of Soviet competition for influence with Pyongyang or for some other reason, Beijing might find itself confronting the United States. This would call into question the basic premises underlying current Chinese foreign policy.

Taiwan and Hong Kong. Political and economic trends in Taiwan remain problematical for the PRC. As the growth in the standard of living in Taiwan continues to outpace that of the mainland and as island-born opposition politicians displace mainlanders in positions of power, there may be a greater tendency to follow a separatist identity for the island. In particular, the formation of an opposition party on the island in late 1986 that emphasizes Taiwan's right to determine its own future status has strengthened concern in Beijing about possible separatist trends on Taiwan following the passing of President Chiang Ching-kuo (now seventy-six) and his mainland Chinese colleagues who have dominated the government on Taiwan for forty years. Separatism in Taiwan could represent a major challenge to Beijing's sense of national unity that would have important implications for the current peaceful approach of the Chinese to the issue.

Hong Kong, meanwhile, does not appear likely to cause a major reassessment of Chinese policy. The settlement with Great Britain and subsequent negotiations on its implementation have met with general satisfaction on the part of the PRC. While there have been some complaints from residents in Hong Kong, a prevailing view among those who plan to stay in the territory after reversion appears to be a wish to avoid confrontation with Beijing. Rather, these individuals appear determined to make the best of the situation by encouraging Beijing to see it in China's best interest to leave Hong Kong with as much autonomy as possible.

Conclusion

The problem for East Asia posed by China's recent drive toward modernization continues to grow as China increases in strength. But China's interest in getting along well with its neighbors is also growing. A review of factors influencing recent Chinese foreign policy suggests a greater likelihood of continuity than of substantial change in China's generally moderate approach of recent years. Unless provoked, Beijing seems more likely than not to remain focused on the difficult requirements of economic and political modernization, and less interested than in the past in assertive and potentially disruptive behavior in East Asia.

Notes

1. For background on these perspectives, see Harry Harding, ed., *China's Foreign Relations in the 1980s* (New Haven: Yale University Press, 1984); and James W. Morley, ed., *The Pacific Basin: New Challenges for the United States* (New York: Academy of Political Science, 1986).

2. For a fuller discussion, see Robert Sutter, *Chinese Foreign Policy: Developments after Mao* (New York: Praeger Publishers, 1986).

3. It is often the case that ideas such as "nationalism" can direct leaders of countries to behave pragmatically, thereby best serving the development and security of their nation. In the case of China, however, nationalism has been closely tied with the Chinese revolution and the perceived need of Chinese leaders to regain "lost" territory or assert more strongly China's position in Asian and world affairs. With the passage of time, Chinese leaders may moderate the revolutionary nationalism of the recent past. For a perceptive recent study, see Michel Oksenberg, "China's Confident Nationalism," *Foreign Affairs* (January 1987).

4. This logic also implies that improved Sino-Soviet relations in the future could give the PRC more freedom to adopt a tougher approach regarding U.S. ties with Taiwan, although such PRC policy will be governed by a number of variables (policy interest vis-à-vis the United States and Japan, for example) not directly related to Sino-Soviet ties.

5. See, for instance, Robert Sutter, "Realities of International Power and China's 'Independence' in Foreign Affairs, 1981–1984," *Journal of Northeast*

Asian Studies (Winter 1984), pp. 3–28. A contrary viewpoint emphasizes U.S. accommodation of Beijing's demands on a range of issues regarding Taiwan, technology transfer, and other questions. See, for instance, Robert Manning, "Reagan's Chance Hit," *Foreign Policy* (Spring 1984).

6. For differing perspectives on this issue, see A. Doak Barnett, "China: Ten Years after Mao," *Foreign Affairs* (Fall 1986), pp. 36–65; testimony by Professor Nicholas Lardy, U.S. Congress, Joint Economic Committee, December 12, 1986; articles by A. Doak Barnett, Robert Dernberger, and Harry Harding in "China's Economy Looks toward the Year 2000," U.S. Congress, Joint Economic Committee, 99th Congress, 2d session (Washington, D.C.: GPO, 1986), and John Heinz, "Report on the Visit to China of the Senate Delegation," U.S. Congress, Senate, 99th Congress, 2d session (Washington, D.C.: GPO, 1986).

7. For a full discussion, see Morley, *The Pacific Basin*. For differing perspectives on future trends in the region see: Paul Kreisberg, "The United States and Asia," *Asian Survey* (January 1986); Alan Romberg, "New Stirrings in Asia," *Foreign Affairs* (Winter 1986); Donald Zagoria, "The U.S.S.R. and Asia in 1985," *Asian Survey* (January 1986); Peter Drucker, "The Changed World Economy," *Foreign Affairs* (Spring 1986); Richard Holbrooke, "East Asia: The Next Challenge," *Foreign Affairs* (Spring 1986); and Harry Gelman, "Continuity versus Change in Soviet Policy in Asia," *Journal of Northeast Asian Studies* (Summer 1985).

Commentary

Chang Pao Min

I share Dr. Sutter's cautious optimism about the prospect of China's economic reforms, and I believe the economic reform policy has generated its own momentum and therefore cannot be easily reversed in spite of temporary setbacks. Despite the problems now emerging in China, I think the Chinese leadership will continue to pursue its policy of reform. The problems have arisen not because of the nature or direction of such economic reforms but because of their pace and magnitude.

I find it slightly difficult to accept Dr. Sutter's logic in his forecast of the security implications of China's economic reform. He argues that too much economic progress, just as much as failure of reform or too little economic progress, may lead to radicalization of China's foreign policy. One could dispute this argument on logical grounds. The argument is that the current moderate Chinese foreign policy can only be sustained by limited economic progress, but limited economic progress could well generate a higher degree of frustration, resulting in a radicalization of foreign policy.

There is a positive link between economic development and national power. But whether China would use its national power aggressively depends to a large extent on the presence or absence of major issues of contention between China and its Asian neighbors and between China and the superpowers.

If we examine the history of Communist China, we could argue that Chinese foreign policy, particularly toward its Asian neighbors, has been basically reactive to a perceived threat from external sources. *Regardless* of the domestic situation and of the level of economic progress or development, China has taken great risks in trying to safeguard what it considers its vital national interests by asserting its territorial integrity when threatened.

Throughout the 1950s China was very hostile toward the United States and almost all the other Asian countries, mainly because the

United States pursued a policy of containment against China. Economically speaking, however, the first decade of the Communist regime was recognized as the golden period. So I do not think there is a necessary cause-and-effect relationship between the level of economic progress and the degree of assertiveness or aggressiveness in Chinese foreign policy.

We can say the same thing about the 1960s. During the 1960s China was hostile toward both the Soviet Union and the United States, partly because of the continuing military confrontation between China and the United States in Indochina. Economically, the 1960s were also bad years for China. In the 1970s the Soviet Union became the archenemy of China, because the Soviet Union was perceived as the major threat to China's security. If this line of thinking is valid, perhaps the question can be raised, Are not external factors more crucial and more important determinants of China's foreign policy, particularly its policy toward its Asian neighbors, than internal factors?

If history can serve as a guide, one could argue that China has not been much concerned about what smaller nations in Asia could do to it. Rather, China has been preoccupied with the superpowers and with the smaller countries' being used by the superpowers against China. Chinese policy toward its Asian neighbors has been mainly a function of Chinese policy toward the two superpowers.

The question can be asked, Will issues of contention continue to exist in the year 2000 between China on the one hand and the two superpowers on the other hand as a result of either superpower's involvement with smaller Asian countries? If there are such issues, what will they be? Which superpower is likely to be perceived as constituting a greater threat to China?

Dr. Sutter has mentioned three major obstacles standing between China and the Soviet Union that carry almost the same weight as the one obstacle standing between the United States and China—Taiwan. It may be asked whether, in the coming decade or so, it would be easier for the Soviet Union to remove the three obstacles than for the United States to remove one obstacle.

Would a more powerful China be more accommodating on the issue of Korea, particularly with respect to the continuing U.S. military presence in Korea, as well as more accommodating on the issue of Soviet involvement in Indochina? Assuming that China's national power will continue to increase, would China go beyond its immediate preoccupation with national security and territorial integrity and try to project its military power in other parts of Asia, particularly in Southeast Asia? What kind of influence would a more powerful China try to exert in East Asia and Southeast Asia?

Mr. Sutter has identified all the changes that may occur in the next decade or so. He has not, however, identified or predicted exactly what kind of change is most likely to occur or in what sense or to what extent such change is likely to affect China's policy in East Asia and in Southeast Asia.

David M. Lampton

It seems to me that Americans have a fairly relaxed view about what Chinese power means for Southeast Asian people. I was particularly caught by a statement in this paper that the dilemma is that economic growth seems to moderate Chinese behavior but also increase Chinese capacity to act. It seems the Southeast Asians are not so sure that moderate behavior will necessarily result from economic growth or what kinds of influence China might be able to exert as we approach the year 2000.

Second, to the list of factors that affect Chinese international behavior and seem to be driving Chinese policy, I would add the element of nationalism, particularly if I were thinking about Japan and Taiwan. Nationalism is a wild card in this deck, and I am never quite sure when it is going to rear its head in an important way. Certainly, the anti-Japanese disturbances in 1985 give one some pause, and the whole Taiwan issue can be affected by nationalism.

Third, in the discussion of the Soviet Union's strategy of expansion on the periphery, there is a 50 percent chance that Gorbachev is serious, at least for the medium term, in trying to reduce expansion, primarily out of concern for internal economic development and the fear that if the Soviet Union does not get on the technological innovation curve fairly quickly, it will be a minor power in all ways except, perhaps, militarily. In short, I am not sure that a straight-line projection of the past expansionist policy of the Soviet Union into the future is warranted.

Fourth, before I came here, I spent a few days in Taiwan, and I came away from those talks and presentations somewhat optimistic about Taiwan's capacity to maintain its economic stability and its capacity to manage the transition toward a more pluralistic polity while also managing the self-determination issue. I would like your thoughts about the ability of the leaders on Taiwan to manage all these quite difficult transitions.

Finally, what are the variables, in your view, that will determine the level of Japanese military expenditure, in light of the fact that they have broken the 1 percent budgetary ceiling? My own feeling is that the bureaucracies' aversion to military power stemming from the Second World War and the constitutional prohibitions may diminish in importance over time. The question is, What other factors will determine what the Japanese spend for military power?

Discussion

DAVID M. LAMPTON: Let's begin our discussion by letting the members of the audience address their questions and comments to us. Then we will try to respond to them.

QUESTION: The year is 2000. Communists are now running the Philippines. What is China's response to a Communist regime in the Philippines? My understanding is that the Philippine Communists would be rather independent and nationalist vis-à-vis the Soviets, the Chinese, or any other Marxist ideological brethren. I would be interested in your response. Second, how does China view Japanese support of the Strategic Defense Initiative (SDI), since China itself opposes the SDI, particularly in relation to Japan's recent incorporation into SDI research?

QUESTION: I am interested in the question of Korean instability. You say a great power confrontation would pit China against the United States. Is that really the way you think it would come out now? Or would that alignment change to the degree that China might find itself pushing up from the south a little bit to keep that situation under control?

QUESTION: Here is a hypothetical situation. It is the year 2000, and five years earlier Gorbachev has returned islands north of Japan to Japan; they have settled amicably. There is a Communist government in the Philippines. Japan has rearmed because the United States cut off its surplus rather dramatically and encouraged Japan to reflate its economy within. That was done most easily through the buildup of an arms industry, which the Soviet Union was delighted to help purchase from to enhance its own capabilities. At the same time Taiwan has declared its independence and found itself supported militarily, to some degree, by the resurgent Japanese military capability. Thus there is an axis or a necklace around China from the Soviet Union down through Japan, Taiwan, and the Philippines through Vietnam. How haywire is that?

COMMENT: I would like to follow up on the statement that with economic success at a high level China might pursue its interests in the region with less regard for the concerns of other countries. Even given Albert Keidel's very optimistic projections of China's economic growth by the year 2000, bearing in mind that we are going to see a tremendous continued growth by other countries in the region, it seems to me that China's relative position is not going to be that good or its power or its economy that great. The need for technological cooperation with the rest will certainly be as great as it is today. Therefore, the radicalization simply would not make a great deal of sense for China, even under those most optimistic assumptions.

QUESTION: I was struck by your drawing a parallel between the Soviet modification of its behavior on the three obstacles and Nixon's modification of our policy on Taiwan. I would like to ask your comment on that.

ROBERT G. SUTTER: I think it is very dangerous to take too legalistic a view of these conditions, whether the conditions that China imposed on improving relations with the United States or the three conditions with the Soviet Union. To the Chinese the key issue on the Taiwan problem was the intention of the United States. Did the United States intend to interfere in the internal affairs of China? Did the United States intend to follow a one-China, one-Taiwan policy or a two-China policy?

Once it was clarified (at least the Chinese were satisfied until the confusions of 1980) during the normalization negotiations that it was not the intention of the United States to split Taiwan off from China, the Chinese were prepared to be quite flexible on the detailed arrangements. They even went so far as to agree to a statement in the normalization agreement saying that Taiwan no longer was an issue in bilateral relations between the United States and China.

On the Soviet Union's three conditions, I submit that the Chinese are not naive and will not be satisfied by token withdrawals of force from Afghanistan. In fact, we cannot even think of Afghanistan as the real obstacle. The obstacle is Soviet intentions. If those three conditions stand for a policy of surrounding and isolating China, the condition on the border will not be satisfied by a token withdrawal by the Soviet Union. As far as Southeast Asia is concerned, as Deng Xiaoping pointed out, it is China's major concern. I cannot imagine anything that the Soviet Union could do down there. The Soviet Union's global concerns, its Indian Ocean interests, and its interest in the American bases in the Philippines are so strong that I cannot imagine that Gorbachev—even if he were foolish enough to try it himself—could get the support of the Soviet military to sacrifice that tremendous strategic advantage for the possibility of some improvement in relations with China.

On the relationship between economic development and assertive Chinese policy, the main point I was trying to make was of a preoccupied China. If China is preoccupied—which Dr. Chang posits that it is—its foreign policy will be more reactive. But some specialists look at Chinese foreign policy as springing from an internal dynamic. I do not see a direct causal relationship between internal politics and external policy. We see a China that is preoccupied with economic modernization. That is what is important to it and what it wants to continue.

As to the questions about the obstacles that have been raised, there is a fundamental difference between these two sets of obstacles. We must keep in mind that the Soviet obstacles reflect, from the Chinese point of view, a threat to China. The Nixon Doctrine of the late 1960s showed the Chinese that the United States was no longer a threat to China.

We are at a stage of looking not at the Taiwan issue, but at the issue of U.S. containment. In the Nixon period, containment came first; Taiwan came second. Nixon first reassured the Chinese, "Look, my intentions to you are sincere, and I'm withdrawing these troops." That was not the reason he withdrew the troops, but he did, in fact, withdraw them. That got China's attention. The strategic problem they had faced for twenty years was being moved away. Nixon withdrew 600,000 to 700,000 troops from East Asia. It was an enormous performance.

If for some reason Gorbachev were to do the same thing, that would withdraw the threat from around China's periphery and would change China's foreign policy orientation fundamentally. Obviously, there are many reasons why it would be very difficult for him to do so.

ROGER W. SULLIVAN: Let me just add a footnote. That is interesting, but it was not so much the withdrawal of the troops as it was that the Chinese were convinced that the United States had changed its policy in some fundamental way. What I am saying is that token withdrawal by Soviet forces would not indicate a fundamental change in Soviet policy and I do not think the Chinese believe that policy is changing or is likely to change.

MR. SUTTER: If the Soviets did follow through with troop withdrawals, I think the Chinese would take due account of that and would be quite interested in talking, but I don't think that is going to happen. There are very serious dilemmas for the Soviet Union in carrying out these troop withdrawals, and I do not think the Soviet Union has reached the point where the United States was in 1968. That is the key difference here. That is the Soviet obstacle. Meanwhile, our obstacle, of course, is Taiwan, which is much more of a concern for Chinese sovereignty than for Chinese security.

I would like to address Japan's role because I think it is very important. The main impediment to Japan's military power in the region is that the Japanese people do not yet feel threatened. Therefore, they are not willing to spend much money on defense. That is the thing that Mr. Nakasone finds himself up against right now, as he has tried to increase the defense budget a little bit while keeping total budget spending down. He has tried to raise taxes, but he is taking a beating politically in Japan. This has been tried by other Japanese prime ministers, and they have taken a beating every time. It is just not a popular issue to spend a lot of money on defense because that constituency in Japan is not strong. This blocks the efforts on the part of the United States to encourage the Japanese to share more of the defense burden.

On the factor of nationalism in Chinese policy, if China is preoccupied internally and has to respond to what it sees as a provocative action from outside, yes, nationalism will come forward. But China does not want to disrupt its modernization effort or to disrupt the environment, which is important to the modernization effort. Its reaction would be carefully calculated. The ideological motives that have been important in Chinese policy in the past, I think we will find, will not be allowed to reach such a point as to disrupt the economic development programs or the stable environment that the Chinese have worked so hard to build up in East Asia over the past fifteen years.

A Communist regime in the Philippines would be a very serious matter. If the United States were forced to withdraw from its bases in the Philippines, we really have nowhere to go that would allow us to maintain a strong position in Southeast Asia. The Soviets in Vietnam with a Communist regime in the Philippines would be extremely interested. They would be interested in getting in those bases, and they would do whatever they could to get there.

If the Soviets got access to those bases, the East Asian order would be very different. So China would probably do what it could to keep the Soviets out of those bases. I think they would try to improve relations with the new Philippine regime to try to keep the Soviets out. But I don't think Beijing would go to bat for us to keep us there, particularly if the Communists took over, because they are a very independent and anti-American group of Communists.

On the question, To what degree is China's economic success likely to change Chinese society? I don't know the answer, and I don't think it matters much. We have a long way to go, and they are preoccupied internally. We can worry about changes in the society in the year 2050, I think, rather than 2000.

As to Korean instability, I was referring to the current situation, the leadership transition in both North and South Korea and the alignment that would take place. Even now, of course, people are well aware that the Chinese are trying to moderate the situation and establish communication between the United States and North Korea and between North Korea and South Korea. If push came to shove, China would be very worried about North Korea's being totally dependent on the Soviet Union. It would put them in an awful position. Whether they would side with the north in the event of an attack against the south, I do not know, but it would put them in a very serious situation. Since they are militarily aligned with North Korea, that would be a very serious matter for them to consider.

9
Afterword

David M. Lampton

I think the way to close is to summarize four questions, the kinds of questions all of us, no matter where we come out in our particular assessment, need to keep looking at. Our assessment may well change as we see the answers to these questions unfolding.

One of the questions that has permeated the conference—and we all have our individual answers to it—is whether China can separate economic and technical change—the acquisition of technology—from cultural and political change. A number of people suggested that it is absolutely essential that Deng and the Chinese leadership be able to separate these two things. It is an interesting question whether that is feasible.

The question has been dichotomized throughout the conference. When we talk about economic change being linked to cultural and political change, I don't think any of us have the notion that China must become democratic if it is to have our technology. Plenty of economies in this part of the world show that such a link is not there or is tenuous at the very most. But I think the Chinese people must make up their minds soon about how much cultural change they are going to tolerate and the Party must reconcile itself to political changes. It is not feasible to think China can acquire the technology and economic wherewithal without being willing to accept some substantial cultural and political change.

A second question that has permeated the debate here is, What are the lines of division in China's leadership? Yesterday's *Straits Times* said Deng and Chen Yun pretty much agree about the ends. What they are arguing about, we were told, is the means. If that is true, it is important. The more we can find out about what China's leaders think, particularly the coming leadership generation, the better.

The third question concerns urban industrial reforms, the toughest part of the nut to crack. It is there that the interests of the Chinese Communist party are most vitally affected. The critical question to look at in the next year is, Will the Chinese be able to move ahead with significant reforms in that area, and what will be the reaction of the Party?

The fourth question, which came up in the discussion of computers, concerns China's producing primarily for its domestic market. The question is, Will the domestic market provide the engine of competition China needs? If China must place its emphasis on the domestic market, will the forces at work in the domestic economy provide enough competition to keep China from slipping further and further behind? If the answer is that China will continue to slip behind, we must ask what the consequences of that might be for its behavior.

By way of conclusion, since you are all going out into the traffic of Singapore, I am reminded of Adam Pilarski's somewhat facetious question—if you switched the direction of traffic for only 20 percent of the cars, what would happen? Behind Dr. Pilarski's remarks is a serious question: Can mixed economic systems exist? It is clear that they can. Almost every economy in the world is a mixed system. The question is, Will the mixture that the Chinese are likely to come out with be a viable one?

Index

U.S. relations. *See* Trade relations,
 U.S./PRC
Trade policy and position, Taiwan, 117,
 161
 electronics exports, 108
 Japanese relations, 154
 PRC relations, 63–65
 sectoral problems, 42–44
 trends, 45, 47
 U.S. relations, 61, 163
Trade policy, U.S., 61, 163, 213
Trade ratio, 42, 45, 86, 144, 145, 161, 163
Trade relations, U.S./PRC
 Chinese exports via Hong Kong, 164
 economic forecasts, 143–45, 161,
  163–65
 political/strategic concerns, 142, 152–
  60, 162, 165, 167–68
 protectionism, 147–48, 161, 167
 U.S. aid and investment positions,
  150–52, 164, 170
 U.S. export controls, 148–50, 162,
  164, 166, 168–70
 U.S. share, 108, 145–48
Trade surplus, 47
Transportation industry, 152
Tsiang, Sho-chieh, 41

United Kingdom, 106, 108, 130, 151, 169
 Hong Kong issue, 209, 216–17
 national defense, 172–74, 176, 182
Urban economic reforms, 75–77, 82, 84,
 86, 228–29

Very large scale integrated (VLSI) circuits, 95, 105, 110
Vietnam, 195, 199–200, 205, 207, 208,
 214, 215
Voting systems, 3–4, 54–55

Wages, 134
Wang Co., 106, 120
Wang Renzhi, 19
Wang Ruowang, 19
Wang, Tso-yung, 41
Wan Li, 99–100
Warsaw Pact countries, 149, 150
Weinberger, Caspar, 171, 202
Westinghouse Electric Corp., 132
Wong, John, 162–64, 167
World Bank
 development assistance funds, 151,
  170
 studies, 68–69, 71, 81–82, 84, 86, 116
  145
Wu, Chung-lih, 35–54, 64–65, 83–84
Wu, Friedrich, 27–29, 32
Wuxi, 97, 99, 100, 105, 106, 118
Wu Xueqian, 185

Xinjiang, 180
Xu Xin, 10

Yang Dezhi, 199
Yang Shangkun, 199
Yangtze River Computer Group Corp.,
 101
Yen, C. K., 41
Yoshida letter, 59, 154
Young China party, 51
Youthification *(nianqinghua)* campaign,
 177, 195
Yunnan province, 107

Zhang Jianzhi, 171, 172
Zhang Jingyi, 179
Zhao Ziyang, 18–20, 158
Zhou Enlai, 74, 153, 204
Zhu Houze, 19

A NOTE ON THE BOOK

This book was edited by Dana Lane,
Trudy Kaplan, and Janet Schilling of the
Publications Staff of the American Enterprise Institute.
The index was prepared by Patricia Ruggiero.
The text was set in Palatino, a typeface designed by Hermann Zapf.
Coghill Book Typesetting Company, of Richmond, Virginia,
set the type, and Edwards Brothers Incorporated,
of Ann Arbor, Michigan, printed and bound the book,
using permanent acid-free paper.